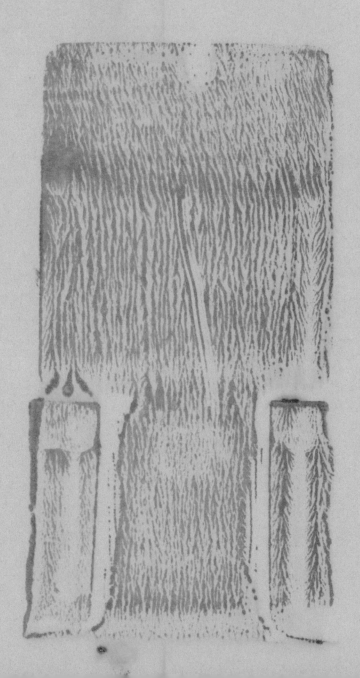

THE CONCEPT OF THE PRIMITIVE

ASHLEY MONTAGU, *Editor*

The Concept of
the Primitive

THE FREE PRESS, NEW YORK
COLLIER-MACMILLAN LIMITED, LONDON

First Printing

Dedicated to Erich Kahler

Preface

GOETHE, in his play *Faust*, makes one of his characters say that where an idea is wanting a word can always be found to take its place. This is not only true where ideas are in short supply, but especially so where the ideas are confused and confusing. A good rodlike term in such circumstances compensates for all the insecurities one may occasionally feel about reedlike ideas upon which it is quite impractical to lean for support. That is why words, especially technical words, can be so comforting. *They,* at least, stand for something. Indeed, they may very well do so, and what they stand for may be entirely erroneous, and what is even worse, confused. Truth grows more readily out of error, opined my Lord Bacon, than out of confusion. Words may not only obscure the fact that there is a complete absence of ideas behind them, but they may also serve as devices to conceal the confusion from which their users suffer. Still worse, words, and especially technical terms, may embody prejudices and pseudological rationalizations based on unanalyzed systems of values. Stereotypes of this kind can be worse than merely confusing.

The term "primitive" is such a cliché, and it is a damaging word. Not only confusing and damaging, but obfuscating, corresponding to nothing in reality, and obstructive of progress in understanding the meaning of the great variability presented by man in all his manifold variety.

There is a perfectly sound sense in which the term "primitive" and the concept for which it stands may be used, but not until we have disembarrassed ourselves of the unsound ways in which the word is employed shall we usefully be able to employ it at all.

Among the terms that have been suggested as substitutes for "primitive," are "primary," in Cooley's sense as referring to groups "characterized by intimate face-to-face association and cooperation." [1] Edwards has argued in favor of this term on the ground that it tends to mesh with the traditional areas of anthropological, as opposed to sociological, endeavor. While the sociologist deals with complex modern (secondary) societies, the anthropologist is concerned with noncomplex (primary) societies.

But the inherent error here is the assumption that so-called "primary" societies are noncomplex. Edwards is on stronger ground when he urges that by limiting the reference of these terms to a single dimension of culture, namely, the nature of social interaction, a priori implications are avoided concerning the degree of technological, religious, artistic, and so on, complexity of any particular culture. Edwards believes that "primary" would avoid the pitfall of "primitive," leading to such misconceptions as "primitive language" and "primitive mentality," generalized from one trait, such, for example, as technology.[2]

Unfortunately, it is difficult to see why such a term as "primary" could not be equally misgeneralized.

1. Charles Cooley, *Social Organization*. New York, 1909.
2. R. H. Edwards, "Primitive." *Current Anthropology*, vol. 2, 1961, p. 396.

A similar difficulty besets Haring's plea for the use of Thurnwald's "peripheral." "Peripheral" peoples have a way of rapidly ceasing to be so.

Other terms, equally unsuccessful in establishing themselves, are considered elsewhere in this book.

I shall not anticipate here what is to be repeatedly said in the body of this volume concerning the deficiencies of the concept "primitive." For many years increasing numbers of anthropologists and others have found that concept unsatisfactory. I launched an attack upon the term in 1945 in a paper, somewhat revised, reprinted in the present volume. In more recent years the concept has come under increasing criticism from a number of anthropological quarters. It has seemed to me that it might in many ways be useful to bring these criticisms together within the covers of a single volume.

Finally, to the authors and publishers who made this volume possible, many thanks.

Ashley Montagu

Princeton, N. J.

Contributors

Catherine M. Berndt is a lecturer in the Department of Anthropology, University of Western Australia. Dr. Berndt is the author, jointly with her husband Ronald M. Berndt, of many books and monographs on the Australian and New Guinea aborigines and their cultures.

Stanley Diamond is Professor of Anthropology at The New School for Social Research in New York.

Edward P. Dozier is Professor of Anthropology at the University of Arizona.

Katherine George teaches at United College, Winnipeg, Manitoba.

Jules Henry is Professor of Anthropology at Washington University, Saint Louis, Missouri.

Francis L. K. Hsu is Professor of Anthropology at Northwestern University, Evanston, Illinois.

Ashley Montagu was formerly Professor of Anthropology at Rutgers University, New Brunswick, New Jersey.

Marshall Sahlins is Professor of Anthropology at the University of Michigan, Ann Arbor, Michigan.

Sol Tax is Professor of Anthropology and Dean of the Social Sciences at the University of Chicago, Chicago, Illinois.

Contents

THE CONCEPT OF THE PRIMITIVE

ASHLEY MONTAGU

The Fallacy of
the "Primitive"

F ROM the rather self-conscious heights of our own state of equivocal civilization and of that of the community to which we belong, we men of the latest period of human development have traditionally taken the view that whatever has preceded us was by so much the less advanced. Since we are the latest bearers of human development we reason, therefore, that we are the most fully developed. This rather ortholinear view of development is widely held, and it is, of course, widely believed to be in harmony with the evolutionary facts.

Reprinted from *The Journal of The American Medical Association,* March 24, 1962, Vol. 179, pp. 962 and 963. Copyright 1962, by American Medical Association.

The truth is that evolutionary processes do not proceed in straight lines but are more accurately observed to assume a reticulate form. And so it has been in the evolution of man, both physically and culturally. So entrenched, however, have our beliefs become concerning the ortholinear evolution of man that our conceptions of "progress," "development," and "evolution" have rendered the assumption automatic that what developed later in time must therefore be more "advanced" and more "evolved" than that which developed earlier. From this the "logical" inference followed that what was less developed must be earlier than that which was more developed, and therefore the earlier was the more "primitive" and the later the more "advanced." Furthermore, since straight-line evolution is taken for granted by so many, it followed that the more advanced developed from the less advanced, from the "primitive," and that the former was "superior" to the latter.

Since evolution from the less advanced to the more advanced or from the simpler to the complex (not quite the same thing) is a fact beyond dispute (although the reverse has sometimes occurred in evolution), it has been easy to fall into the habit of assuming that the later developed is not only the more evolved but also the better. "Better" is, of course, a value judgment, and value judgments are a quagmire in which one may become inextricably bogged. And this seems to be the condition into which civilized man has fallen, with respect to those whom he chooses to call "primitive."

We speak of "primitive" peoples—the nonliterate peoples of the earth. What do we mean when we use the term? We mean that such peoples are, in comparison with ourselves, undeveloped; in many respects that is true. For example, it would be true of reading and writing, of technological progress, and in various cultures it would be more or less true of certain aspects of moral and institutional development. But it is very necessary to point out that, in certain respects, such cultures are more highly developed than are most civilized cultures. By the standards of values in these matters prevailing in civilized societies, "primitive" cultures are "better" than cvilized cultures.

For example, Eskimos and Australian aborigines, to take two of the so-called most "primitive" cultures known to anthropologists, are very much more generous, loving, and cooperative than are most of the members of civilized societies. By the standard of our own values in these matters, Eskimos and Australian aborigines are better than we are. Members of these "primitive" cultures are honest, dependable, cheerful, and courageous, in all these respects to a degree which comparatively few civilized men manage to be. Who is more developed in these respects? Those who pay lip-service to these qualities or those who live them out in their lives?

An additional assumption widely made is that "primitive" peoples are "nearer" and more closely resemble prehistoric man than the so-called "more advanced" peoples. This, too, is a very questionable assumption. The fact is that nonliterate peoples have as long a history as civilized ones. Despite references to "living fossils," no human population can, even by the most violent torsion of the imagination, be considered to be a fossil. All human societies change. The rate of change undoubtedly varies, the rate being slower in some than in others, but changes must occur. They occur in language, religion, custom, and technology, and the changes will be considerably influenced by the varying experiences which each society undergoes. Those that are isolated from the mainstream of cultural change will change slowly; those that are exposed to the fertilizing effects of cultural interchange with other peoples will change rapidly. But even in the absence of such cultural stimulation, the very nature of cultural life involves more or less continuous adjustment to and encouragement of change to meet the requirements of changing conditions. We can, therefore, be certain that no culture, as we know it today, is as it was in prehistoric times. It may even be that some of the so-called "primitive" cultures are much less like those of prehistoric times than some that appear to be more advanced. It cannot be questioned that, in some respects, some non-literate cultures are closer to the conditions as they prevailed in prehistoric times than are civilized cultures. This, however, does not mean that they are so in all, or even most, respects.

Each culture in the course of time makes the progress necessary to enable its members to live as comfortably as possible in the environment in which the culture functions. The environment generally sets certain limits beyond which it is impossible for the culture to develop unless radical changes are introduced from the outside. Metal tools, for example, will not be developed in an environment in which metal ores are unknown. As I have already said, cultures differ from one another in the history of the experiences they have undergone and, therefore, in the kind of development they have realized. This does not mean that any culture, i.e., the human beings through whom the culture is expressed, is—given the same history of conditions—incapable of realizing or achieving the same degree of development as any other culture, but merely that most cultures have not had the same or similar opportunities to do so, and largely for that reason differ culturally from one another.

Too often we identify "primitive man" with contemporary nonliterate peoples when the only legitimate use of the phrase "primitive man" is when it is applied to prehistoric man. But even here there are dangers in the use of terms which are so loaded with erroneous ideas. Primitive man, that is, prehistoric man, is too often thought of as a beetle-browed monster, with little brain, a bull neck, knock-knees, and a nasty habit of dragging his womenfolk around by their hair. Sad to say, all these ideas were perpetrated upon an innocent public by leading scientists of their day. Beetle-brows there undoubtedly were, but it should have been explained that behind those beetle-brows beat a brain of considerable power and, as in the case of Neanderthal man, larger in size than our noble own! The monster, the bull neck, the knock-knees, and the hair-dragging of women are all figments of the imaginations of those who wished to see these things the way they thought they ought to be. But the true scientist endeavors to see things the way they are, not the way they ought to be or what is considered desirable.

One of the consequences of the belief that primitive man was so much less developed than ourselves is the failure to understand that prehistoric man of 15,000 years ago was, in some aspects of his life, capable of achievements which have scarcely been surpassed by men since. An outstanding example of this is prehistoric art, especially the art of the Upper Old Stone Age. When this was first discovered at the beginning of the century, it was at first attributed to modern artists who, for some unexplained reason, were alleged to have crept into a natural crypt and decorated its ceiling in the manner of Michelangelo in the Sistine Chapel. But, as other discoveries were made in the dark recesses of caverns and caves under conditions which pointed to an extreme antiquity, the weight of evidence could no longer be resisted, and prehistoric man was finally acknowledged as the creator of these wonderful works of art, paintings, sculptures, and engravings. As Sir Herbert Read has said, "The best paintings in the Altamira, Niaux, and Lascaux caves exhibit a degree of skill which is not less than that of a Pisanello or a Picasso." Anyone who has seen the originals or even reproductions will agree that this is no overstatement. In addition to the technical skill displayed by the artists, their work exhibits a vitality and expression which has seldom been equalled in any age.

Be that as it may, in the works of art of prehistoric men who lived between 15,000 and 30,000 years ago, we have the clearest evidence that these men, as artists, were as accomplished as any who have lived since. When it is remembered that these works were not really executed as works of art but as a part of magico-religious rituals calculated to yield success in the hunt, that the conditions under which these works were created were usually of the most difficult kind, high up on walls and ceilings, often with the artist lying on his back, and doing his work by the uncertain light of a smoky oil flame, the achievement becomes all the more remarkable. There can be little doubt that individuals capable of such skills were endowed with an intelligence potentially no less great than that possessed by contemporary civilized man. Because the term "primitive" not only tends to obscure that fact, but also militates against the possibility of understanding the true significance of the facts, it will readily be understood why, if the term is used at all, it should be used with the greatest caution.

Primitive man as prehistoric man is most certainly a reality, and the more we learn to understand him, the better we understand ourselves. But to identify existing nonliterate peoples with prehistoric man is an egregious error when it is not an expedient fiction, a fiction which is rather bathetically calculated to provide a lift for the faltering ego. In the rapidly developing world in which we live, in which the underdeveloped regions of the world will witness their most spectacular advances in the areas of human development, it is of the first order of importance that the civilized peoples of the world understand and act upon these facts.

CATHERINE H. BERNDT

The Concept

of Primitive

IN THIS tenth anniversary year of the new series of
Sociologus, it seems appropriate to look again at the term "primitive," to consider briefly both its meanings and its implications.
The relevance here is two-fold. On the one hand the founder of
this journal, Professor Richard Thurnwald, was firmly convinced

Reprinted from Sociologus, *Vol. 10, No. 1, 1960, pp. 50–69. This paper
was provoked by the ways in which a number of Anthropology students in
the University of Western Australia used the term "primitive," in essays and
in seminar discussions, and the reasons they gave for doing so. They held that
because the term appeared so frequently in anthropological and other literature
there could be no reasonable objection to it ("Everybody says it"), and certainly no need to define it ("We all know what it means"). Some of them
treated it as a polar opposite to "contemporary," which they restricted to Western European-type society: in other words, peoples called "primitive" were, by*

that despite wide divergencies mankind was essentially one: that there was no inherent cleavage between peoples often called primitive, and those often called civilized. On the other hand *Sociologus*, following in this tradition, is centrally concerned with relations between peoples, and the problems arising from contact between different ways of living. The views which members of any given society hold about those who belong to others (and, conversely, about themselves) influence both the nature and the content of interaction between them. They represent a charter or guide to behavior, which may or may not be modified by what takes place in the actual situation. Assumptions, or stereotypes, about "other people" are notoriously persistent even in the face of contrary evidence. They are part of an ideological framework within which "facts" are examined, or a screen through which "facts" are perceived. These frameworks or screens are inevitable up to a point in social affairs, when the peoples concerned may be evaluating one another in accordance with very different criteria. Nevertheless, they constitute barriers both to communication and intercourse among them, and to relatively objective statements about them.

There are thus two facets to this question. One is the theoretical issue, the place of the concept of primitive in generalizations about human society and culture, its usefulness in the ordering of data on a comparative basis. Efforts to classify or explain differences between peoples and ways of living have been going on for a long time, and have taken a number of forms. But perhaps the most persistent and most popular is the approach in which a category labeled primitive is separated out from another or others, with or without specifying criteria for doing so.

---

definition, not "contemporary." A few students inferred from this that generalizations relating to one type of people or society, that is, "primitive," could have no relevance to the contrasting type, that is, "contemporary" or "Western." There was some confusion as to where non-"tribal" Asian societies fitted into this scheme, and in fact when they were under consideration labels of this sort were often dropped. On the whole, however, the tendency was to make a clear-cut division between "primitive" on the one hand, and "contemporary" or "Western" on the other.

The other issue is one of expediency. Objections to either the term or the concept, or both, may be such that they cannot lightly be disregarded. But merely changing the term may not satisfy either its protagonists or its opponents. In the first place, the contention may be that the label itself doesn't matter; that it merely points to a conceptual, objectively ascertainable reality, which exists independently of any name that may be applied to it. In the second place, this point of view itself may be challenged, as an attempt to distort the "facts" for political or other reasons.

Since it is not possible to engage here in an exhaustive discussion on the subject, nor to do more than touch on the relevant literature, this paper will be confined to outlining a few of the points which should be borne in mind in regard to it.

MEANINGS OF THE TERM "PRIMITIVE"

(a) In a general sense, it suggests crudity, lack of development, roughness, inferior quality.

(i) In some contexts it connotes inadequacy of means in relation to stipulated or inferred ends. This has special reference to the technological sphere, but is just as relevant to conditions within a society as it is in cross-cultural comparisons. For example, a digging stick is "primitive" in contrast to a machine such as a tractor; a hand-worked pump, to a system of obtaining water through pipes and taps; a tent or shack, to a house; an open fire or a wood-stove to gas or electric appliances for cooking—and possibly the last two in turn will one day be called "primitive" in contrast to devices which draw on solar heat, or atomic energy. And so on. "Primitive" modes of transport are laborious, time consuming or uncomfortable, as against those which are both speedier, and designed to afford passengers the minimum of inconvenience in reaching their destination.

(ii) Sometimes it is taken to mean "simple," or undifferentiated, as the polar opposite of "complex." Conversely it may mean "complex," as the polar opposite of simplicity; that is, differentiated in respect of certain features which are negatively evaluated. Language is a notable example (cf. R. R. Marett, 1912/1923: 139–45; M. R. Cohen and E. Nagel, 1943–1949: 389; H. Good, 1958: 17–18). The loss of inflections in English is sometimes seen as a move toward clarity (simplicity positively evaluated), as against retention of inflections in such languages as Latin and German.

(b) In accordance with its etymology it may imply a point on a time scale, that is "early" or "first" or, more dramatically, "primeval," "primordial," "pristine." It has to do with the "beginning" of things, the "dawn" of human society. In the unilinear-evolutionary framework which is still fairly widely accepted, the same term embraces societies remote in time and accessible only through archeological exploration, and present-day societies said to resemble them in a number of significant respects, for example, use of stone tools, and a hunting or slash-and-burn-agricultural economy. The latter are then taken as living representatives of "early man," and therefore more or less straightforward examples of prehistoric culture and society (cf. C. von Fürer-Haimendorf, in W. L. Thomas ed., 1955: 149–68). An offshoot of this view, not entirely abandoned even today, was the "recapitulation theory," the suggestion that the development of human society through time paralleled the growth of individual human beings from childhood to physical and social maturity. There were references to the "childhood of man," to the immaturity of prehistoric man and his living counterparts, and their naive, unadult approach to reality.[1]

1. S. Langer (1942–1954: 121) speaks of arrested development at an "adolescent" stage. See also A. L. Kroeber (1952: 224) for a parallel between "primitive culture" and children's play. In a different setting, it has even been suggested that "primitive" peoples in the process of becoming "civilized" need to personalize authority before they can reach this goal, just as children in a "civilized" society must do if they are to achieve social maturity. G. Freyre (1959: 50).

In all such cases the term primitive suggests the persistence of certain features over long periods, with the minimum of change. In this sense it has a "timeless" quality. People or societies so labeled are conceived as being, as it were, outside time. As physical organisms, it is conceded, such people are contemporary with ourselves: but this is an anomaly. They are in our time, but not of it because they belong to another world, the world of the past.

It is not, however, accepted unquestioningly even by all of those who continue to use it. Its vagueness has led to difficulties at times in the realm of "practical," nonacademic affairs.

A topical example, in Australia, is a proposal put forward by the Commonwealth Government as part of the 1959 Federal Budget. The relevant section was reported in the local Press (*The West Australian,* Perth, August 12, 1959): "Under proposed legislation, Australian aborigines, unless they are nomadic or primitive, will be eligible to receive pensions and maternity allowances on the same basis as other people." The Western Australian State department responsible for handling the scheme, once it had been legally finalized, immediately raised the question of "What does the word primitive really mean? How do we interpret it in actual situations?" They had some general idea of what was involved, but this was not enough to guide them in making decisions on individual cases. On the one hand it has been applied to semi-nomadic Aborigines with a minimum of outside contact. On the other it has been used in a blanket way for all people of Aboriginal descent, ranging from those who speak little or no English to part-Aborigines who closely resemble the Australian-Europeans among whom they live; some of the latter too have been labeled "primitive," though in this case the criteria are usually poor living conditions, carelessness about hygiene, and so on.

PERSISTENCE OF THE TERM

Among the intangibles sometimes associated with "civilization" are a broadening of conceptual horizons, an extension of the notion of humanity to include peoples outside one's own social environment, and tolerance or appreciation of other ways of living. A contrast is drawn between this and the closed society of the noncivilized world, with its arrogant rejection of "foreigners" and "foreign" customs, its jealously ethnocentric definition of humanity, its indifference to any moral claims except those of its own members. This distinction, however, is more of an ideal than a reality. The unit of membership in today's world is wider than it was, and so is the acknowledgement of humanity, but it is sometimes a grudging acknowledgement (cf. R. Berndt, 1959: 60–77). Although ethnocentrism in some degree is a feature of most societies, as part of the process by which social boundaries are maintained, the dominance of Western European nations in world affairs meant, also, the dominance of their particular varieties of ethnocentrism. The gulf between their living standards and values and those of the nonliterate people they encountered on other continents was perceived by most of them as far-reaching and almost unbridgeable—far more so than the differences between themselves and the settled peoples of Asia (India, China, and Japan for instance), with their textiles and other material equipment for living, and their tradition of literacy at least among the elite. The discovery of the nonliterate world may have reinforced the belief in an essential opposition between civilized city-dwellers and the nomads who threatened them from without, a belief deriving perhaps from man's early history in the Middle East and kept alive by the popular conception of the "Fall of Rome."

Much of what has been written about the people and societies of the nonliterate world is not easily explained except in terms of some such framework of assumptions. In the early days of contact with them, a certain insensitivity in such matters was only to be expected. Anthropology and empirical Sociology were barely developing. In spite of the wealth of literature dealing with Europe and its traditions, the people of that continent (as of others at that time) were not accustomed to a systematic, relatively objective scrutiny of their institutions and values. At the risk of oversimplifying, one might say that the position of Europe in the Nineteenth Century, not seriously or consistently challenged by the rest of the world, may well have supported the view that only the "lower" races, like the "lower" classes, were a proper subject for this kind of scrutiny. In reading some of the accounts of that period relating to nonliterate peoples, one cannot help being impressed by their lack of "self-awareness" in social-cultural terms. Herodotus-type reporting was still very much in vogue. Partly because of the very nature of their subject matter, the social sciences were slower in systematizing their methods and their handling of data than the natural and physical sciences; and the evolutionary framework built up after the Darwinian model, although later qualified to some extent, seems to have had in some quarters almost a petrifying effect.

Increasing sophistication in methodology and techniques, in the reporting and analysis of social and cultural events, have led anthropologists to be more cautious in accepting at face value the "facts" reported by early ethnographers, missionaries, and travelers. The assumptions underlying their reporting in the first place, and in the second place the use made of their statements by others, have not always been treated so critically. Many of them affirmed their belief that all contemporary peoples, however odd some of them might seem, shared a common humanity; but this was counterbalanced by the suggestion of an equally fundamental cleavage, between "civilized" and "noncivilized" man. The linkage here, where one was admitted, was often claimed to be so tenuous as to be almost negligible for most practical purposes. As reporting became less obviously subjective, similarities assumed increasing importance. The framework within which they were perceived, however, has remained very much as before.

One difficulty in social research is that "hunch" statements often take much the same form as generalizations which have undergone a certain amount of empirical testing, and on the face of it the two are not always easy to distinguish. Deductive systems built up with the help of a few "facts" may appear very much like carefully considered accounts of actual phenomena. Synthesizing statements designed to "map out" areas on which information is scanty are undeniably useful, as part of the two-way relationship involved, in theory-building, between empirical "facts" and idea-systems. The danger lies in treating them as more than tentative formulations, as statements of actuality rather than as hypotheses for testing.[2] The "halo" associated with some writers tends to perpetuate them as authoritative statements, especially but not only among persons within their particular fields of interest. The words of Marett and of Tylor, in the same or a slightly different form, have been repeated over the years in a variety of contexts as reliable empirical generalizations: ". . . in primitive society . . . , in a general way of speaking, no one dreams of breaking the social rules"; "Custom is king, nay tyrant, in primitive society" (R. R. Marett, 1912/1923: 182–3); "life in the uncivilized world is fettered at every turn by chains of custom" (E. B. Tylor, 1930: 137); "one might almost say that the savage sees himself so consistently through the eyes of the rest that he thinks of himself as "so-and-so" rather than as "I." . . . Self-consciousness, in the sense of self-criticsm based on an analysis of motive, is quite beyond his reach." [3]

The evolutionary scheme which classified people in such terms as "savage" and "barbarian" has had, indirectly, a far-reaching impact. Among present-day anthropologists the word "savage" is no longer in vogue, although Malinowski used it as

2. One example, among many, is Talcott Parsons' account of the "Kinship System of the Contemporary United States" (Talcott Parsons, 1949–1954: 177–96). In spite of the author's qualifying remarks, this is often treated as a firmly grounded empirical account of that subject.

In regard to this general point, especially where earlier writers were concerned, see Furfey's remarks on "the fallacy of speculation plus illustration" (P. H. Furfey, 1953: 174).

3. R. R. Marett (1927/1928: 77); see also p. 8, for a summing up of "savagery" as a state of "Intellectual confusion combined with physical discomfort."

one substitute for "primitive." Its appeal, however, has not been confined to the "popular" field. It appears as a descriptive label in a wide range of settings.[4]

Stereotypes of this sort seem to remain unaffected by the accumulation of data; or rather, such data are used selectively within the preferred conceptual setting. In extreme instances they are drawn upon to build up a self-supporting or self-perpetuating system, as in a recent study by Kelsen.[5] The earlier generalized assertions have a well-merited place in the history of anthropological methodology and theory, as provisional syntheses which served to order such material as was available, and so contributed to the refinement of conceptual frameworks and techniques. Their influence, however, has been more extensive and more pervasive than this. To take the case of a writer who made considerable use of ethnographic material, the interpretations of Lévy-Bruhl have had a tremendous influence on both academic and popular views about "primitive thought." Because his earlier works on this subject have been available for some time in English translations,[6] as his later reformulations are not,

4. S. Langer (1942/1954: *passim*. See index references, but especially pp. 83–4); J. Huizinga (1950/1955: e.g., 25); J. Dewey (1922/1950 and 1955/1956): e.g., 9–10; J. Paiget (1955: 26–7, in reference to "the language of savages, imbeciles and young children"; H. and H. A. Frankfort et al. (1949–1951: e.g., 12).

5. H. Kelsen (1946: e.g., 24.): "The savage cannot project his ego upon the external world because he has not yet discovered his ego." To support his thesis, on the development of the "idea of causality," he draws most heavily on earlier secondary accounts, of the type already mentioned. Cf. footnote 21 on page 271, where the reference is to D. Brinton (1897: 68), as saying of "the savage": "His language has no word meaning 'to die,' but only 'to be killed'."

6. See e.g., L. Lévy-Bruhl (1926), (1923). For an example of the author's bias in favor of a special category of "primitive thought," clouding his own assessment of what it involved, it is interesting to contrast two statements in this last volume: on the one hand the missionary's complaint (quoted on p. 23) that some South Africans refused to believe in God unless they could actually see him (they "only believe what they see"), on the other the author's comment on "primitives" (p. 31): "We cannot rid their minds of the belief that an infinite number of invisible beings and actions are actually real. Livingstone tells us that he often found wonder in the incontrovertible faith of the negroes of South Africa in beings whom they had never seen."

these "second thoughts" seem to be less widely known.[7] In them he rejected the term "prelogical," and acknowledged that there were common qualities inherent in all human thinking. For instance, that the "law of participation" was not confined to the "primitive" world. Nevertheless he continued to employ the dual characterization of "primitive" as contrasted with "ourselves," and inferred that only "primitive" man was a predominantly social being, unable to separate himself as a distinct individual person from his social and natural environment (Lévy-Bruhl, 1949: e.g., 247, 250–1).

Even studies designed to challenge or to controvert allegations of difference in kind between "primitive" and "civilized" mentality have tended to use the same schema of classification. Boas called his volume on this topic *The Mind of Primitive Man* (1938). Driberg gave his the title of *The Savage as He Really Is* (1929: cf. his reference on p. 2*n.* to the categories "primitive" and "savage"), evidently taking it for granted that there were human beings who could legitimately be categorized in this way. We no longer speak of the "ruder" peoples, as some earlier writers did, perhaps because the word has a different connotation in present-day English usage. Nor do we speak so readily of "lower" or "inferior" peoples, although "Stone Age" remains a popular label. The assumptions which underlie this kind of distinction, however, in other words the emotional as against the rational "reasons" for retaining it, are still with us.

PERSON, OR ENVIRONMENT?

A distinction occasionally drawn here has a partial parallel in the "nature-nurture," "heredity-versus-environment" controversy. It is suggested in the contrast between such titles as "The

---

7. L. Lévy-Bruhl (1949). He had already suggested earlier that "prelogical" thinking was not confined to "primitives": see e.g., Lévy-Bruhl (1931: 26).

Religion of the Primitives" or "The Mind of the Primitive" and "Primitive Religion," "Primitive Mentality" or "The Primitive Mind." The first two point to the social dimension, implying that there are specific persons or societies which can be so labeled. The others might be expected to focus on the cultural dimension, dealing with certain ways of thinking or behaving but not necessarily relating them to any specific social units.

(a) *Primitive Man* has become almost a mythical figure in the literature of most European languages, and not just in that part of it conventionally labeled "anthropological." He is a convenient peg on which to hang a variety of views, but this is variety only within a rather narrow range. At one extreme, in his "uncontaminated" state he is seen as a noble character,[8] exemplifying all or most of the virtues which less fortunate human beings have lost or been deprived of, in a word, Adam, before his "fall" and expulsion from the Garden of Eden. More often he is shown in a less favorable light. In this guise he often appears as a "marginal man" in the most fundamental sense, human only by definition or extension of definition. His intelligence or "mental ability" is limited, if not "childish." His world is not only restricted, but framed almost wholly in anthropomorphic terms. He is unable to differentiate between personal and non-personal, animate and inaminate, living and dead. He is incurious, content to accept without question the traditions handed on to him from the past, bound by custom, mystical, nonrational, uncritical, given to confused symbolizing, improvident, dirty, irresponsible, swayed by emotion and habit, incapable of discursive reasoning, and incapable too of achieving more than a limited development in his moral standards. The picture, even without further elaboration, is a depressing one.

Anthropologists today, on the whole, handle this label of "primitive man" more warily than they did a few years ago. Extravagant characterizations persist, but they are mainly in other fields, especially those in which there is a preference for the

8. For a recent example, where the word primitive is used "as a term of respect," see V. Elwin (1959: 15).

sweeping but confident impressions of the past rather than for the more sober accounts which are increasingly demanded within the profession.

(b) *"Primitive Culture"*: Even writers concerned with "the mind of primitive man," or "the primitive mind," mostly took the cultural setting into account as either a limiting or a determining factor. At the present time, however, it is generally accepted that there are no innate differences in "mental ability" or in "intelligence" on the basis of race—or, rather, that no such differences have been satisfactorily established. What is more, this issue is not a popular one in many parts of the world. To raise it is to question the creed that, in this respect at least, all but the physically brain-damaged are potentially equal; that hereditary handicaps, where such exist, do not take this form. The cross-cultural validity of tests designed to measure "intelligence" has been repeatedly challenged. At the same time the political implications of ranking or grading different peoples in these terms, and the possibility of manipulation to suit politically framed ends, have become more obtrusive, and more a matter of international concern.

This means that "primitiveness" is no longer regarded as an individual or personal attribute in quite the same way or to the same extent that it was. There is rather more emphasis on the flexibility and malleability of human material, rather less on rigidity and inherent inequalities. This is in line with the view adopted by a number of writers, in the last century as well as in this, that there is no such thing as "primitive man" or a "primitive mind," merely man living in a "primitive" culture or society. Responsibility for lack of "progress" is then attributed to absence of opportunity rather than to innate incapacity. Isolation, for instance, equivalent to lack of cross-fertilization of ideas, infrequent contact with other peoples who might have stimulated changes in various fields of living, has been seen as a major factor here. The "primitive isolate" (see e.g., R. Redfield, 1956: Chapter I) is contrasted with "folk" or "peasant" or urban societies.

The current trend is to speak less in terms of "primitive man" as such, and more in terms of the society or culture, or religion, or art which is said to be associated with him. The major problems involved, however, have not been allowed to lapse. They have merely been formulated in slightly different ways.

ASSESSMENT OF "DIFFERENCES"

In the study of social affairs, much use has been made of conceptual divisions as a means of understanding or explaining uniformity and diversity, conservatism and change. Usually they are framed in terms of two basic types, occasionally three: Gemeinschaft-Gesellschaft, or "Community-Association"; folk-urban, rural-urban, or folk-peasant-urban; mechanical solidarity-organic solidarity; sacred-secular; society of status-society of contract; traditional-value rational-purposive rational; tradition-directed inner-directed, other-directed. All these have some features in common, approaching the same broad set of problems from varying angles.

Two methodological points are relevant in connection with all of them. Firstly, there is the question of whether they are heuristic devices for exploring the empirical situation, or descriptive labels which correspond to certain aspects of that situation. Secondly, there is the question of what is involved in each case: a dichotomy or a continuum. Although opinions differ, in practical as well as in ideal terms the weighting does seem to be in favor of treating them as logical or fictional constructs, "ideal types" which abstract from the real situation in order to explore significant relations within it, but have no exact counterparts there. Recently there have been attempts to reconcile the two approaches and show that they are not mutually exclusive.

Freeman and Winch (1957: 461–66), for instance, holding that such "polar ideal types" are all concerned with the same "unidimensional phenomenon—societal complexity," selected as indicators of this eight characteristics, framed as "paired oppo-

sites." Because six of them could readily be arranged on a Gutt-man-type scale, they concluded that such constructs were empirically as well as heuristically applicable to social phenomena. (The remaining two characteristics they found to be unscalable. This is not surprising. One, concerned with exogamy, was phrased in terms of "range of incest tabus"; the other, concerned with criteria of mate selection, contrasted "beauty," alone, with "beauty" plus consideration of fertility and working ability.)

In another example [9] twenty "cultures" [10] listed in the Human Relations Area Files were taken, and scaled for "developmental ratings" in terms of "primitivism" and "modernity." The last two terms were used in a more or less arbitrary way, reinforced by the fact that eight of the cultures had been categorized by the Human Relations Area Files as "primitive," the other twelve as "more advanced." Of the 72 categories which the authors tried to scale in these terms, only 16 responded satisfactorily. Among those excluded as nonscalable were social stratification and communication, two features sometimes regarded as critical in discussions of this sort. Moreover, the authors point out (Rose and Willoughby, 1958: 481) that had they chosen a different source for their information on Indonesia, "a completely different cultural profile would obtain" for that country. One of their concluding comments is of direct interest to us here, in connection with the meanings attached to the term "primitive": noting Freeman and Winch's concern with "increasing complexity" they observe that they themselves, on the contrary, "were impressed by a narrow range of emphases among modern cultures that could well be regarded as a sort of simplicity."

There have been other endeavors, over the years, to find valid indexes for comparing and scaling human societies. Some,

9. E. Rose and G. Willoughby (1958: 476–90). Another recent effort to investigate "levels of development," in this case in an evolutionary framework, is afforded by R. Naroll (1956: 687–715).

10. Cf. discussion of "units of comparison" by I. Schapera (1953: 353–62). In Rose and Willoughby's study (1958), the "cultures" treated for their purpose as single units included such disparate entities as the Soviet Union, China, India, Copper Eskimo, northern Paiute, and Tasmania.

like these two, have employed statistical techniques. Others have proceeded more impressionistically, and others again have drawn on a wealth of more or less systematic empirical data. The basic criteria vary. Pater Schmidt's criterion of the presence or absence of a "high god" is well known. So are the evolutionary stages centering on means of subsistence; the criterion of industrialization, or use of machines, comes under the same broad heading. As has often been said, techniques and material equipment are perhaps the easiest of all cultural features to assess on a unilinear scale.[11] Another kind of demarcation was suggested by Kroeber (1952: 317–9),[12] who took as one criterion a social or ritual focus on physiological aspects, as against a diminishing social concern with them in "civilized" societies.

It is perhaps useful to have a shorthand label which summarizes a number of features not easily compressed under some more specific heading: smallness in scale; relative self-sufficiency; simple technology; stress on kinship, and on interpersonal relations; absence of a money economy and so on. But this usefulness is far outweighed by its disadvantages, particularly in regard to applying it in actual situations.

Conceptualizing the human world into two broad categories, however subdivided, is widespread in space and time, ranging from moiety systems to more fluid or ambitious formulations. Where the line of cleavage is taken as a shifting one, with societies or cultures classified in different ways for different purposes, or where a series of such lines is suggested, there is less likely to be a hardening of divisions between them and less danger of assumptions about essential or generic differences. To insist on a "difference in kind" (cf. F. S. C. Northrop, 1956: 1953) be-

11. For a recent comment see J. Cazeneuve (1959: 102–24). He suggests that in purely technical matters two stages of human development can be delineated, the first comprising those peoples "whose technical method is oriented toward direct acquisition and simple manufacture." Less specifically, he speaks of "societies which stagnate in archaism and those which open up to history."

See also R. Firth, in E. Evans-Pritchard et al. (1956: 15–16); S. F. Nadel (1956: e.g., 170).

12. Also D. Riesman (1954: 301–2).

tween one type of society and another, as a fundamental and far-reaching distinction which extends into all areas of living, is to speak in normative terms, to underestimate similarities for the sake of highlighting differences. It carries to an extreme the distinction often drawn (e.g., S. Tax, 1950; J. H. Rowe, 1950) between scientific and nonscientific (or "prescientific") thinking. A number of writers have warned against making too much of the assumed cleavage (e.g., F. Kaufmann, 1944: 33; A. Macbeath, 1952: 261; R. Merton, 1949–1957: 560), pointing out for instance that such a distinction is relevant *within* Western industrialized societies, and not just between them and others.

There is a tendency to play down this point, by asserting that the existence of "nonrational" features in Western-type societies has been adequately documented, and that this is already acknowledged as a matter of degree rather than of mutually exclusive alternatives. Such differences in degree are, however, often held to be so massive as to override similarities for comparative purposes. Nevertheless, the material dealt with by psychiatrists and psychoanalysts, for instance, and the field of religious belief as such (i.e., apart from considerations of complexity, or the logical structuring of that belief) indicate plainly enough that "rational," "scientific" thinking remains largely an ideal, more relevant to certain categories of persons (e.g., "scientists") and of culture (e.g., technology) than others. High-pressure advertising, most notably in North America, can draw on a wide range of technical and social scientific developments; but in this sphere, the consideration of how to "catch" and "hold" customers, one finds statements strikingly similar to those so often made about "primitive" man. We are told that most people ordinarily tend to think in "concrete" rather than "abstract" terms (cf. D. B. Lucas and S. H. Britt, 1950: 123) and are of only "average intelligence"; that "the average person" can take in only four or five points at a time (*ibid.*, 42); that the simplest and most direct appeals are the most likely to suceed (W. Albig, 1956: 81); that the language used must be fairly elementary if it is to be understood by the majority of readers (Lucas and Britt, 1950:

50–1, 426); that verbal language alone is less easily understood and remembered than pictures or objects (cf. J. Ruesch and W. Kees, 1956: 30, 102, 191; also L. Doob, 1948–1949: e.g., 445–7); that potential customers cannot be reached by persuasion through "logic and argument," but only through such means as constant repetition (M. Mayer, 1958: 43–4, 57), and the arousing of an emotional response.

Fluctuation between two extremes is exemplified too in the current dichotomy of "East" versus "West," which in this sense points less to spatial than to cultural or political or ideological positioning. Kipling's portentous assertion that the two could "never meet" is still echoed in some quarters today, more especially perhaps in sections of the mass media. Against it is the stand that cultural and other differences are entirely irrelevant, that "human nature is the same everywhere" regardless of superficial divergences. This duality, wavering between "mystical incomprehensibility" and almost intuitive understanding, is directly comparable to the kind of attitudes often expressed in regard to "primitive man."

CONCLUSION

On the one hand, then, there is growing recognition of the similarities and common features which can be found among all human beings, and all human societies. In one context this takes the form of acknowledging that the racial differences between them are of a minor sort, seen against the long period of man's evolution. On the other hand, there are perhaps equally strong and more obtrusive claims of essential dissimilarities. In the generic sphere, an extreme but deviant position was taken at least until quite recently by Ruggles Gates, who postulated differential development for the principal races of mankind (which he labels "species"). In the social and cultural sphere, it is illustrated in statements to the effect that "primitive" societies are so clearly unlike modern "civilized" societies that the study of the one can have no bearing on the other. Proponents of this view are in some respects following in the intellectual footsteps of earlier writers, who based their arguments on impressions rather than on sustained empirical analysis. But even these earlier writers were not as consistently dogmatic as they often appear to be.

Marett (1912–1923: 206), for instance, observed cautiously: "I think that we may easily exaggerate the differences in culture and, more especially, in religious insight and understanding that exist between the ruder peoples and ourselves." He went so far as to suggest that contact between peoples with different ways of living could lead to the "widening of horizons" often associated with "civilization," in a much broader sense than is sometimes understood by this phrase. In other words, he envisaged it in relation not just to the nonliterate peoples coming into contact with the Western world, but to that Western world itself. Although he prefaced his statement with the qualifications inevitable in his day and age, he nevertheless hoped that: "with fuller experience of the rich content of human intelligence, we shall become more tolerant of diversity, more inclined to widen our own tastes, as in matters of fine art, than to curtail those of our neighbors" (Marett, 1927–1928: 10).

Tolerance of diversity is of course, like conformity, a relative matter, varying in accordance with the type of behavior or subject matter involved and its social and political context. It is perhaps significant that Marett selected the case of "fine art" to illustrate his point, since this is often taken as a sphere remote from controversial issues in the political sense. This is not the place to discuss the question, which is relevant here only in relation to the contention that use of the term "primitive," as an heuristic tool or a descriptive label, encourages intolerance of diversity by taking certain differences as "given" but concealing the premises on which the assumption is based.

Despite the confusion attaching to it, some writers despair of any prospect of abolishing it. After pointing to its vagueness, its emotional aura, or the distortion of reality which it encourages with its connotation of crudeness and distance in time, they conclude that it is nevertheless too deeply ingrained in European thinking to be dislodged (cf. M. J. Herskovitz, 1940/1952: v–vi, 25–8; R. B. Inverarity in W. L. Thomas, ed., 1955: 376–77), or that there are no convenient labels to take its place (Macbeath, 1952: vi). Even Lévy-Bruhl (1923: 13) was not wholly in favor of it; and Tylor (1930: Vol. 1, 25) suggested that it should not be applied to the stone-age hunters whose remains were found at Abbeville or Torquay, because "this might be understood to mean that they were the first men who appeared on earth, or at least like them."

Substitutes which have been tried are all open to criticism on one ground or another. Some point openly to differences in time. "Stone-Age" man is a device for exciting popular interest, and like talking of "archaic" [13] or "old" societies or cultures is misleading where contemporary peoples are concerned. Preliterate, pre-agricultural, pre-industrial, imply staging on a fixed evolutionary scale. "Exotic," which has become quite popular lately, is reminiscent of the kind of appeal made by travel agencies. Terms like backward, naive, retarded, unsophisticated, stunted, or vegetative, even "Nature-folk," have a pejorative ring. Speaking of "arrested development" or even of undeveloped or underdeveloped societies implies much the same tone of superiority, even though the last two are often specifically applied to countries or means of production rather than to social or cultural phenomena. With "agrarian" societies we enter a more clearly neutral realm of discussion, but with the danger of slipping into the easy scheme of labeling peoples simply in accordance with such economic categories as "hunters," "food-collectors," and so on. Although "nonliterate" (M. J. Herskovits, 1948: 74–5) has obvious shortcomings, it does draw attention to the most im-

---

13. Cf. M. Eliade (1954: *passim*). He also uses the terms "premodern," "traditional," and "primitive"; under the latter heading he evidently includes Japan, which he refers to (p. 70) as having "an eccentric culture." See also K. E. Boulding (1956: 126, 49).

portant single criterion of difference as between one human culture and another, and one underlying the further demarcation hinging on the development of the machine. It has the advantage of being a neutral term, which at the same time indicates in a straightforward way what criterion is being employed.

"Primitive" has been employed as a contrast or a polar opposite to "Western," or "civilized," or "advanced," [14] or "historical," or "prosperous," or "modern," or even "contemporary." [15] Despite attempts to tighten up its application by the use of more systematic techniques than were available in the past, it carries an emotional aura of disparagement or negative evaluation which cannot so readily be eliminated. The plea which Dozier (1955: 187–202) has made for relinquishing it in favor of less "loaded" terms is both cogent and timely. The reasons he gives are twofold. There is the ethical question of applying it to peoples who may regard it as degrading and offensive. Equally important are the practical problems stemming from their reaction: on the one hand the political connotations in the present state of world affairs; on the other, on a smaller scale, their objections to being studied by members of a discipline, Anthropology, which is popularly associated with the study of "primitives"—often equated with "subject peoples," under "colonial" domination.[16]

It is true that some persons who continue to use the word primitive do so in a relatively neutral way, with no evidence of emotional prejudice. But this does not mitigate its impact on peoples who are aware of its evaluative bias, especially in pop-

14. For a fictional society which superficially appears to be "primitive" but is actually "advanced" see Chad Oliver (1955: "Rite of Passage"): in this case technological achievements are concealed, but nonetheless present.

15. Although both "modern" and "contemporary" are of course relative terms, it is interesting to notice the change in meaning associated with them in some contexts. Contemporary "means" existing at the same time, and modern is sometimes taken as a little ahead of this, in the sense of "new" or "up-to-the-minute." But in regard to the construction and sale of houses, at least in Australia, their meanings are sometimes reversed. "Modern" popularly refers to a house which is not quite up-to-date or only just abreast of the latest developments. In effect, it points to the past. "Contemporary" refers to a house design which is, if anything, in advance of current trends, often impressionistically assessed. It points, that is, to the future.

16. See G. J. Held (1953: 25).

ular or sensational interpretations. With the spread of literacy and the increase in political awareness on an international basis, people so designated are coming to realize something of what it involves, and to incorporate this new knowledge into their own assessment of other societies and cultures. The labels which people apply to one another acquire "meaning" in the course of being used; their "flavor" comes from the contexts with which they are associated. Even the word native, which in a general sense has no derogatory meaning, has come to be linked in some regions (India, for instance) with "colonial" rule, and to be rejected as a sign of unfavorable discrimination. Such changes in meaning are part of a familiar and universal process; but in the sensitive area of international relations, with dealings between peoples a more public and also a more large-scale affair than they used to be, it is as well to remember that the need for objectivity in social research is a matter of practical and not just of theoretical concern.

A third point, noted at the beginning of this paper, is worthy of attention too. Social scientists, including anthropologists, are concerned with the development of a body of theory relating to social and cultural phenomena generally, and not in a merely local or regional sense. The suggestion of crucial differences distinguishing one "kind" of society or one "kind" of people from another [17] has a direct bearing on this matter, limiting the range within which generalizations can be applied or tested, implying that there are no pan-human phenomena appropriate to such study.

Man is an evaluating animal, given to ordering his preferences on unilinear rather than on multilinear scales; but there is the danger that highlighting dramatic differences, by means of blanket-categories (or "weasel-words") such as "primitive," will obscure equally important similarities.

Two partly contradictory trends have gathered momentum

17. This is what Bierstedt implies: R. Bierstedt (1948: 22–30), and the attached "Comment" by C. Kluckhohn. See also R. Redfield (1953: e.g., Chapter VI, "The Transformation of Ethical Judgement").

in the past decade or so. On the one hand there is the tremendous increase in technological achievements, accompanied by growing emphasis on the natural and physical sciences. The current respect for developments in this sphere (earth satellites, for instance) and desire to surpass them, is widening the conceptual distance between nations capable of participating in this race and nonliterate or nonindustrialized peoples with poor material equipment and inadequate financial resources. The gap between specialists and nonspecialists within such nations is frequently deplored, but it is even more marked between them and others. On the other hand, the post-war period has seen the intensification of demands for "freedom," "equality of opportunities," "the rights of man" and so on. Among the foremost in this field have been non-European peoples, including some (for example in Africa) still occasionally labeled "primitive." Pressures toward differentiation among peoples on the basis of technological skills, then, are meeting other pressures rejecting such differentiation on the grounds of fundamental human equality. The clash is, so far, more incipient than actual, but it is likely to have far-reaching effects which cannot be confined to the sphere of technology.

LITERATURE

Albig, W. *Public Opinion* (rev. ed.), New York: McGraw-Hill (1956).

Berndt, C. H. "Social and Cultural Change in New Guinea: Communication and Views about 'Other People,'" *Sociologus,* Vol. 7, Part 1. (1957).

Berndt, R. M. "The Global Spread of Western Europeanization," *The Australian Quarterly,* Vol. XXXI, No. 1. 1959).

Bierstedt, R. "The Limitations of Anthropological Methods in Sociology." *American Journal of Sociology,* Vol. LIV, No. 1. (1948).

Boas, F. *The Mind of Primitive Man* (rev. ed.), New York: Macmillan (1938).

Boulding, K. E. *The Image,* Ann Arbor: University of Michigan Press (1956).

Brinton, D. *Religions of Primitive Peoples* (quoted by Kelsen 1946) (1897).

Cazeneuve, J. "Technical Methods in the Prehistoric Age," *Diogenes,* 27, (English ed.) (1959).

Cohen, M. R. and E. Nagel. *An Introduction to Logic and Scientific Method,* London: Routledge and Kegan Paul (1943–1949).

Dewey, J. *Human Nature and Conduct,* New York: Holt. Extract reprinted in Columbia University Contributions to Knowledge, *Man in Contemporary Society* (1955–1956), Vol. I (1922–1950).

Doob, L. *Public Opinion and Propaganda,* New York: Holt. (1948–1949).

Dozier, E. P. "The Concepts of 'Primitive' and 'Native' in Anthropology," in W. L. Thomas, ed., *Yearbook of Anthropology 1955,* New York, Wenner-Gren (1955).

Driberg, J. H. *The Savage as he Really is,* London: Routledge (1929).

Éliade, M. *The Myth of the Eternal Return,* New York: Pantheon Book, Bollingen Series XLVI (1954).

Elwin, V. "Tribal Life in other Planets," *The Illustrated Weekly of India,* LXXX, 28 (1959).

Firth, R. In E. Evans-Pritchard et al. *The Institutions of Primitive Society,* Oxford: Blackwell (1956).

Frankfort, H. and H. A. et al. *Before Philosophy. The Intellectual Adventure of Ancient Man,* Penguin Books (1949–1951).

Freeman, L. C. and R. F. Winch. "Societal Complexity: An Empirical Test of a Typology of Societies," *American Journal of Sociology,* Vol. LXII, No. 5 (1957).

Freyre, G. "Ethnic Groups and Culture," *Diogenes,* 25 (1959).

Fürer-Haimendorf, C. von. "Culture History and Cultural Development," in W. L. Thomas, ed. *Yearbook of Anthropology 1955,* New York: Wenner-Gren (1955).

Furfey, P. H. *The Scope and Method of Sociology,* New York: Harper (1953).

Good, H. *Language in History,* Penguin Books (1958).

Held, G. J. "Malaysia," in W. L. Thomas and A. M. Pikelis, eds. *International Directory of Anthropological Institutions,* New York: Wenner-Gren (1953).

Herskovits, M. *Economic Anthropology,* New York: Knopf (1940–1952).

——. *Man and His Works,* New York: Knopf (1948).

Huizinga, J. *Homo Ludens* (English trans.) Boston: Beacon Press (1950–1955).

Inverarity, R. B. "Primitive Art," in W. L. Thomas, ed., *Yearbook of Anthropology 1955,* New York: Wenner-Gren (1955).

Kaufmann, F. *Methodology of the Social Sciences,* New York: Oxford University Press (1944).

Kelsen, H. *Society and Nature,* London: Routledge and Kegan Paul (1946).

Kroeber, A. L. *The Nature of Culture,* Illinois: Chicago University Press (1952).

Langer, S. *Philosophy in a New Key. A Study in the Symbolism of Reason, Rite, and Art,* New York: Mentor Book ed. (1942–1954).

Lévy-Bruhl, L. *Primitive Mentality,* London: Allen and Unwin (1923).

——. *How Natives Think,* London: Allen and Unwin (1923).

——. *La Mentalité Primitive,* Oxford: H. Spencer Lecture (1931).

——. *Les carnets de Lucien Lévy-Bruhl,* Preface de Maurice Leenhardt, Paris: Presses Universitaires de France (1949).

Lucas, D. B. and S. H. Britt. *Advertising Psychology and Research,* New York: McGraw-Hill (1950).

Macbeath, A. *Experiments in Living,* London: Macmillan (1952).

Marett, R. R. *Anthropology,* London: Williams and Norgate (1912/1923).

——. *Man in the Making. An Introduction to Anthropology,* London: Benn (1927–1928).

Mayer, M. *Madison Avenue, U.S.A. The Inside Story of American Advertising,* London: The Bodley Head (1958).

Merton, R. *Social Theory and Social Structure,* New York: Free Press (1949–1957).

Nadel, S. F. "Understanding Primitive Peoples," *Oceania,* Vol. XXVI, No. 3 (1956).

Naroll, R. "A Preliminary Index of Social Development," *American Anthropologist,* Vol. 58, No. 4 (1956).

Northrop, F. S. C. "Man's Relation to the Earth in its Bearing on his Aesthetic, Ethical and Legal Values," in W. L. Thomas, ed. *Man's Role in Changing the Face of the Earth,* New York: Wenner-Gren (1956).

Oliver, C. *Another Kind,* New York: Ballantine Books (1955).

Parsons, T. *Essays in Sociological Theory,* New York: Free Press (1949–1954).

Piaget, J. *The Language and Thought of the Child,* New York: Noonday Press, Meridian Books ed. (1955).

Redfield, R. *The Primitive World and Its Transformations,* Ithaca: Cornell University Press (1953).

———. *Peasant Society and Culture,* Chicago: University of Chicago Press (1956).

Riesman, D. Review of B. Bettelheim, *Puberty Rites and the Envious Male,* in *Psychiatry,* Vol. 17, No. 3 (1954).

Rose, E. and G. Willoughby. "Cultural Profiles and Emphases," *American Journal of Sociology,* Vol. LXIII, No. 5 (1958).

Rowe, J. H. "Thoughts on Knowledge and Ignorance," *Kroeber Anthropological Society Papers,* No. 2, Berkeley (1950).

Ruesch, J. and W. Kees. *Non Verbal Communication,* Berkeley: University of California Press (1956).

Schapera, I. "Some Comments on Comparative Method in Social Anthropology," *American Anthropologist,* Vol. 55, No. 3 (1953).

Tax, S. "Animistic and Rational Thought," *Kroeber Anthropological Society Papers,* No. 2, Berkeley (1950).

Tylor, E. B. *Anthropology. An Introduction to the Study of Man and Civilization,* London: Watts (Thinkers' Library) (1930).

Washburn, S. L. "Thinking about Race," reprinted in E. A. Hoebel, J. D. Jennings and E. R. Smith, *Readings in Anthropology,* New York: McGraw-Hill (1955).

FRANCIS L. K. HSU

Rethinking the
Concept "Primitive"

IF THERE is one term which is consistently identified
with anthropology it is "primitive," an adjective used to describe
the data found by anthropologists all over the world: primitive
science, primitive religion, primitive economics, primitive mentality, primitive peoples, primitive societies and cultures. According to Webster, the term "primitive" is defined as "pertaining to
the beginning or origin or to early times, or characterized by the
style, simplicity, rudeness, etc., of early times; old-fashioned, as,
primitive tools." There is no doubt that the idea of being "inferior" was what E. B. Tylor, the first major anthropologist in

Reprinted from Current Anthropology, *June 1964, Vol. 179, pp. 169–178.*

the world, had in mind when he spoke of the three stages of cultural evolution in his *Anthropology* (1881), first published just ten years after his *Primitive Culture* (1871): (1) a "savage" stage, characterized by subsistence on wild plants and animals, and the utilization of stone age implements; (2) a "barbaric" stage characterized by agriculture, metal work, and some form of community life in villages and towns; and (3) a "civilized" stage which began when men acquired the art of writing (Tylor 1881:1–18).

Alexander Goldenweiser has perhaps given the most concise and explicit definition of the term "primitive" in his *Early Civilization* (1922:117–18). Although he speaks of "primitive" as being small, isolated, etc., there seems to be no doubt that he also equates it with "inferior." For in a later work, *Anthropology: An Introduction to Primitive Culture* (1937), he expresses himself as follows:

People in general, and primitives in particular, do not think or analyze their culture—they live it. It never occurs to them to synthesize what they live or reduce it to a common denominator, as it were.

Or again:

A sad commentary on the psychological limits of diffusion is presented by the disheartening failure of White civilization to either leave primitives alone or pull them *up* to its own level (1937:47 and 490) (Italics mine).

Over the years the connotation of inferiority and other difficulties have often troubled many scholars. For this reason there have been attempts at reform along two lines. On the one hand some scholars have suggested other kinds of dichotomies to take the place of the primitive-civilized one. Sapir's (1925) Genuine versus Spurious cultures as well as Redfield's (1941) Folk-Urban continuum are notable examples of this trend.

Herskovits explicitly suggested substituting the term "non-literate" for the term "primitive," the first such need eloquently voiced. After showing that all those called "primitives" or "savages" are much more diverse in their cultural characteristics than the groups which are called "civilized," he says:

> In anthropological works, the words "primitive" or "savage"—the latter being used mainly as a synonym for "primitive" by English writers—do not have the connotation they possess in such a work as Toynbee's, or in other nonanthropological writings. As for the word "barbaric," most anthropologists do not employ it at all. Anthropologists merely use the word "primitive" or "savage" to denote peoples outside the stream of Euro-American culture, who do not possess written languages. By reiterating this meaning, it was hoped that all other connotations might be sloughed off, and that it would no longer convey such meanings as simple, or naive, or serve as a catch-all to describe, except in the single matter of absence of writing, such differing civilizations as those of the Siberian reindeer herders or the Luanda empire of the Congo (1958:75).

He then goes on to suggest the use of the term "nonliterate" for "primitive" because the former is "colorless, conveys its meaning unambiguously, and is readily applicable to the data it seeks to delimit, [and] is thus to be preferred to all the other terms we have considered" (1948:75).

On the other hand, some scholars are determined to search for greater precision in the use of the term. In this regard Radin (1953) has contributed greatly, but lately Stanley Diamond (1963) has done more than others in finding what he calls "a positive definition" of the term primitive by observing that:

> all primitive peoples are marginal to the mainstream of modern history, primarily because of "accidents" of habitat. In the sense already noted, contemporary primitives can be roughly perceived as our contemporary, pre-civilized ancestors (Diamond 1963:79).

Diamond then proceeds to enumerate ten characteristics of the "primitive," from "communalistic economic base" to the role of "ritual drama" as "a culturally comprehensive vehicle for group and individual expression at critical junctures in the social round or personal life cycle. . . ." The over-all purpose of Diamond's redefinition is perhaps indicated by his tenth characteristic which is: ". . . if the fulfillment and delineation of the human person within a social, natural, and supernatural (self-transcendent) setting, is a universally valid measure for the evaluation of culture, primitive societies are our primitive superiors," and by his plea that "we cannot abandon the primitive; we can only outgrow it by letting it grow within us" (Diamond 1963:103 and 111).

A few years ago Sol Tax sounded the bugle against use of the term "primitive" (1960:441). His objections to it were supported by a "Memorandum on the Use of *Primitive*" by a research assistant Lois Mednick (1960:441–45) which shows how the term has been used by a variety of scholars, primarily anthropologists. The many enthusiastic responses to these two pieces (CA 2:396–97 and 3:206) reflect fairly the above-mentioned division of opinion in our profession today. Some, including Sol Tax himself, are opposed to its continuation except to "men who have been extinct since the late Pleistocene," while a majority seem to prefer either redefining it or substituting it with some other terms such as "primary," "peripheral," "ethnological," or even "anthropological."

The thesis of the present paper is that a dichotomy of the world's peoples and cultures into two varieties, no matter under what disguise, presents large difficulties. In particular the primitive-civilized dichotomy is replete with undesirable psychological connotations and scientific consequences which cannot be avoided by redefinition even of the most positive kind. Furthermore, by his plea that we not "abandon" the primitive but let it "grow within us," Diamond has distinctly left the path of science and entered the door of charity, for the problem is neither one of turning the tables (by stressing that the primitives are our "superiors") nor of permitting or wishing the nurture of the primitive in us.

Lois Mednick's "Memorandum on the Use of *Primitive*" (1960) referred to before already provides us with an excellent panorama of the "ambiguous and inconsistent" way in which the term "primitive" is used. But in order to ascertain the extent to which this state of affairs exists in anthropological works of a general nature, especially introductory texts, Nancy Schmidt, a research assistant, and I examined a total of thirty books published in the last ten years (except for Murdock 1949, Evans-Pritchard 1951, Kroeber 1952 and Levy 1952).

The following table summarizes the results:

THE USE OF THE TERM "PRIMITIVE" IN TEXTS ON ANTHROPOLOGY (IN THE ENGLISH LANGUAGE BUT EXCLUDING PHYSICAL ANTHROPOLOGY) PUBLISHED IN THE YEARS 1953–63.

Explanation of Table: When the word "primitive" is italicized, the author has used it himself; whereas, when it is not italicized, he has used it in reference to the way it has been used by someone else. Most of the definitions following the word "primitive" are paraphrases, or else were obtained from the general context in which the word appears. Only when the definitions appear in quotation marks are they the authors' exact definitions. The page numbers indicate the pages on which the meaning of the word "primitive" is found; they do not in all cases correspond to the pages on which the word "primitive" itself appears. There is no correlation between the number of pages following a category and the frequency with which the word "primitive" occurs in the text. The word that the author uses the most or prefers is marked with an asterisk (*); or when the word "primitive" is rarely used, this is noted.

(Beals and Hoijer 1959)
nonliterate peoples: those studied by ethnologists, formerly called primitives (2)
primitive people: calendars of (2)
primitive culture: subject matter of ethnologists (2), in references to Tylor's work (15–16)
primitive art: art forms of nonliterate people (598–99)

(Bohannan 1963)
*most often uses *folk* (11, 51, 284, 263)
primitive peoples: those into whose languages the Bible was translated (42 ff.), those whose political systems are studied by anthropologists, in reference to Lévy-Bruhl's comparisons of mentality (321, 322)
primitive society: in reference to Lowie's theory of nonkinship groups (147–48), in reference to Tylor's theory of magic (319)
primitive economics: economic analyses by anthropologists (233)

"primitive" warfare: as conducted by warriors in contest, not by whole
societies (305)
primitive culture: in discussing works of Tylor and other early anthropologists (311)
primitive man: in reference to Lévy-Bruhl's and others' works on mentality (321)
primitive religion: rejects the traditional study of animatism, fetishism,
and totemism (313 ff.)

(Coon 1962)
primitive culture: culture of men before modern times (appears in title,
definition based on context, not specific citation)
primitive people (of today): simple, not civilized (1)
primitive arts: skills of living primitive peoples (93 ff.)
*primitive society: small in scale in terms of numbers, territory, and social
contacts, have simple technology and little specialization of social
functions, often have no literature (8) used throughout book,
anthropological concern with (8–10), manner of studying (15–
18), philosopher's consideration of (25 ff.), study of religion in
(90)
*primitive peoples: institutions of (39), role of ethnologist in studying
(48 ff.), functional study of (55)
primitive science ⎱
primitive art ⎰ specialized studies
primitive technology of anthropology (14)
primitive family: in reference to theories of Bachofen (29)
primitive institutions: not related to mentality (35)
primitive society: Durkheim's contribution to theories of (51 ff.)
primitive man: speculations about (65 ff.)
primitive languages: need for anthropologists to learn (79–80)

(Firth 1956)
*primitive: used extensively in the following ways:
primitive people: those who retain tribal ways of life, distinguished from
peasants, those in simple societies, savage tribes (39)
primitive communities: have comparatively simple material equipment
that is not integrated into industrial organization (71), lack wide
intercommunication with each other (72), not part of world
market (72)
primitive economics: study of technology, arts and crafts, and basic principles that control the work and wealth of "native societies" (72)
primitive group: as distinguished from purely individual activity (73)

primitive transaction: "the equivalent of buying and selling on a non-price level" (80)

primitive distributive system: gives reward for social advantages of participating in production (81)

primitive money: objects other than coins, with a relatively standard value, used in exchange (92)

primitive society
primitive culture } used as synonym for primitive people (93, 97, 47)
primitive tribe

primitive behavior: as regulated by custom (132)

primitive law: rules expected to be obeyed, and normally kept through some means for insuring obedience (137)

primitive thinking: used in discussion of Lévy-Bruhl's theory (152)

primitive life: in reference to the role of dreams in lives of primitive people (174)

primitive religion: beliefs of (171 ff.), rites of (182–85)

(Gleason 1961)
not used, distinctions between written and unwritten languages, the specific language referred to is usually named

(Goldschmidt 1959)
*primitives: contrast to moderns (223, 224), comparative not absolute term (223, 224), uses by anthropologists (224), circumlocutions for (223, 224), in reference to historical theories (43)

primitive man: in reference to work of Radin (223)

primitive people: means of social control among (153), in reference to works of Herskovits (223)

primitive cultures: in reference to Boas' works (39)

primitive state systems: discussion of Steward's criteria (208)

living primitives: in reference to data collecting (43), evolution (153)

primitive level of social systems: contrasted to civilized systems (155–57)

primitive conditions: of social forms (153)

(Goldschmidt 1960)
[Analysis only of articles by Goldschmidt]
*primitive: contrasted to modern, all people outside Western civilization, is a comparative, not absolute, term, "preliterate" not an adequate term (664, 665)

primitive people: those with technology fundamentally like those of prehistoric times (122, 123, 125)

primitive: contrasted to civilized (172)

primitive society: division of labor in (173), affiliations in (268, 275), child-training practices in (177)

primitive people: residence patterns of (223), spatial groupings of (275, 419), clans in (225, 277), status relations among (317), government an extension of kinship (226 ff.), religion among 475 ff.), moral rules of (529 ff.), private property of (545)

primitive level: of family development (277, 279, 280)

primitive tribes: lack of government in (368), comparative ethics of (544 ff.)

primitive man: religious rituals of (476 ff.)

primitive art: contrasted to European art (586)

(Hawkes 1954)

primitive: contrasted to civilized (17, 103), used very seldom, the book is historical and specific names are usually used

(Herskovits 1955)

*nonliterate used throughout book, not defined, but a substitute for primitive (123, 363, 522, 367–68)

primitive culture: as opposed to civilized (358, 359), contrasted to folk culture (521), synonym for primeval (435), synonym for savagery and barbarism (360), problem of defining (360, 362), rejection of term (363)

primitive people: simple people (360), those traditionally studied by anthropology (368–69)

primitive society: in discussing *Kulturkreis* (464, 465)

primitive man: synonym for contemporary ancestor (358, 359), in discussing theories of culture change (448 ff.), in reference to works of Tylor and Morgan (434–36)

(Hill 1958)

primitive not used: refers to *speech communities* (4)

(Hockett 1958)

not used: occasional reference to savages (4) and aboriginals or aboriginal times (8, 479)

(Hoebel 1960)

*primitive: preliterate or non-literate (defined 657), used throughout book in all contexts

primitive man: *use of caves by* (202), husband-wife relations of (334–36), weapons of (512), religion of (526 ff.)

primitives: hunting techniques of (185), traps used by (202), marriage among (301 ff.), kin terms of (357 ff.), divorce among (314 ff.), polygyny among (325)

primitive peoples: domestic animals of (196), houses of (206), stone tools of (217), effect of culture contact on (590), status among (357), stock ownership of (445)

primitive communism: in reference to the theories of Morgan (201)

primitive art: art of primitive peoples, not crude art (253 ff.)

primitive society: marriage in (301 ff.), women's groups in (402), classes in (415 ff.), slavery in (425 ff.)

primitive world: role of the aged in (391–92), inheritance in (460)

primitive law: contrast to European (468–69), systems of (471 ff.)

primitive warfare: tactical operations of (511–12)

primitive mythology: stable core of (539)

(Honigmann 1959)

* most often uses *culture* without any adjectives (25)

primitive ancestors: reference to concern of early anthropologists (23)

primitive stage of human existence: reference to the fallacy of such labels (24)

primitive cultures: isolated ways of life investigated by anthropologists traditionally (23 ff.)

primitives: as used by Lévy-Bruhl (679)

(Honigmann 1963)

*"*small scale*" used throughout book (25, 28, 94, 202)

primitives: in reference to current disuse of the term (21)

(Keesing 1958)

primitive, *nonliterate, *simpler: distinguishable from civilization, not survivals from an earlier time (45–46)

primitive societies: most today are nearly peasant societies or well on the way (46), in reference to evolutionary theories (139 ff.), in reference to psychic unity of mankind and comparative method (141, 142), in reference to historicalism and *kulturkreise* (146), in reference to works of Durkheim (153), organization of life cycle in (247 ff.)

primitive law: in reference to theories about noncodified law systems (305–6)

primitive culture: in reference to theories of religion (325 ff.)

primitive science: in reference to Frazer (332)

primitive arts: difference from civilized arts (348)

(Kroeber 1952)

The term "primitive" is not used much. In the 50 essays, the word appears in the title of 1; most essays are of a general theoretical nature.

primitive culture: contrasted to European culture (47, 49), in reference to works of Tylor et al. (19 ff., 144 ff.), in reference to work of Roheim and Freud (303, 304)

primitives: contrasted to civilized (219 ff.), in reference to theories of Morgan (169, 170), psychoses of (310 ff.)

primitive life: social organization of simple peoples (219 ff.)

folk culture: occasionally used as synonym for primitive (310)

primitive man: less civilized peoples with important kinship organization (219, 224)

(Levy 1952)

*usually uses *society or social system* (6 ff., 18 ff., 111 ff.), contrast between industrialized and *nonindustrialized societies* (97), contrast between *traditional* and modern societies (131, 320 ff.), "primitive," *nonliterate* compared to modern societies (132), a self-sufficient social system (132), contrast between "simple" and modern societies (166)

"primitive" society: in reference to prerational nature of (376)

(Linton 1955)

*usually uses culture prefixed by a place name (African culture) (431) or occupation (dairying culture) (438)

primitive languages: unwritten languages (9)

primitive cultures: in reference to theories of arrested development (41)

primitive women: those who have simple cultures, like those in the Stone Age (71)

modern "primitives": people with simple culture, esp. simple tools (84)

primitive pattern of life: in reference to Neolithic (174)

"primitive" areas: those inhabited by simple people, esp. in reference to Polynesia (183)

primitive group: simple tribes, esp. reference to Indian influence in Southeast Asia (187)

primitive art: an inaccurate designation when applied to African sculpture (438)

primitive man: prehistoric man (593)

(Mead and Calas 1953)

Mead (1953) savages, nonliterate (xvii ff.)

primitive peoples: savages (xix ff.)

Nicholas Calas (1953) unknown peoples (xxvi ff.)

Engels (1884) barbarians: as opposed to civilization (14–15)

T. Reik (1919) *primitive peoples:* those who practice the couvade (26)

E. Crawley (1902) *primitive culture* ⎫ characterized by homogeneity
              primitive society ⎭ (29–30)

R. Marett (1911) *primitive* [appears in title, but not defined (32)]

L. Lévy-Bruhl *primitives:* those who regard artificial likenesses as real
         (33), natives (34), those who regard their names as concrete,
         real, and sometimes sacred (37), uncivilized races (41)

primitive peoples: in reference to Hill Tout's work on Salish (38)

E. B. Tylor (1871) *primitive culture:* that of tribes "low on the scale of
         humanity" (49)

savages (primitives): distinguished from civilized men (50–51)

D. Lee (1949) *primitive society:* those among whom being is identical
         with the objects (53 ff.) (selection refers to Trobriands)

R. Benedict (1932) *primitive peoples* ⎫ homogeneous groups as differ-
              primitive tribes ⎬ entiated from modern statified
                                  ⎭ groups (80 ff.)

P. Radin (1927) *primitive man:* one endowed with overpowering sense
         of reality (258)

primitive community: where everyday facts have religious and ritual
         covering (259)

G. T. Emmons (1911) *primitive people:* those who endow all nature
         with spirit life.

(Murdock 1959)

*usually uses *society* or *social unit* without adjectives, makes compari-
         sons by saying "our society—other societies" (56)

primitive society: (occasional use, not defined) in reference to adjustment
         of co-wives (31)

primitive man: in reference to 19th century theories of evolution (58)

primitive times: in reference to theory of matriliny (185)

(Nadel 1957)

primitive society: (not used often, not defined, but apparently synonym
         for tribal), different number of roles in (61 ff.), linkage of roles
         in (65 ff.), coherence of role systems in (72 ff.), current work
         of anthropologists in (146)

(Piddington 1950–1957)

Vol. 1

Primitive is used with great frequency, but only a few examples are
         given for each category

primitive communities: usually literate, have small social groups, low level of technical achievement, social relations based on kinship most important, lack of economic specialization, but not sharply divided from civilized communities (5), social status in (189), political authority in (190), voluntary associations in (216), land tenure in (287)

primitive culture: "material and spiritual or social" culture of primitive communities (14), need for functional analysis of (45), discussion of theoretical approaches to (14–17), emphasis on variety of (31–33), past and present study of (26), in Asia (60), in India (65), in Pacific (71)

primitive society: groups with primitive culture (272), production in (267), economic exchange in (271), idea of property in (282), social structure of (107 ff.), place of women in (169 ff.), initiation ceremonies in (175), education in (179 ff.), law and customs in (319 ff.), hunger and famine in (257), belief in immortality in (375), taboos in (379)

primitive people: members of primitive societies, cultures and communities (11), descent systems of (151), local groups among (167), totemic groups of (200), mythology of (370)

primitive communism: all property belongs to the community (270–71), reference to use by Engel's (267), fallacy of the term's application (287), questionnaire to test peoples' view of its meaning (416–19)

primitive economics: material production of primitive societies (266 ff.), applicability of modern economic concepts to (267)

primitive education: conditions of (187)

primitive law: the whole normative system of a primitive community (351), compared to modern law (355)

primitive promiscuity: in reference to Engel's theory of social development (315)

primitive religion: magico-religious institutions of primitives (356), ethical implications of (381)

primitive man: in reference to idea of the noble savage (393)

Vol. 2

primitive art: artistic embellishment of objects with social utility or significance (516), meaning associated with (518), difference from our own (520)

primitive trade: examples of (459)

primitive ceremonial: importance of feasting and food distribution in (470)

primitive technology: reasons for primitiveness (485), why advance
    occurs (486)

(Radcliffe-Brown 1952)
*primitive society: living, nonliterate societies that can be studied only
    by direct observation and contact, have no historical records, con-
    trasted to advanced (used very frequently), preliterate (2, 3, 18,
    25)
primitive people: those with very important kinship relations (15, 2, 153)
primitive myth and ritual: in reference to totemism (130)
primitive times: in reference to Robertson Smith's religious theories
    (156)
primitive law: social control by application of force among primitives
    (212 ff.)

(Radcliffe-Brown 1957)
*usually uses *society* or *human society*
primitive people: early distinctions between primitive and civilized (33–
    34)
savage tribes: territorially delimited groups studied by anthropologists
    (60)
"primitive": use of words in typing societies (74 ff.)
primitive society: simple society, gift giving in (114 ff.), ritual pollution
    in (135)

(Radin 1953)
*primitive civilization: aboriginal civilization in which is respect for the
    individual, amazing degree of political and social organization,
    and strong concept of personal security (ix ff., 184 ff., 260 ff.,
    286)
*primitive: and aboriginal are used interchangeably throughout the book
    (4, 5), contrasted to civilization (7, 8)
primitive man (ix): must be studied in terms of positive achievements
    (x), life permeated by magic and religion (26), analysis of Ego
    by (57), knowledge of legal principle (114 ff.), philosophizing
    of (233)
primitive people: have efficient tools (32), the thinker among (43),
    economic structure of (105 ff.), anti-social behavior of (120),
    puberty ceremonies of (168–69)
primitive man: in reference to theories of Lévy-Bruhl (49)
primitive religion (103–4)

primitive communities: in reference to Malinowski's theory of reciprocity
(111)
primitive economics: characterized by intricate transfers (117)
primitive tribes: inadequate description of religion of (138), localized
authority among (232)
primitive societies: change in (192), real authority in (245)
primitive tribal lore: in reference to theory of Jung (309)

(Thompson 1961)
*mankind: all men, all human phenomena of all times and places (xxvi),
anthropological study of (xxiii ff.) used throughout book
nonliterate people ⎫
primitive culture ⎭ in reference to ethnographic survey (5–6)
primitive economics: in reference to early theories (27–28)
aboriginal community: synonym for primitive or nonliterate (112 ff.),
more frequently uses *human community* (126, 28 ff., 156 ff.)
primitive peoples: in reference to works of Mead (137)
primitive and folk communities: contrasted to civilized communities
(201 ff.)

(Titiev 1959)
*primitive peoples: aim of anthropologists to understand their customs (19), distinguished from nonprimitive (used throughout
book)
*primitive society: in reference to Neolithic society (209), in reference
to societies before acculturation (387), relatively isolated group
of racially similar people that work together for common goals,
usually has relatively uniform language and religion, usually
nonliterate (208–9) (used throughout book)
primitive customs ⎫ use of analogies to in archaeological
primitive religions ⎭ interpretation (118, 131)
primitive community: members of a primitive society living in one area
(208, 333)
primitive world: all primitive societies (332)
primitive kinship: prime importance of in understanding (283–85)
primitive law: used as Hoebel does (208 ff.)
primitive religion: different definitions and functions (333 ff.)
primitive folk: nonliterate folk (272)
primitive personage: in reference to seeking supernatural aid (339 ff.)

(Titiev 1963)
primitive: "nonliterate, . . . relatively small in numbers, relatively iso-

lated, comparatively homogeneous in culture, and racially and linguistically alike" (386)

primitive society: preliterates studied by archaeologists (5), desire for children in (442), plural marriage in (454), mother-in-law taboo in (458), cross-cousin marriage in (461), institutionalized friendship in (472), classificatory terms in (478), model for national character study (498), sacred songs in (548), connection between dancing and verbal arts in (557)

primitive contemporaries: groups studied by early anthropologists (3)

primitives: cultures used for archaeological analogy (196)

primitive people: interest of anthropologists in (387), differentiation among religions in (463), linguists' concern with (539), art of (553–554), games of (569)

primitive tribe
primitive life } interests of anthropologists in (387)

primitive group: relation of subsistence to religion in (278), ethnologists' contact with (389), kinship in (458)

primitive folk: difficulty in making contact with (388), accumulated knowledge of (516)

primitive culture: personal reports of (391)

primitive law: as Hoebel uses it (464 ff.)

primitive religion: sociocultural aspects of (501 ff.)

primitive man: beliefs in the supernatural of (511), knowledge of the seasons among (525)

primitive customs: study of in relation to our own mores (576)

(White 1954)

*primitive man: native societies, uncivilized, nonurban, savages (10–11) (used throughout), anthropological study of small, compact groups of (13)

primitive man: size of communities compared to those of man-apes (47), synonym for early man (48)

primitive tribesman: senses of (83)

primitive mind: theories of (83 ff.)

primitive community: characteristics of (94–95), stages in development of (118 ff.)

primitive world: life in early times before there were many inventions (101–2)

primitive people: cultural environment of (108)

primitive economy: those without money and price system (119 ff.)

primitive life: communistic traits of (125 ff.)

primitive population ⎫
primitive family   ⎬ traits of (129 ff.)

primitive marriage   ⎫
primitive social structure ⎬ kinds of (134 ff.)

It is clear from this table that the term "primitive" enjoys wide currency in introductory and general works and the meanings attached to it are as "ambiguous and inconsistent" as Lois Mednick found them to be in her briefer survey. In general the following meanings are attached to it:

nonliterate, lower, simple, simple tools, not civilized, pertaining to technology fundamentally like that of prehistoric times, small-scale, isolated, arrested in development, folk, all peoples outside western civilization, less civilized, lacking in historical records, low level of technical achievement, pertaining to societies in which social relations are based primarily on kinship, distinguished from nonprimitive, aboriginal, nonindustrialized, savage, contrasted to civilized, law contrasted to European system, lacking in literature, relatively homogeneous, nonurban and tribal, general lack of abstract time reckoning, below the general level of the state of civilization, with all pervasive religion, moneyless, peasant, traditional, lack of economic specialization, one endowed with over-powering sense of reality, where everyday facts have religious and ritual covering, those who endow all nature with spirit life, civilization with respect for the individual, amazing degree of political and social organization, strong concept of personal security, isolated, society in which cooperation for common goals frequent, language and religion uniform, all human phenomena of all times and places.

Several things emerge from this tabulation. First, although a few speak of salutary characteristics like "strong concept of personal security," or "frequent cooperation for common goals," or of neutral ones like "social relations . . . based primarily on kinship," or "relatively homogeneous," a majority give the term the meanings of simpleness, antiquity, undesirableness, and undisguised inferiority.

Second, many of the meanings attached are not only multifarious and uncoordinated, but generally slapdash and conflicting.

Third, some seem to use the term through force of habit as

when Thompson (1961) refers to all men and all human phenomena of all times and places which she deals with in her book as "primitive."

Fourth, even though some do not use the term "primitive" for categorizing their own data, they make no attempt to evaluate its use in other works which they quote or to which they refer.

Lastly, in particular the use of the term "primitive" does not seem to have any significant intellectual or analytic advantage. It cannot be shown from these surveys how the use of the term has given us any noticeable advantages in theory-building. On the contrary, I think it can be shown that its continued use may be an effective bottleneck against further advances in our discipline.

In the science of man, as in all sciences, terms or concepts are essentially means of classifying data or points of reference around which the data may be organized so as to achieve an empirically descriptive picture to enable one to grope for some theoretically based insights into the data. The major criterion for the introduction or the continuance of a concept should be, therefore, that it has empirical validity (e.g., when we employ terms to designate categories used by the natives themselves) or theoretical utility (e.g., when we describe one system of economy as characterized by barter and another by money, using this contrast to reveal the different extents to which kinship or other ties affect economic transactions). My contention is that the concept "primitive," as it has been and is used in a majority of anthropological works, has neither empirical validity nor theoretical utility, and that this is why our use of this term has been so miscellaneous and intellectually unproductive.

The concept of "primitive" is scientifically applicable to prehistorical phenomena, and was functional during the early stages of development of our science, but it is now like a worn out old shoe, to which we are still attached seemingly for sentimental reasons or from sheer inertia, but which will do no more for us than clutter up our anthropological closet and catch dust. There is no longer an empirically or theoretically defensible ground for dichotomizing all cultures or societies into the two broad categories "primitive" and "civilized."

First let us look at the empirical picture. There are small societies that are very highly urbanized in Europe. There are predominantly rural societies of enormous scale such as China. The kinship system of the Americans of the highly complex industrialized society of the United States is extremely simple but the kinship system of the Australian aborigines, whose main tools for production are the digging sticks and the boomerang, must be rated in general among the most complex in the world. There are societies with highly organized political structures such as that of Uganda and Dahomey which share the lack of written language with others with no trace of centralized government whatsoever such as those of various branches of Eskimos or Kaska Indians. Barter as the main form of trading is found among the Toda with their polyandry and among diverse other peoples including Chuckchee of Siberia, Congo pygmies, Bantus, Melanesians, and many Indians of the New World. As for the importance of the sense of personal security and cohesiveness of communal life, compare such peoples as Dobuans and Alorese, on the one hand, and Zuni and Fox Indians, on the other. Religion and religious rituals are far more homogeneous and important among Catholics in the world as a whole than among the widely divided and various Protestants as a whole. This contrast holds true whether we compare them intrasocietally or intersocietally. Who among us have observed that Catholics are therefore more primitive than Protestants? Even the criteria of abstract thinking versus concrete thinking are not foolproof for differentiating the primitive from the civilized. Is the Arunta or Murngin type of social organization less abstract than the Arab or Chinese traders' profit calculations?

The most troublesome meaning of the term "primitive" is that connected with various shades of inferiority. Sometimes we can unquestionably determine that some single items or usages of a culture are more inferior or less inferior than others in the same culture or in other cultures. In this sense, we can describe hand-pushed carts as more primitive than horsecarts and horsecarts as more primitive than automobiles. We are not likely to run into serious disputes here. In the same sense we can speak of a more primitive way of crime detection and a less primitive one, a more primitive way of transmitting messages and a less primitive one, a more primitive teaching aid and a less primitive one. But the primitiveness of other single items is by no means so easy to settle. For example, is the custom of sending children to boarding school or to summer camp more or less primitive than that of continuous parental supervision of the children at home? Is a totalitarian system of government more or less primitive than tribal rule or benevolent despotism? Is a religious system based upon monotheism with a history of heresy persecution, witch hunting, and holy crusades more or less primitive than another with a *laissez faire* attitude toward different creeds and ritual practices? Is the custom of taking care of aged parents at home more primitive than that of leaving them to themselves or in institutions?

Though satisfactory answers to such questions are difficult to come by, our difficulties become much greater when we attempt to determine the inferiority or superiority of whole societies or cultures. Why, despite the scientific indefensibility of applying the concept "primitive" to contemporary cultures and societies, have so many anthropologists tolerated such lack of precision? In a previous paragraph I alluded to sentiment or inertia. But I think there are more complicated factors at work.

First, there is probably a reluctance on the part of some scientists to subject their own cultures to the same kind of scrutiny applied to those not their own. As long as they are analyzing the strange and the exotic they can be emotionally uninvolved. But the same type of analysis applied to their own ways of life may be too painful, especially if such analyses threaten to turn up customs and practices and thought patterns which may not only be unsalutary but even similar to those they have, for whatever reason, labeled "primitive" with its many inferiority connotations.

In this connection it is interesting to note that, though some of Margaret Mead's works are referred to in almost every general book on anthropology, her study of the American family, child-rearing practices, psychological orientation, etc., namely *And Keep Your Powder Dry* (1942), is not usually mentioned. As a matter of fact it is only barely referred to in three of the books we have examined (Hoebel 1958, Honigmann 1959, and Keesing 1958) and quoted in a short selection in only one of them (Goldschmidt 1960). Mead's credentials as an expert on American culture are at least as good as hers on the Manus, Arapesh, and Mundugumor, or Lowie's (1935) on the Crow Indians. Yet while Mead's work on the South Seas is among anthropological classics, her work on the United States enjoys no such esteem among her colleagues.

Another phenomenon is also worth noting in this connection. We have many studies on acculturation. But whether, in general, works on the subject dealing with theories of acculturation built on facts from many cultures (Herskovits 1938), or in more limited works dealing with the acculturative processes of single societies (Linton 1940, or Hallowell 1955), we usually obtain a one-sided picture. We read about which tribes or which sections of a tribe are more acculturated; we also know something about the effects of acculturation on tribal culture and personality; but we find only sporadic or passing mention rather than serious and systematic analysis of the cultures to which the tribes under scrutiny are acculturating. Yet acculturation is certainly a two-sided affair. If we are analysing the impact of acculturation among the Ojibwa or the Menomoni, we should have systematic treatments of the White American cultures as much as of the Indian cultures. For example, many are the statements that the social acceptance of the Negro depends upon the extent of his acculturation. Sociologists of the importance of Hauser continue to make statements such as: "But as the Negro becomes acculturated he will become acceptable and will be accepted" (Moore 1964). But how many social scientists have actually attempted to harmonize the contradictory nature of many reasons given for discrimination against minority groups by considering the possibility that there is an inherent need for prejudice on the part of many self-reliant Whites irrespective of the professed reasons (Hsu 1961a:216–29)? Fred Gearing's work on the Fox in Iowa is the only study on Indian-White contact I know of so far which has attempted seriously and systematically to analyse the White image of the Indian as much as the Indian image of the White (Gearing n.d.). For both affect Indian acculturation.

All this, it seems, is not accidental. There is perhaps an aversion on the part of anthropologists to study their own cultures. How deepseated is this aversion may perhaps be gauged in the attitude expressed by A. L. Kroeber, dean of American anthropologists, in connection with irrational taboos and beliefs:

Quite likely our civilization has its share of counterparts, which we cannot segregate off from the more practical remainder of the business of living because we are engulfed in this civilization of ours as we are in the air we breathe. Some centuries may be needed before the full recognition of our own non-rational couvades and totems and taboos become possible (1948:307).

There are many obvious flaws in this statement, but only two need be dealt with here. On the one hand, if "some centuries" are needed to understand the Western cultures, the same or similar length of time will evidently be required to understand many non-Western cultures. In that case a majority of nonliterate cultures must be left unstudied, for few of them have a historical depth of even one hundred years.

On the other hand, fortunately, we do not have to wait for "some centuries" to study any culture. For the essential contribution of anthropology to the science of man lies in its cross-cultural perspective. The Melanesians, the Africans, the Hindus, and all other non-Western peoples are understandably too "engulfed" each in their own particular civilization as they are in the air they breathe, but anthropologists (a majority of whom have been Westerners so far) who are not so "engulfed" have been able to achieve relatively more objective views of these non-Western ways of life. Does it not logically follow that non-Western anthropologists could also conceivably scrutinize the nonrational couvades, totems, and taboos in the Western ways of life in a more objective light than native Westerners without waiting for some centuries to come? In fact, the study of Western cultures by non-Western anthropologists is a methodological necessity. It is inconceivable that a scientist of Kroeber's stature should fail to see this point. The only explanation for his statement would seem to be that he was unwilling to subject his own culture to the same kind of scrutiny that he has applied to others—at least not for "some centuries" yet.

The second reason why anthropologists have been unwilling to forego the unsatisfactory concept of "primitive" to designate a conglomeration of diverse cultures and societies is a methodological one. Here the difficulties are real and the main problem is coverage.[1]

The difficulties are not obscure. In dealing with materials from the so-called "primitive" societies possessing no written histories, the researcher can usually obtain relatively complete coverage of the data. Thus if he is comparing the political systems of sub-Saharan Africa, he can usually be fairly sure of having examined all the significant ethnographic reports concerning the societies in his study. None of these societies has great historical depth, and the writings on each are highlighted by the major works of one or a few authorities. Even if he wants to compare these African systems with the political systems in Polynesia, he can still proceed on the same basis and with the same assurance of reasonable coverage.

However, suppose the researcher wants to compare the African and the Polynesian systems with those of China and Japan, or of India. The problem of coverage at once seems overwhelming, for these literate and historical societies have been studied and written about by specialists in diverse fields for many generations, and the anthropologist is immediately confronted with mountains of material, the study of a small part of which tends to become a lifetime work for many a scholar. Under such

1. In assessing these difficulties I have greatly benefited from a discussion with my colleague, Dr. Raoul Naroll.

circumstances what part of this mountain of material is the comparative scholar going to use without being attacked left and right by the many sinologists or indologists, not to say historians and art specialists, who have spent their lives on one limited phase of life or culture of one of these large societies?

This is an aspect of the methodological problem for which we have at present indeed no completely satisfactory answer. But our ability and determination to solve this problem will have a most significant bearing on the future of theoretical anthropology. And the prevailing state of affairs in which the students who study the historical and literate societies and the students who study the nonliterate societies generally go their separate ways is certainly not bringing us nearer its solution.

In this situation we can proceed by letting the methodological difficulties dictate our theoretical direction, or we can devote some time and energy toward overcoming the methodological difficulties in order to attain our theoretical goal. I have no doubt that if we decide upon the former course we shall be allowing the tail to wag the dog. For there is no scientific justification whatsoever for confining ourselves to one kind of society and not all societies. Physical anthropology and linguistics have never been confined to data among "primitive" peoples. Physical anthropologists deal with the physical characteristics of all branches of mankind just as linguists deal with all types of languages. These are, of course, as they should be. No zoologist deserving of his title can confine his deliberations to horses and cows or lizards and fish. Any science of society and culture must similarly be based on the data found in all mankind wherever they occur.

Given this major premise, we shall note that the difficulties in the path of those students who wish to compare all peoples with no regard to whether they do or do not possess historical depth are far from insurmountable. For one thing, some groundwork has been laid by anthologies such as *Societies Around the World* (Sanders et al. 1953) and cooperative field projects on specific aspects of culture such as *Six Cultures: Studies of Child Rearing* (Whiting 1963). The works of Chapple and Coon

(1942) and Homans (1950) are valiant attempts to construct theory on the basis of data from all types of societies without fitting them into the primitive-civilized categories or other forms of dichotomy. The technical problems of such comparative studies are real and probably will not be solved to anyone's satisfaction for a long time. But this is simply one area where more anthropologists will have to make more intensive efforts, unless we insist that adequate theories of man's ways can be derived from a particular variety of mankind.

However, over and above the empirical and theoretical reasons just outlined, there is a practical necessity today for pause before using the term "primitive" in describing cultures and societies. There was a time when anthropologists from a Western society could write about the "primitive" Bantu or the Maori without the fear of being challenged. The peoples who were objects of study could not read the ethnographic reports, nor were they in any position to challenge them even had they read them. Today many of these once voiceless peoples have become members of independent nations taking their places as equals with their most powerful brothers in the international arena. To a majority or to all of them we have sent ambassadors, and we receive their ambassadors. Among every one of these newly independent peoples the zeal for national pride runs high. None of them will regard with delight the designation of "primitive" applied to any aspect of their culture, far less to their way of life as a whole, no matter how the concept is defined. The overall psychological and political climate of the world today is simply unfavorable to the continued application of this term to any people who have a voice. We need only recall the incident involving the American girl serving as a Peace Corps member in Nigeria who wrote a postcard to one of her friends at home deploring the conditions in which she found herself. The Nigerian students' reaction was prompt and explosive. One can almost say with certainty that similar incidents will occur in many parts of the world with similar or other kinds of provocation. On the other hand, one can also say with certainty that such incidents were not likely to have occurred before World War II.

For this reason even the more descriptive term "nonliterate" proposed by Herskovits (1948) is not going to be useful for long. For as national states emerge from among previously non-literate peoples, the leaders of each new state will be anxious to adopt or create a written language suited to their particular circumstances. Ghana has adopted English as its *lingua franca*. Tanganyika has adopted Swahili as its *lingua franca*. Indonesia has adopted Bahasa based on Malay spoken in Sumatra and some Pidgin Dutch. Other new nations are either adopting existing languages or creating their own with the aid of some Indo-European alphabet. Judging from historical examples from the Japanese and the Manchus to the Russians and the Mongols, this transformation of a people without a written language into one with a written language is well within the grasp of any organized society so determined. It will not be long before a majority or all of the presently nonliterate peoples become literate. Then the term "nonliterate" as distinguished from "literate" will be meaningless unless it is used with qualifications such as "nonliterate until 1961."

Nor will interesting efforts such as that of Stanley Diamond (1963), already discussed, appreciably help to restore the concept of primitive to the central place it once unquestionably occupied in anthropology. Diamond's work in this connection embodies and may even be regarded as a synthesis of three lines of antecedental thought in our discipline. One is that represented by Goldenweiser (1922:117–18), in attempting clearly to formulate criteria of primitiveness as contrasted to civilizedness, and by others of the folk-urban dichotomy sort. A second line is represented by Herskovits (1958:61–78) in his formulation of cultural relativism, the central theme of which is the need for avoiding judgment of one culture by the standards of another. A third line is both older and younger than either of the two already noted. This is the idea of the noble savage prevalent in the West years and even centuries ago, tarnished by later discovery of savage inferiority and the White Man's burden, but, in more recent years, gaining importance once again because of the stress on racial equality and the dignity of the individual.

Diamond's effort has not restored the concept of "primitive" to its former greatness but has, instead, I believe, clearly shown how incompatible the "superior" characteristics of his "primitive" are with modern developments such as industrialization and the building of political states motivated by nationalism. Industrialization and nationalism are today the twin goals that most or all peoples want to achieve, either by their own bootstraps or through some form of aid from capitalistic or communistic sources. But these goals are not possible unless peasants are willing to leave the security of their small plots of land to work in mass-producing factories, unless believers are willing to ignore the dictates of gods and oracles to accept the verdicts of market analyses and scientific medicine, and unless most natives are willing to forget or suppress their kinship obligations and replace them by impersonal and cold-blooded considerations such as efficiency and capacity to produce. Finally, when Diamond pleads for letting the "primitive grow in us," he has left behind most of the characteristics of the "primitive" as he has defined them and concentrated on the *community* aspect of it as an antidote to the increasing alienation of men from each other which, according to him, accompanies civilizational development. Diamond has pointed out a wish, a desirable wish, but how he proposes to reach that end, or whether it is feasible, is not at all clear from his writings on the subject (Diamond 1960; 1963; and 1964). My view is that as long as Western men and the rest of the world pursue the objectives they do now, Diamond's wish will remain a beautiful wish. Glorification of the concept "primitive," or some phase of it, is likely to be unattractive to mankind, most of all to those whose behavior patterns exemplify the "primitive." For whether we assume the "inferiority" of the "primitive" vis-a-vis the "civilized" or protest the "superiority" of the "primitive" vis-a-vis the "civilized," the anthropologists will be dichotomizing the world's societies and cultures with little or no allowance for other histori-

cal cultures and societies but with their own Western variety of
societies and cultures as the central point of reference (unless
they wish to make the unconvincing and unlikely claim that
their central point of reference is the "primitive"). This suggests
the very kind of ethnocentrism which anthropology as a profession has been trying to eliminate or at least reduce.

Above all, however, we must not allow the tremendously
wide spectrum of differences among the societies and cultures to
be concealed by the concept "primitive." These differences are
crucial not only from the point of view of scientific curiosity but
also in terms of their dissimilar reactions and adjustments to the
impact of the modern industrial and nationalistic West. Anthropologists, after painting themselves into a corner by their unwill-
ingness to discard the concept "primitive," have no alternative
to using it in so many differing, imprecise, conflicting, or meaningless ways because it is a grab bag. Even Diamond, after
defining this concept by a list of ten specific characteristics, is
forced to resort to such vague and scientifically useless statements
as "primitives possess . . . the immediate and ramifying sense
of the person . . ." and that "primitive society at its most positive, exemplifies an essential humanity" (Diamond 1963:111),
when he tries to show what it is that his "primitive" can offer to
his "civilized."

The grab bag nature of the concept "primitive" makes this
inevitable. Each user must either impute some particular meanings to it without regard to what other students do, or resort to
statements about it too general to be scientifically usable. Continued elaboration of and preoccupation with this concept can
only obscure rather than clarify what we hope to analyse, and
seriously hamper our endeavors in building a science of man.

In this paper my purpose is to show the empirical, theoretical
and practical obsolescence of the concept "primitive" except in
some most restricted sense referring to specific items of culture or
to certain prehistorical forms of development. But I do not deny
the need for classification of man and his works in other ways.
In fact, classification is essential to all sciences, but the usefulness

of the classificatory categories is dependent upon the extent to which they do or do not correspond to the facts or yield significant insights into the facts so classified.

We must be flexible enough with our classificatory categories at any one time so that they will serve primarily as convenient tools to shift and tie facts together but not as invariable points of reference so that our thinking is molded and predetermined by them. As our knowledge increases we must refine our classificatory categories to suit the new developments. I firmly believe that we have come to a time when we must go beyond the concepts of "primitive" and "civilized," or other forms of simple dichotomy, and move to more refined modes of classification.

There are already many such new modes of classification at our disposal. For example, different kinds of descent, inheritance, and succession provide us with one basis for classification. Different varieties of economic practices and organizations provide us with another basis for classification. We can classify societies according to the extent to which they exhibit the characteristics of an organized state as distinguished from those which are stateless. We can classify them into those which, to borrow David Riesman's terms (1950), are predominantly tradition-directed, inner-directed, or other-directed, or, to use my terms (Hsu 1963), according to patterns of interpersonal interaction, into those which are characterized by mutual dependence, unilateral dependence, or self-reliance. Societies could be classified on the basis of a few precise traits, such as language, territorial contiguity, and political organization, into Hopi, Flathead, Aztec, and Tarascan types (Naroll 1964). Or they could be classified according to what I designate as the dominant attributes in the kinship content, which serve as keys to their wider psycho-cultural orientations (Hsu 1959; 1961*b*; 1964).

Each of these modes of classification may, of course, only elicit particular kinds of results which may not be entirely relevant to those elicited by others. As the science of man moves forward, the scientifically less productive classificatory schemes will be replaced by scientifically more meaningful ones. We will also have to find means of integrating some of them or relating them to each other. But to stagnate at the level of a "primitive" versus "civilized" dichotomy and its substitutes is to block our paths to progress.

ABSTRACT

This article shows the empirical, theoretical, and practical obsolescence of the concept "primitive" except in some more restricted sense, such as application to peoples and cultures in prehistorical times. A survey of thirty basic books in anthropology written during the last ten years reveals that the concept still enjoys a high degree of currency in an ambiguous, inconsistent, or scientifically meaningless way.

The reasons for this insistent use of the concept by anthropologists despite its obsolescence are discussed. One of these reasons is the seeming reluctance of anthropologists to examine their own societies and cultures. Another is the difficulty in comparing large societies with extensive historical records and relatively small ones with shallow pasts. But whatever the reason, the continued use of and preoccupation with the concept "primitive" (through such efforts as redefinition or substitution), will hamper the further progress of our science.

REFERENCES CITED

Beals, Ralph L., and Harry Hoijer. 1959. 2d edition. *An introduction to anthropology*. New York: Macmillan.

Bohannan, Paul. 1963. *Social anthropology*. New York: Holt, Rinehart & Winston.

Chapple, E. D. and C. S. Coon. 1942. *Principles of anthropology*. New York: Holt, Rinehart & Winston.

Coon, Carleton S. 1962. 2d edition. *The story of man, from the first human to primitive culture and beyond*. New York: Knopf.

Diamond, Stanley. 1960. "Plato and the definition of the primitive," in *Culture in history: Essays in honor of Paul Radin*. Edited by Stanley Diamond, pp. 118–41. New York: Columbia University Press.

———. 1963. "The search for the primitive," in *Man's image in medicine and anthropology*. Edited by I. Galdston, pp. 62–115. New York: International Universities Press.

———. 1964. "Introduction: The uses of the primitive," in *Primitive views of the world*. Edited by Stanley Diamond. New York: Columbia University Press.

Evans-Pritchard, E. E. 1951. *Social anthropology*. London: Cohen and West.

Firth, Raymond. 1956. *Human types*. London: Nelson.

Gearing, Fred. n.d. *The public face of the Fox Indians* (in press).

Gleason, Henry A. 1961. Revised edition. *An introduction to descriptive linguistics*. New York: Holt, Rinehart & Winston.

Goldenweiser, Alexander, 1922. *Early civilization*. New York: Knopf.

———. 1937. *Anthropology: An introduction to primitive culture*. New York: F. S. Crofts.

Goldschmidt, Walter. 1959. *Man's way*. Cleveland: World.

———, Ed. 1960. *Exploring the ways of mankind*. New York: Holt, Rinehart & Winston.

Hallowell, A. L. 1955. *Culture and experience*. Philadelphia: University of Pennsylvania Press.

Hawkes, Jacquetta. 1954. *Man on earth*. London: Cresset Press.

Herskovits, M. J. 1938. *Acculturation: The study of culture contact*. New York: J. J. Augustin.

———. 1948. *Man and his works: The science of cultural anthropology*. New York: Knopf.

———. 1955. *Cultural anthropology*. New York: Knopf.

Hill, Archibald A. 1958. *Introduction to linguistic structures*. New York: Harcourt, Brace & World.

Hockett, Charles F. 1958. *A course in modern linguistics.* New York: Macmillan.

Hoebel, E. A. 1960. 2d edition. *Man in the primitive world.* New York: McGraw-Hill.

Homans, George C. 1950. *The human group.* New York: Harcourt, Brace.

Honigmann, John J. 1959. *The world of man.* New York: Harper & Row.

———. 1963. *Understanding culture.* New York: Harper & Row.

Hsu, Francis L. K. 1959. Structure, function, content, and process. *American Anthropologist* 61:790–805.

———. 1961a. "American core value and national character," in *Psychological anthropology: Approaches to culture and personality.* Edited by Francis L. K. Hsu, pp. 209–30. Homewood, Ill.: Dorsey Press.

———. 1961b. "Kinship and ways of life: An exploration," in *Psychological anthropology.* Edited by Francis L. K. Hsu, pp. 400–56. Homewood, Ill.: Dorsey Press.

———. 1963. *Clan, caste and club.* Princeton: Van Nostrand.

———. 1964. Dominant attributes in kinship and social grouping: a hypothesis. Revised paper read at American Anthropological Association Meetings, San Francisco, November 1963.

Keesing, Felix. 1958. *Cultural anthropology.* New York: Holt, Rinehart & Winston.

Kroeber, A. L. 1948. *Anthropology.* New York: Harcourt, Brace.

———. 1952. *The nature of culture.* Chicago: University of Chicago Press.

Levy, Marion Joseph. 1952. *The structure of society.* Princeton, N.J.: Princeton University Press.

Linton, Ralph, Ed. 1940. *Acculturation in seven American Indian tribes.* New York: Appleton-Century.

———. 1955. *The tree of culture.* New York: Knopf.

Lowie, R. H. 1935. *The Crow Indians.* New York: Holt, Rinehart & Winston.

Mead, Margaret. 1942. *And keep your powder dry.* New York: Morrow.

Mead, Margaret, and Nicholas Calas. 1953. *Primitive heritage.* New York: Random House.

Mednick, Lois. 1960. Memorandum on the use of *primitive. Current Anthropology* 1:441–45.

Moore, Ruth. 1964. Hauser rejects area projections patterned on past. *Chicago Sun Times* (January 26), p. 22.

Murdock, G. P. 1949. *Social structure.* New York: Macmillan.

Nadel, S. F. 1957. *The theory of social structure.* New York: Free Press.

Naroll, Raoul. 1964. On ethnic unit classification. *Current Anthropology* 5:283

Piddington, Ralph. 1950–1957. *An introduction of social anthropology.* 2 vols. Edinburgh, Scotland: Oliver and Boyd.

Radcliffe-Brown, A. R. 1952. *Structure and function in primitive society.* London: Cohen and West.

——. 1957. *A natural science of society.* New York: Free Press.

Radin, Paul. 1953. *The world of primitive man.* New York: Schuman.

Redfield, Robert. 1941. *Folk culture of Yucatan.* Chicago: University of Chicago Press.

Riesman, David. 1950. *The lonely crowd.* New Haven: Yale University Press.

Sanders, I. T., R. B. Woodbury, F. J. Essene, T. P. Field, J. R. Schwendeman, and C. P. Snow. 1953. *Societies around the world.* New York: The Dryden Press (2 vols.).

Sapir, Edward. 1925. Spurious and genuine cultures. *American Journal of Sociology* 29:405.

Tax, Sol. 1960. "Primitive" peoples. *Current Anthropology* 1:441.

Thompson, Laura. 1961. *Toward a science of mankind.* New York: McGraw-Hill.

Titiev, Mischa. 1959. *Introduction to cultural anthropology.* New York: Holt, Rinehart & Winston.

——. 1963. 2d edition. *The science of man.* New York: Holt, Rinehart & Winston.

White, J. E. M. 1954. *Anthropology.* London: English Universities Press.

Whiting, Beatrice, ed. 1963. *Six cultures: Studies of child rearing.* New York: Wiley.

SOL TAX

"Primitive" Peoples

LIKE many other anthropologists, I have used the term *primitive* with increasing misgivings. A textbook published in 1958, called *A Profile of Primitive Cultures* (Service), includes descriptions of the Arunta, Yahgan, Andamanese, Eskimo, Tungus, Cheyenne, Nuer, Navaho, Jivaro, Nootka, Trobrianders, Tahitians, Kalinga, Maya, Inca, Ashanti, and villages in Yucatan, Morocco, China, and India. Here, and in earlier books like *Our Primitive Contemporaries* (Murdock 1934), the term seems to mean only "peoples that anthropologists study." Then, why *primitive?*

This is not only a matter of semantics. In recent travels, it became evident to me that our tolerance of this term will be

Reprinted from Current Anthropology, *Vol. 1, Nos. 5–6, Sept.–Nov., 1960, pp. 441–445.*

harmful to anthropology. An anthropologist is defined as "one who studies primitive peoples"; but by the dictionary meanings of *primitive*, there are no such groups—or, at least, the peoples that we study are not primitive as they understand the term. In the world emerging today, scholars who study "primitive" groups are out of subject-matter.

I undertook to write a paper on this subject for the Central States Anthropological Society's meeting in Bloomington, Indiana (U.S.A.), in May, 1960, and asked a research assistant, Lois Mednick, to prepare some material on uses of the term *primitive* in Anthropology. Her memorandum is reproduced here for its general interest.

Meanwhile, it became evident to me that the reason we have never found an acceptable substitute—such as *preliterate, native,* etc.—is that the anthropological use of *primitive* is not a legitimate concept deserving a single term. We lump together all of the peoples of the world, past and present, except those which are part of Western Civilization and its ancient progenitors. Anthropologists, of all people, should know that this is not a legitimate class. If an oak tree should demand a term for all other trees, leaving out only oaks, should one be surprised if no suitable answer can be found? The truth is that all these peoples we call *primitive* have nothing in common that is not also shared by all human societies and cultures. Such a quality would have to be something (1) characterizing equally Andamanese, the Arunta, Ashanti, Cheyenne, Chinese, Eskimo, Inca, Indians, Jivaro, Kalinga, ancient and modern Maya, Moroccans, Navaho, Nootka, Nuer, Tahitians, Trobrianders, Tungus, and Yahgan; and (2) distinguishing all of these from Ikhnaton's Egypt, Pericles' Athens, Cellini's Florence, Shakespeare's England, Napoleon's Europe. We have not discovered any such quality; rather, we have concluded that there is no such thing. But we carry on with a word for the first group because they are the peoples who became our special subjects for study (the second group was already well-known).

Although any single term would be inappropriate, the one

we happened to choose—*primitive*—is peculiarly so, because of its connotations. It is a curious irony that when cultural relativists abandoned the invidious terms, *Savage*, *Barbarian*, and *Civilized*, they applied the even more invidious misnomer *primitive* to those whom the evolutionists had called savages and barbarians, and in addition used it for those "civilized" peoples not well-known to Europeans. Anthropologists tend to use *primitive* less often in theoretical contexts (where, of course, it has no genuine referent) than in titles of courses and of books, and in ordinary parlance, where—greatest irony of all—our influence is greatest! We put the term in quotes, and we know it is not true; but can others be blamed for saying that, in the division of labor, anthropologists are the persons who study primitives?

MEMORANDUM ON THE USE OF *PRIMITIVE*

Webster's Unabridged Dictionary lists the following usages for the word *primitive* [F. *primitif*, fr. L. *primitivus*, fr. *primus* first]:

(1) Of or pertaining to the beginning or origin; earliest in time; first; original; as *primitive* ages of religion; our *primitive* ancestors.

(2) Of or pertaining to the earliest ages, as of man or civilization, or the earliest period, as of Christianity or an art; as, *primitive* tools or morals; the *primitive* church; *primitive* lack of perspective.

(3) Original; primary; radical; not derived; as, a *primitive* verb in grammar.

(4) Characterized by a quality or qualities belonging or ascribed to the original state of man, an institution, etc., as naturalness, mildness, simplicity, etc.; as, to live in *primitive* fashion.

A really *primitive* people nowhere exists.   *McLennan.*

(5) Of or pertaining to the denomination or denominations of Primitive Baptists, Methodists, etc.

Originally, perhaps, members of some *primitive* sect, they were now in the natural course of things members of the Church of England.
                                                              Galsworthy.

(6) *Biol. a.* Primordial. *b.* Ancient, archaic, little evolved, persistent;—said of species or groups whose structure more or less closely approximates

that of their early ancestral types; as, the opossoms are *primitive* mammals; the tuatara is a *primitive* type of reptile, etc. Cf. PROMORPH.

(7) *Geol.* Earliest formed; fundamental;—applies esp. to the crystalline rocks of the Archean.

Syn.—First, pristine; aboriginal, ancient, antiquated. See PRIMARY
Ant.—Modern, recent, contemporary, present.

A search of present-day anthropological literature soon makes it clear that the use of *primitive* by anthropologists does not accord with its dictionary definition. Several recent books whose titles include the word *primitive* class together under this term (1) such diverse societies as those of Philippine headhunters and Hindu peasants (Service 1958); (2) the laws of the Indians of the North American Plains, and those of the Ashanti (Hoebel 1954); (3) the religion of the Murngin and that of the people of Dahomey (Goode 1951). In *Primitive Heritage* (1953), Mead and Calas include articles ranging from Aztec human-sacrifice to Pawnee war parties. The selections in these four volumes appear to have been chosen for contrast of material and diversity of locale; the only common denominator uniting the various cultures and societies seems to be the fact that all of them have been studied by anthropologists.

In *The Primitive World and its Transformations* (1953), Redfield draws on contemporary data in order to understand what cultures were like before the rise of *literati* and cities. He uses the term *primitive* as synonymous with *preliterate* (p. xi), but his "primitives" range through time, encompassing peoples who were primitive in the etymological sense of the word and peoples who recently have become literate.

Not only is it hard to define *primitive* as the term is used by anthropologists, but sometimes an author who uses the word in a book title scarcely refers to the concept in his text. The series of essays and lectures by Radcliffe-Brown collected in *Structure and Function in Primitive Society* (1952) is a case in point. His essay, "Primitive Law," makes no use of the word in the entire exposition; and the eleven remaining articles use the word only four times—twice in one address to a lay audience.

The illusiveness of *primitive* is attested to by the many authors who feel it necessary to explain or justify the manner in which they have used the word.

I have used here throughout the term "primitives" without further explanation. I hope this has not conveyed the impression that I consider these tribes as living in an original state of nature, such as Rousseau imagined. On the contrary, we must remember that every primitive people has had a long history. It may be descended by decay from a stage of higher development or it may have arisen to its present state battling against vicissitudes. There is no primitive tribe that is not hemmed in by conventional laws and customs. The more primitive it is the greater is the number of restrictions that determine every action (Boas 1888; reprinted in Boas 1948:633).

. . . They are not old. But they are nevertheless primitive. The point to be grasped is that among contemporary societies primitiveness does not necessarily mean antiquity, in spite of the fact that primary means first. What it does mean is that the cultural forms of primitive societies are more similar in their general characteristics to those that presumably prevailed in the early cultures of the infancy of mankind (Hoebel 1954: 289–90).

"Primitive," to be sure, is not a good word for the peoples investigated by social anthropologists, though we use it because it has become customary. Primitive societies are not always primitive in the sense of "simple." . . . Primitives are better called nonliterates; but besides their failure to develop written languages, they have another characteristic in common. In these societies, more activities are carried on by organizations, membership in which is determined by kinship, than in any modern Western Society (Homans 1950:192).

Leslie White (1949:241) has still another definition to add:

. . . Primitive society: tribes based upon kinship ties, free access to the resources of nature for all, relatively little social differentiation and specialization, and a high degree of social equality.

These quotations exemplify a few of the different meanings that social and cultural anthropologists attach to the word *primitive*. Actually, however, *each* of the five sub-fields of anthropology (archaeology, linguistics, physical anthropology, social anthropology, and ethnology) has redefined *primitive* in terms of its own interests and needs, in much the same way as has been done with the word *culture*. This is perfectly satisfactory, if there is agreement within each field as to what the word means. Unfortunately, this is not the case.

For example, one linguist (Greenberg 1953:265) talks about "primitive" languages and means unwritten languages; while Beals and Hoijer (1954:508–11), in their discussion of primitive languages, also put the word in quotation marks and then proceed to demonstrate the fact that there are no such languages.

In archaeology, Caso (1953:228, 230) equates his Middle American Primitive Horizon with the Old World Neolithic; Movius (1953:189) definies it differently:

> For during prehistoric times, just as in the historic range, environmental factors played a dominant role in conditioning the behavior of various early (or primitive) groups of mankind.

In physical anthropology, the situation is just as confused. Simpson (1950:101), adhering to a strict biological definition, uses *primitive* to mean "slowly evolved," contrasting it with advanced, or rapidly evolved, organs or organisms. Washburn (1944:70) declines to use the word and warns that it "changes its meaning constantly." Three quotations from Hooton (1954) demonstrate the aptness of Washburn's warning:

> In [whites] the presumably primitive wavy hair form predominates (p. 581).
> In the Iron-Age, an Upper Paleolithic or Combe-Capelle type of primitive Mediterranean penetrated into South India (p. 615).
> The pygmies are scattered in small groups through the Congo, have no language of their own, and are usually attached as hunters or pets to the full-sized agricultural negroes in their districts. They know no agriculture, have no domesticated animals and are generally in about as primitive a state as can be imagined (p. 623).

An examination of the literature of ethnology and social anthropology adds to the growing confusion. Twenty-three different meanings for *primitive,* some used in combination, and others frequently standing alone, were compiled during a few hours search. Most often, *primitive* means.

> *Noncivilized* (Calas 1953: xxvi; Coon 1948: v; Firth 1951: v, 80; Kroeber 1953; xiii; Mead 1953: xviii).

Simple (Homans 1950:192; Radcliffe-Brown 1952:153).

Small (Fortes and Evans-Pritchard 1950:5; Nadel 1951:52).

Pre-literate or Nonliterate (Homans 1950:192; Mead 1953: vxii; *Notes and Queries* 1954:28; Radcliffe-Brown 1952:3; Redfield 1953: xi).

Non-Western (Coon 1948: vi; Firth 1951:10; Herskovits 1940:237, 246, 261, 264).

Static (Firth 1951:80–81; Malinowski 1936:80).

Tradition-bound (Boas 1948:633; Malinowski 1936:80).

Some of the less frequently encountered meanings are:

Exotic (Kroeber 1953: xiii).
Unprogressive (Firth 1951:80).
Backward (Radcliffe-Brown 1952:2).
Tribal (White 1949:241, 377).
Isolated (Redfield 1953: xi).
Homogeneous (Redfield 1953: xi).
Nonmonetary (Firth 1951:133–34).
Uncritical, Prescientific (Bidney 1953:332, 334).
Pseudo-scientific (Malinowski 1936:80).

This does not exhaust the usages, but to list more, or to cite other than representative sources, would prolong this memorandum needlessly. The point should be clear. The use of *primitive* is ambiguous and inconsistent within each separate field of anthropology, and between the fields of anthropology; above all, one wonders what meaning *primitive* has when the larger public is addressed.

Unfortunately, confusion in the use of *primitive* does not stop at the threshold of anthropology, since any scholar from any discipline is free to borrow the already amorphous concept for his own use. Freud (1913) makes use of it in these ways:

Another trait in the attitude of primitive races towards their rulers recalls a mechanism which is universally present in mental disturbances, and is openly revealed in the so-called delusions of persecution (p. 807).

Primitive man is known to us by the stages of development through which he has passed . . . moreover, in a certain sense he is still our contemporary: there are people whom we consider more closely related to primitive man than ourselves, in whom we therefore recognize the direct descendants and representatives of earlier man. We can thus judge the so-called savage and semi-savage races; their psychic life assumes a particular interest for us, for we can recognize in their psychic life a well-preserved, early stage of our own development . . . a comparison of the psychology of primitive races as taught by folklore, with the psychology of the neurotic as it has come to be known through psychoanalysis, will reveal numerous points of correspondence and throw new light on subjects that are more or less familiar to us (p. 846).

In fairness, it is interesting to compare this second quotation from Freud with an anthropological work written forty years later: Margaret Mead (Tax et al. 1953:174) makes the following statement:

The other problem that Dr. Caudill raises, which is important at the primitive and the ethnological level (and we will not be able to get information out of already accumulated material), is the one raised by all the psychiatrists as to whether there is some kind of deeper layer in man that is unaffected by culture. There is supposed to be something going on inside, sometimes called the "unconscious" or the "deeper impulses," that is equated by psychiatry everywhere with a human nature invariant, unaffected by culture. We probably can solve this important problem far more quickly with primitive than with civilized material.

Jung (1929), in *The Psychology of the Unconscious*, makes this statement:

Primitive thinking and feeling are exclusively concretistic; they are always related to sensation. The thought of primitive man has no detached independence but clings to the material phenomena. The most he can do is raise it to the level of analogy. Primitive feeling is always equally related to the material phenomenon. . . . The primitive does not experience the idea of divinity as a subjective content, but the sacred tree is the habitat—nay even the deity himself (p. 534).

Additional references in this same vein could be cited; but the case should not be overstated, for several more recent writers show a more modern tenor in their use of anthropological data. Erikson (1950) writes:

Finally we turn to cultural primitiveness as the apparent infancy of humanity where people seem, to us, to be at one moment as naive as children, at another, as possessed as lunatics. . . . We now know that primitives have their own adult normality, that they have their own brands of neurosis and psychosis and, most important, that they too have their own varieties of childhood (p. 95).

The discovery of primitive child-training systems makes it clear that primitive societies are neither infantile stages of mankind nor arrested deviations from the proud progressive norms which we represent: they are a complete form of mature human living often of a homogeneity and simple integrity which we at times might well envy (p. 96).

However, later in the same book, one reads:

The system underlying Sioux education is a primitive one—i.e., it is based on the adaptation of a highly ethnocentric, relatively small group of people, who consider only themselves to be relevant mankind (p. 139).

Turning from psychiatry to economic history, we find the following quotations in Polanyi (1944):

To start with, we must discard some nineteenth-century prejudices that underlay Adam Smith's hypothesis about primitive man's alleged predilection for gainful occupations. Since his axiom was much more relevant to the immediate future than to the dim past, it induced in his followers a strange attitude towards man's early history. On the face of it, the evidence seemed to indicate that primitive man, far from having a capitalistic psychology, had, in effect, a communistic one (later this also proved to be mistaken) (p. 44).

Developing the topic, "The motive gain is not natural to man," Polanyi (p. 45–46) cites the following anthropological sources:

The characteristic feature of primitive economics is the absence of any desire to make profits from production of exchange (Thurnwald 1932). Another notion which must be exploded, once and forever, is that of the Primitive Economic Man of some current economic textbooks (Malinowski 1930). We must reject the *ideal types* of Manchester liberalism which are not only theoretically, but also historically misleading (Brinkmann 1924).

In concluding the section on primitive economics, Polanyi states:

Primitive economics as studied in the preceding pages is not far distinguished from any other form of economics, as far as human relations are concerned, and rests on the same general principles of social life (p. 53).

Here is an example of how a legal historian, William Seagel (1941:33–35) uses *primitive*. Under the fourth chapter heading on primitive law, entitled, "Custom is King," he writes that primitive societies are lawless and live under an "automatic sway of custom" that seems to suffice. Therefore, "there is no law until there are courts." And if people who are ordinarily recognized as primitive have courts, then *ipso facto* they are not primitive, for "to speak of the law of some African peoples as 'primitive' although they have courts and have invented many complex forms of legal transactions which compare not unfavorably with those of the ancient Babylonians is to abuse the natural meaning of the term."

Two examples from philosophy use *primitive* to denote peoples with a different emotional and mental outlook from that of modern man:

. . . A high degree of civilization was always first necessary for the animal man to begin to make those much more primitive distinctions of "intentional," "negligent," "accidental," "responsibility," and their contraries, and apply them in the assessing of punishment. That idea—"the wrong-doer deserves punishment because he might have acted otherwise," in spite of the fact that it is nowadays so cheap, obvious, natural, and inevitable, and that it has had to serve as an illustration of the way in which the sentiment of justice appeared on earth, is in point of fact an exceedingly late, and even refined form of human judgment and inference; the placing of this idea back at the beginning of the world is simply a clumsy violation of the principles of primitive psychology (Nietzsche 1929 ed.:19).

Primitive man expresses his feelings and emotions not in mere abstract symbols but in a concrete immediate way. We may speak of a tension between stabilization and evolution. . . . In myth and in primitive religion the tendency to stabilization is so strong that it entirely outweighs the opposite pole. Mythical thought is, by its origin and by its principle, traditional thought. . . . From the point of view of primitive thought the slightest alteration in the established scheme of things is disastrous. . . . Primitive religion can therefore leave no room for any freedom of individual thought (Cassirer 1944:280–82).

Interestingly enough, the sociologist Mannheim (1960:542), commenting on Weber, writes:

Max Weber observed that even in primitive communities the psychopathological types usually become the prophets, saviors, and reformers, changing the old ways of life and breaking down the old magical attitudes. In his view, this is because in societies whose customs are sanctified mainly by magic it is the psychopath who is unadjusted and who therefore dares to break these old habits, which are no longer fitted to the changed situations, and is able to discover new and better adjusted attitudes.

A final example is the classic Primitivism of Rousseau, which Muller (1957:51) characterizes as follows:

. . . men looked to primitive societies to discover human nature in its "pure" state. In fact, however, we cannot find such a universal state of nature. We find instead a fantastic diversity in design for living, with often an outrageous disregard of the reputed laws of human nature. And this commonplace of modern anthropology is pertinent because first of all we have to deal with primitivism—the familiar idea that civilization is a disease, and that the only possible cure for it is to return to nature and the simple life. The myth of the noble savage is at least as old as Homer . . . while later Greek and Roman literature is full of homilies on the happier, more virtuous life of rude peoples. . . . Primitivism is based on a misunderstanding of primitive life, whose apparent simplicity is complicated by rigid taboos and black magic. The primitivists cherish an impossible desire. They wish to appreciate the simple life with all the self-consciousness and sensitivity that only civilization makes possible; they wish to be children of nature and also poets and philosophers celebrating nature.

It is now quite clear why *Notes and Queries on Anthropology* (1954) abandoned use of the word *primitive* with this statement:

The word native is used in this volume because it is presumed that investigations will be made in the vast majority of cases among peoples in their native habitat. The terms primitive, savage, and aboriginal are avoided because these words have all been used too loosely. It would be difficult to define what any author means by primitive (p. 28).

But after demonstrating the confusion beclouding the word *primitive,* one still wonders how anthropologists departed so far from its dictionary meaning. In the earliest anthropological literature, one finds the concept of primitive a little clearer. Boucher de Perthes (1846) entitled his treatise on prehistoric implements *De l'Industrie primitive,* obviously meaning that these were the tools of the first men. Likewise, McLennan's first essay on *Primitive Marriage* (1865) was an attempt to reconstruct the early development of mankind on the basis of cultural survivals. McLennan and the other practicing anthropologists of that period were primarily caught up in the formation of what was to become the British Evolutionist School.

Most of those actively engaged in the anthropological arguments of the day rather consistently used *primitive* in the sense of "primeval" or "original"; and most of the confusion over the meaning of the word seems to have stemmed from the newness of the discipline. Concepts were being formed, definitions were being hammered out, data were being garnered, and there was as yet no world-wide communication among scholars. Under these circumstances, it is surprising that there is not more disagreement in the literature.

In *Primeval Man,* the Duke of Argyll (1872) writes:

> It has not, however, been sufficiently observed that the inquiry into the Primitive Condition of Mankind resolves itself into three separate questions. . . . First, the Origin of Man considered simply as a Species . . . second, the Antiquity of Man. . . . Third, His Mental, Moral, and Intellectual Condition when first created (p. 24–25).
>
> . . . The creature "not worthy to be called a man," to whom Sir J. Lubbock has referred as the progenitor of Man, was, *ex hypothesi,* deficient in those mental capacities which now distinguish the lowest of the human race (p. 67).
>
> Sir J. Lubbock speaks of Primeval Man as having been in a condition of "utter barbarism" . . . it affords no presumption whatever that barbarism was the Primeval Condition of Man, any more than the traces of Feudalism in the laws of modern Europe prove that feudal principles were born with the Human Race (p. 131–33).
>
> Sir J. Lubbock's theory is, that in these Savages we see something rather above than under the Primitive Condition of Mankind (p. 69–70).
>
> Sir J. Lubbock seems to admit that this loathsome practice was not primeval, probably because he considers it as unnatural. . . . Cannibal-

ism is only an extreme case of a general law, and it is a crucial test of the
fallacy of a whole class of arguments commonly assumed by those who
support the Savage-theory respecting the Primeval Condition of Mankind (p. 134–36).

And here it is important to observe that even if savage races be taken
as the type of man's Primeval Condition, the evidence afforded by those
races is all in favor of the conclusion that as regards his characteristic
mental powers, Man has always been Man, and nothing less (p. 150).

The Duke of Argyll precedes the classic formulation of the
Evolutionist theory and nomenclature. With the publication of
Tylor's *Anthropology* in 1888, most of the early ambiguities
were dispelled for the main ranks of British anthropologists. For
Tylor, *primitive* meant exactly what the root denoted; he used
it to refer to that long-gone original population of mankind about
whom one could only speculate. In his descriptions and charac-
terizations of living and historical populations and their cultures.
Tylor used the familiar, and now almost discarded, hierarchy of
Savage, Barbarian, and Civilized.

Going back as far as philology can take us, we find already existing
a number of language groups, differing in words and structure, and if
they ever had any relationship with one another no longer showing it
by signs clear enough for our skill to make out. Of an original primitive
language of mankind, the most patient research has found no traces
(p. 12).

No competent anatomist who has examined the bodily structure of
these apes considers it possible that man can be descended from any of
them, but according to the doctrine of descent they appear as the nearest existing offshoots from the same primitive stock whence man also
came (p. 40).

. . . the Andaman tribes may be a remnant of a very early human
stock, perhaps the best representatives of the primitive negro type which
has since altered in various points in its spread over its wide districts of
the world (p. 88–89).

The original tongue whence these are all descended may be called
the Primitive Aryan (p. 156).

The primitive shield was probably the parrying shield (p. 222).

But though there was a consistent use of *primitive* by the
British Evolutionists, one cannot deny that the literature periph-

eral to the main currents of anthropological thought contained
the loose, ill-defined, use of the word. The first volume of the
Journal of the Royal Anthropological Institute (1871), for example, included an article by C. S. Wake entitled "The Mental
Characteristics of Primitive Man as Exemplified by the Australian Aborigines," in which he used a slightly different interpretation of *primitive:*

> I wish, primarily, to establish what are the real mental phenomena
> exhibited by the native of Australia; and secondarily, to show approxi-
> mately the conditions in which man generally must have existed in the
> primeval ages, not necessarily when he first appeared on earth, but so
> soon as the struggle for existence between man and man commenced,
> and the selfish instincts of humanity had had time to become fully de-
> veloped (p. 74).

Also, the early American, French, German, and Italian journals of this period—1871–1900—reveal a growing tendency to
use the word *primitive* loosely. The *Bulletin de la Société d'An-
thropologie de Paris* (1875) contains two articles: D. Eichthal's
"Sur le texte primitif du premier récit de la création," and Abbé
Petitot's "Sur la contemporanéité de la pierre taillée, de la pierre
polie, du bronze et du fer chez les peuplades primitives de la
Scandinavie, de la Bretagne, et des Gaules." Although the German journals of this period do not seem to use the words *primitive* or *Primitivität*, they abound with such words as: *ursprüng-
lich, altertümlich, Urmensch, Urzeit,* and the like, all of which
the English translations render as "primitive," "primitive man,"
"primitive era," etc. Since the German prefix *Ur-* means "primeval" *or* "primitive," the suspicion might be entertained that the
German usage is in the Tylor tradition.

The Italian journals also list a variety of articles that use
primitive in their titles; but for the most part, these are reports
from travelers or missionaries, or represent peripheral researches,
most of which are by persons with some special point of view
—e.g., Caesar Lombroso's article (1896), "L'uomo primitivo e
l'atavismo."

The first volume of the *American Anthropologist* (1888) includes an article by J. W. Powell entitled "From Barbarism to Civilization," which shows the influence of the evolutionists in its title, if not in its total content:

. . . another set of writers have discovered among such peoples only evidence of primitive innocence and the happiness of primitive simplicity, and such people have been pictured as angels (p. 99).

It is doubtful, however, whether we can trace our current difficulties either directly or solely to such sources as these which for the most part represent fringe interests of anthropological theory. Instead, it seems that our difficulties stem from the demise of the Evolutionist School. It appears that in our anxiety to scuttle unilineal evolutionary theory, we also felt it necessary to disavow the use of Savage, Barbarian, and Civilized. This left us with no term, then current, other than the loose, non-evolutionist usage of *primitive*. Thus, *primitive* at first became the blanket word for savage and barbarian. Today, however, now that anthropologists have also studied Mexican, Mayan Andean, Hindu, and Chinese cultures, these are also called *primitive*, even though anthropologists would be the first to uphold their status as civilizations.

Lois Mednick

REFERENCES CITED

Argyll, George Douglas Campbell, 8th Duke of. 1871 *Primeval Man.* New York: DeWitt C. Lent.

Beals, Ralph L., and Harry Hoijer. 1954. *An Introduction to Anthropology.* New York: Macmillan.

Bidney, David. 1953. "Meta-anthropology" in *Ideological Differences and World Order* (ed. F. S. C. Northrop). New Haven: Yale University Press.

Boas, Franz. 1948. *Race, Language, and Culture.* New York: Macmillan.

Boucher de Crèvecoeur de Perthes, Jacques. 1846. *Antiquités celtiques et antédiluviennes. Mémoire sur l'industrie primitive et les arts à leur origine.* Paris: Treuttel et Wurz.

Calas, Nicholas, 1953. "The world as stage" in *Primitive Heritage* (ed. Margaret Mead and Nicholas Calas). New York: Random House.

Caso, Alfonso. 1953. "New World culture history: Middle America" in *Anthropology Today* (ed. A. L. Kroeber). Chicago: University of Chicago Press.

Cassirer, Ernst. 1954. *An Essay on Man.* New York: Anchor Books.

Coon, Carleton. 1948. *A Reader in General Anthropology.* New York: Holt.

Erikson, Erik H. 1950. *Childhood and Society.* New York: Norton.

Firth, Raymond. 1951. *Elements of Social Organization.* London: Watts.

Fortes, Meyer and E. E. Evans-Pritchard. 1950. *African Political Systems.* London: Oxford University Press.

Freud, Sigmund. 1913. "The savage's dread of incest" in *Basic Writings of Sigmund Freud.* New York: Modern Library.

Goode, William J. 1951. *Religion among the Primitives.* New York: Free Press.

Greenberg, Joseph H. 1953. "Historical linguistics and unwritten languages" in *Anthropology Today* (ed. A. L. Kroeber). Chicago: University of Chicago Press.

Herskovits, M. J. 1940. *The Economic Life of Primitive Peoples.* New York: Knopf.

Hoebel, E. Adamson. 1954. *The Law of Primitive Man.* Cambridge: Harvard University Press.

Homans, George C., 1950. *The Human Group.* New York: Harcourt, Brace & World.

Hooton, Earnest A. 1954. *Up From the Ape,* rev. ed. New York: Macmillan.

Jung, C. 1927. *The Psychology of the Unconscious.* New York: Dodd Mead.

Kroeber, A. L. 1953. "Introduction" to *Anthropology Today* (ed. A. L. Kroeber). Chicago: University of Chicago Press.

McLennan, J. F. 1886. "Primitive marriage" in *Studies in Ancient History*. London: Macmillan.

Malinowski, Bronislaw. 1936. "Magic, science, and religion" in *Science, Religion, and Reality* (ed. Joseph Needham). New York: Macmillan.

Mannheim, Karl. 1960. "Types of nationality and organized insecurity" in *Images of Man* (ed. Wright Mills). New York: Braziller.

Mead, Margaret. 1953. "The restoration of wonder" in *Primitive Heritage* (ed. Margaret Mead and Nicholas Calas). New York: Random House.

Movius, Hallam L., Jr. 1953. "Old World prehistory: Paleolithic" in *Anthropology Today* (ed. A. L. Kroeber). Chicago: University of Chicago Press.

Muller, Herbert J. 1957. *The Uses of the Past*. New York: Mentor Books.

Murdock, G. P. 1934. *Our Primitive Contemporaries*. New York: Macmillan.

Nadel, S. F. 1951. *Foundations of Social Anthropology*. New York: Free Press.

Nietzsche, Friedrich. 1887. *The Genealogy of Morals* (1929 ed.) New York: Macmillan.

Notes and Queries on Anthropology. 1954. A committee of the R.A.I. of Great Britain and Ireland. London: Routledge and Kegan Paul.

Polanyi, Karl. 1944. *The Great Transformation*. New York: Farrar and Rinehart.

Radcliffe-Brown, A. R. 1952. *Structure and Function in Primitive Society*. London: Cohen and West.

Redfield, Robert. 1953. *The Primitive World and its Tranformation*. Ithaca: Cornell University Press.

Service, Elman R. 1958. *A Profile of Primitive Culture*. New York: Harper & Row.

Simpson, George G. 1950. *The Meaning of Evolution*. New Haven: Yale University Press.

Tax, Sol, Loren C. Eiseley, Irving Rouse, and Carl F. Voegelin. 1953. *An Appraisal of Anthropology Today*. Chicago: University of Chicago Press.

Tylor, Edward B. 1888. *Anthropology* (1913 ed.). New York: Appleton.

Washburn, S. L. 1944. Thinking about race. *Science Education*. 28: 65–76.

White, Leslie A. 1949. *The Science of Culture*. New York: Grove Press.

SOL TAX

Primitive man vs.

Homo Sapiens

IN THE preceding article I have argued that our continued use of the phrase "primitive" as applied to contemporary
peoples is not only unwise and unjust as casting aspersions, but
it is totally unjustified from any scientific point of view. Those
who still hold to an evolutionary theory of cultures consider
some peoples as culturally or socially less developed in some respects—or possibly even in all respects—than others; but they
do not lump together as "primitives" the wide variety of societies

*With the assistance of Lois W. Mednick, on a grant from the Wenner-Gren
Foundation for Anthropological Research.*

Reprinted from des Actes du VIᵉ Congrès International des Sciences An-
thropologiques et Ethnologiques, Paris, 1960, Tome ll (1ᵉʳ volume), pp. 297–
304

that anthropologists have come to study. Curiously, it is the anti-cultural evolutionist who most frequently does this; since he has abandoned such specific (and also derogatory) terms as "savages" and "barbarians" he lumps all together as "primitives."

Generally speaking, we do this more in titles of books, e.g., *Our Primitive Contemporaries* (Murdock, 1934), *Primitive Society* (Lowie, 1920), *A Profile of Primitive Culture* (Service, 1958), and in titles of university courses ("Primitive Law," "Primitive Religion," etc.) than elsewhere, and we often begin the course or the book by explaining that the use of the word "primitive" is invalid.

In conferences among ourselves we use the word freely, knowing well that it is not to be taken literally. But others who see our titles and listen to our conversation have an image of anthropologists as people who study "primitives." We ourselves define anthropology as the comparative and historical study of all human cultures and societies—European or "Western" as well as American Indian, Oceanian, African, Asian; urban as well as rural. But we have helped create the different image, in part by our adherence to the term "primitive."

This is now much more than a semantic problem since the peoples of the world justifiably resent "being studied" as "primitive museum specimens." People of all continents and cultures are being trained and encouraged to study the societies and cultures of their own and all other continents; the notion that Europeans study others has long been an anachronism. The idea that the peoples studied are "primitives" is thus a survival from an earlier day, a different world, and outmoded theory.

The present paper proposes to make the scientific point clear by 1) defining modern man in behavioral terms, thus 2) showing that the word "primitive" can be legitimately applied only to men who have been extinct since the late Pleistocene, or even much earlier.

The genus *Homo* is now defined not only morphologically but behaviorally as an animal which has "culture" (Oakley, 1957; Spuhler, 1959). Primitive hominids, such as the Australopithecines, presumably had only rudiments of speech, tool-making traditions, and the like, which began to distinguish them from other primates. Development of the ability to communicate and to control nature became then the major mode of human evolution, with morphology, of course, keeping pace with these behaviorial developments.

In 1959, I attended part of a conference at Burg Wartenstein (*Current Anthropology,* July, 1960, p. 332) on "The Social Life of Early Man" where it became evident that one needs to distinguish two phases of human social-cultural development. Early man gradually developed (1) "culture" but historic man lives in communities with (2) *cultures.* Just as the presence of culture may be taken as a criterion of hominid-ness, so the presence or absence of cultures may be considered the specific criterion for modern man or *Homo sapiens.*

Wherever he has been observed "alive," man has lived in communities each of which is distinguished from its neighbors by having its own distinct language or dialect, its own distinct social system, its own distinct value system. Each human community is, thus, both internally unified and externally distinguished from others, and each, furthermore, consciously identifies itself as different, and (usually) superior. Language, social arrangements and values—all, of course, interrelated as abstracted parts of the culture of the human community—have the characteristic of being somewhat "arbitrary." They are divorced from biology—any genetic population can operate equally well with a particular language, a particular set of social relations, or a particular set of "rights and wrongs." They are also largely divorced from the geographic-economic conditions of life, with only the degree of independence in dispute among theorists. The relatively "free-floating" or arbitrary character of language, social and value systems means that they are very changeable. Like a kaleidoscope which with the turn of a hand forms a new design, so with isolation (not to mention changed conditions, peculiar personalities, and accidents) a language or social or moral system quickly changes. So the human communities become distinguished and the circle of change, social isolation, more change, continues. Ethnocentrism acts regardless of the magnitude of the differences, since small differences in word-meanings or ·in etiquette may be functionally even more significant than the deep differences, substituting, as they do, symbolic-emotional barriers for genuine walls of difference.

The point here is only that human communities, wherever they have been known "in the flesh" have had these general characteristics substantially equally. Now-extinct Tasmanian hunters and twentieth-century Englishmen are both equally characterized by living in self-identified communities with their different dialects, social structures, value systems.

If all examples of *Homo sapiens* are so characterized, and no other living genus or species is so characterized, it appears zoologically justifiable to include these as characters which define the species.

Keeping in mind this picture of modern man, then, the question is what were his immediate precursors? If we ask of the paleontological and archeological evidence this question, what is the answer? We do not ask for the presence of speech or language, but of languages and dialects; we do not ask for evidences of the use or control of fire, or of tool using and tool making, or even religion and burial, but of differing "arbitrary" systems, of cultures in the sense that we find them universally in *Homo sapiens*. In the fossil record, which were the last primitives, and which the first full men?

I turned to Lois Mednick, a student of human paleontology, to examine for me the most evidences available; to attempt to develop and apply criteria that might yield answers to the question. The following paragraphs are mainly her words, influenced by our discussions and only editorially modified by me.

I. LATE LOWER PLEISTOCENE

THE AUSTRALOPITHECINES:

THE FIRST TOOL MAKERS.

Abundant Australopithecine bones have been discovered in South and East Africa. The remains of the earlier group (Oakley, 1954), Sterkfontein (Broom and Schepers, 1946; Broom et al., 1950), Taungs (Dart, 1926), and Makapan (Dart, 1948, 1949), were found in caves and limeworks in a semi-arid, upland plains region that has the characteristic scrub and grass cover of the Transvaal (Brain, 1958; Howell, 1960). Morphologically, the Australopithecines were adapting to bipedalism (Washburn, 1950; Mednick, 1955) and their cranial capacities and dental peculiarities (Le Gros Clark, 1952; Robinson, 1952) place them intermediate to apes and man. Despite the fact that, morphologically, these fossils fall in a proto-hominid category, they manipulated and fabricated tools (Dart, 1959; Leakey, 1959). The Sterkfontein remains (and the temporally later Swartkrans fossils) are found in direct association with abundant artifacts of pebble tools and split-bone scrapers, blades, punches, and clubs.

A second group of Australopithecines (Zinjanthropus) was discovered (Leakey, 1959) in an open air site in the Olduvai Gorge in East Central Africa. Later in time than the South African Australopithecines (Oakley, 1959), the Zinjanthropus population has a more elaborate cultural inventory. Their Pre-Chelles-Acheul tools are chunks and nodules of hard, fine-grained rock which were shaped by percussion flaking into choppers or chopping tools. The stone for making these implements was brought to the occupation site, quite often from areas some distance from the workshop. In addition to this Oldowan tool assemblage, there is a mass of bones of other animals such as antelope, carnivores, baboons, pigs, small rodents, birds, reptiles, and amphibians. The presence of these animal bones indicates that the Australopithecines hunted, captured, or scavenged animal food to some degree.

Taking the extreme position of pushing the Australopithecine data as far as possible, the following reconstruction of their behavior is possible:

From the number of Australopithecine bones found in the Transvaal and Tanganyika sites, it is probable that they lived in small groups of twenty to forty individuals (Washburn, 1959) near sources of permanent water (cave pools or lake sites) which would be important in these semi-arid regions. It seems likely that their nuclear groups would usually be extended biological families; the family may equally well have consisted of a mature male and several females with their immature offspring or of a single male and female with progeny, since the evidence for either pattern is conjectural though based upon primate behavioral studies (Sahlins, 1959; Washburn, 1959).

In either case, band size, the level of technology, plus their plains adaptation, would bring these first hunters and gatherers into frequent contact with other groups at the source of water or at "sleeping" areas such as caves or rock shelters. Due to the fact that the animals they hunted were either small and/or new born (Howell, 1960), and consequently could not feed more than a few people at a time, it seems doubtful that the hunting-gathering groups were very large. Their inventory of stone and bone tools would also preclude any efficient exploitation of the fauna available to them and it is more than likely that they were primarily gatherers who satisfied their taste for meat occasionally. Their pursuit of food probably occupied most of their waking period and given another source of water than that found in cave pools, they may have returned to the caves only in inclement weather. It is more than likely that they slept wherever nightfall found them: squatting in the taller scrub of the area or climbing to sheltering rocks that would offer some protection against nocturnal predators such as cats.

Since there is no evidence of their using fire, one must assume that the animals they killed were eaten raw almost immediately after the act. New born or small juvenile animals might have been carried with them or hobbled and later killed and eaten when the need arose.

If, on the other hand, the level of communication made possible a social organization structured to the extent that males cooperated in the day's hunt, which is doubtful, then their hunting techniques may have consisted of beating the brush in a concerted effort to capture and kill the meat necessary for the group. Small animals could be cornered or driven into bogs and larger animals might have been crippled by driving them into fissures or gorges. Hamstringing and stoning may also have been known techniques (Howell, 1960). However, limited by their tools, butchering large animals, or, for that matter, even skinning them, would be almost impossible. Small or new born mammals, rodents, and birds would be much simpler to deal with since they are easily skinned, their heads are simple to twist off to get to the brains, and so forth.

The fact that the Australopithecines transported stone to the caves and open air site implies that they knew the fracturing properties of different rocks and were perceptive enough to look for the types which made the best tools and to gather them for future use.

The finding of two skulls with depressed fractures of the sort that could have been produced by a femur-club (Dart, 1959) could imply deliberate killing of Australopithecine by Australopithecine, but the evidence is equally lacking to conclude that it was for any of the following purposes: (1) cannibalistic; (2) protection against outsiders; (3) punitive; (4) revenge of a "kindred"; (5) ritualistic sacrifice; or (6) removal of the ill or aged.

In regard to language, the inference may be drawn that the Australopithecines must have possessed some means of communication beyond those found in other animals. The level of their technology implies that they were able to pass on a tool-making tradition, to hunt, and to live in small groups. Certainly they had some sort of vocalization and system of gesture, yet the level of their existence casts serious doubt on their having a true language.

MIDDLE PLEISTOCENE:
STANDARDIZED TOOL-MAKING OF HUNTERS.

'At the time of the Australopithecines, there was only alpine glaciation in Europe. The Middle Pleistocene marks the beginning of the first of several extensive continental glaciations in the northern hemisphere. The Mindel and Riss glaciations profoundly influenced the distribution of animals and plant life and, consequently, that of early human populations. Evidently, it was during this period when the first migrations into extra-African areas of southwestern Asia and India were in progress (Howell, 1960).

In eastern and southeastern Asia, Sinanthropus populations provide our next fossil evidence. These hominids produced stone tools of the chopper/chopping tool industry: single edged choppers and chopping tools, rough flakes and small crude flake tools, whose technique of manufacture, if not the finished product, (Braidwood, 1960) resemble the Pre-Chelles-Acheul stage of the Australopithecine tool assemblage. The chopper/chopping tool tradition has not been discovered west of the Ganges floodplain (Movius, 1944, 1948) while the Pre-Chelles-Acheul tools range from Africa to Southwestern Europe and India (Washburn and Howell, 1960).

Peking Man was found in a cave deposit which contained the remains of more than forty individuals. Some of the bones show evidence of cannibalism. Bones of animals that are non-cave-living are also abundantly present and were brought in by Sinanthropus. There is some evidence that this was probably a seasonally occupied site. This might indicate that these forms, in addition to continuing the making of tools, had gained a rudimentary, yet workable knowledge of the migratory habits of animals (Howell, 1960).

Sinanthropus also presents us with our first example of any animal's using fire: There are charred antler and bone fragments, beds of charcoal, and baked clay hearths. Whatever the value of fire to the species (cooking and preserving of food, heat, light, protection against animals), its use indicates a second large step (the first, tools) in the manipulation of nature.

Howell (1960) points out that over most of the inhabited world of this period, the formal tools were all fashioned in standardized ways. He writes: "This standardization of several techniques of manufacture and of characteristic forms of finished implements indicates a considerable *social* (italics mine) tradition among these early groups aside from very considerable manual dexterity and intimate knowledge of flaking properties of various rocks."

So far, in this review of the archeological fossil associations, there has been a universality of the material characterizing the East, on the one hand, and Africa, Europe and India, on the other. This is even more remarkable when we consider that the Australopithecine and Sinanthropus fossils with their artifacts span 800,000 years of man's evolution, yet instead of demonstrating a changing cultural adaptation through time and space, they can only be said to demonstrate an areally homogeneous static adjustment. Except for the addition of the use of fire, however one might interpret its significance, there is no change, and a socio-cultural reconstruction of the Sinanthropus cultural material would be materially the same as that made for the Australopithecines.

This lack of change during the first four-fifths of the Quaternary Period, in itself, strongly cautions against the interpretation we have given for the Australopithecine socio-cultural attainments. Instead, and we feel this is true for Sinanthropus also, it seems more correct to say that what we are seeing during this period of man's past is pure species (grantedly, Eastern and non-Eastern) behavior. Behavior defined by and limited by the biological and psychological nature of the genetic makeup of the hominids and proto-hominids and certainly not "cultural" in the modern sense. Certainly, the stability of attainment and the lack of change cannot ever be taken as characteristic behavior of *Homo sapiens* as we know him, and we must look closer to home for our first representative of *Man*.

EARLY UPPER PLEISTOCENE:
SPECIALIZED HUNTERS AND GATHERERS.

This period began somewhat over a hundred thousand years ago. In the northern latitudes it was heralded by the deglaciation presaging the Last Interglacial. There is evidence of increased populations and also of larger social units, signs of cultural development and *changes* in technology, including certain specializations into environments never utilized by earlier men.

During this period, flake implements come into their own. In Europe, western Asia, and northern Africa, this culminated in the complex of Mousterian stone industries, associated with the Neanderthal populations. With the advent of the Mousterian complex, there is a remarkable diversity of formal, standardized stone tools (McBurney, 1950). Tools no longer are in a single tradition, but differ for western, central, and eastern Europe alone. This is the first time that we have had evidence that Man's capacity for culture had developed to the point where cultures were possible.

The archeological associations of the Early and Classic Neanderthal populations, viewed from the most conservative of positions, will support a claim for a rapidly increasing cultural heritage. Tool traditions differ for sites within continental Europe, Africa, and the Near East. Within continental Europe, for example, cave assemblages are different from open-air site assemblages (Movius, 1944, 1948). There is no universal tool kit which will characterize these populations, nor is there even a similar ecological adaptation to only a semi-tropical environment. The Classic Neanderthals, as Howell (1951) demonstrates, show the results of having been cut off from the rest of Europe by glacial conditions and evolved, morphologically and culturally, partially in response to isolation under conditions of extreme cold.

Also, our first evidence of human burial is found in this period. Again there is no uniformity of practice: flexed and extended burials are found. Grave goods range from shell ornaments and flint tool to animal bones and red ochre. In some instances, the grave is outlined by rocks, in others, the corpse was weighted down by slabs of rock (La Ferrassie I). These funeral practices point to a rudimentary concern for their dead, at least; to an awareness of the life processes and a conscious attempt at religious expression, at best. A maximal interpretation seems the more justified when one remembers the flourishing of cave art which immediately follows the demise of the Neanderthals.

In regard to their possession of language, some anthropologists consider the stylization and variation of burial practices as sufficient evidence that these peoples had more than rudimentary speech and gestures (Howells, 1946). If this were true, then the isolation of the Classic Neanderthals could not but have resulted in linguistic differences separating them from other populations.

Furthermore, Howell (1960) in reviewing archeological evidence from this period assumes a level of development which included ethnocentrism.

Socio-cultural Universal	Australo-pithecines	Sinanthropus	Neanderthals
1. Groups in a bounded territory	1. Evidence for	1. Evidence for	1. Evidence for
2. Language	2. No evidence	2. No evidence	2. Some authorities posit presence
3. Social structure	3. Minimal	3. Minimal	3. Larger units of cooperation
4. Religion	4. No undoubted evidence	4. No undoubted evidence	4. Evidence abundant; burials
5. Value systems	5. No evidence	5. No evidence	5. Evidence scant; speculative
6. Ethnocentrism	6. No evidence	6. No evidence	6. Some evidence; We-*vs.*-They intergroup conflict
7. Rate of change through time and space	7. None	7. Tool technology static, fire present	7. Evidence of rapid change

". . . there are several instances of lance wounds and signs of severe blows in skeletal remains of this period, not only in Europe and western Asia, but also in sub-Saharan Africa. This has suggested to some workers the possibility of organized group warfare, perhaps related to the defence of territorial rights infringed upon by other shifting groups."

The chart above summarizing the evidence here brought together by Lois Mednick, shows clearly that the word "primitive" can be applied only to men who have been extinct since the late Pleistocene. At least, since Aurignacian times, all populations of *Homo* have been fully *sapiens,* differing only in the content of their cultures. Quite posibly even Neanderthals in Mousterian times were already men living in communities with languages, with social systems and with value systems as much as any present population; if this proves so, the term "primitive" would be applicable only to people extinct since the end of the mid-Pleistocene, about 100,000 years ago.

DISCUSSION

Mrs. M. EDEL.—What is the relevance of "culture" among monkeys to the distinction between primitive and modern man through cultural variation?

Dr. E. MULLER.—In Germany, the term "primitive" has been abandoned for a long time. In Germany the term "Naturvölker" is used, but it will nearly mean the same. Professor Mühlmann has proposed the term "ethnological cultures," but I would propose the term "ethnic culture" and "ethnic people" which will be suitable if we understand by the term "ethnos" groups which are not peoples in the modern sense, but communities, as described by Professor Tax, i.e., groups characterized by common value systems, common language, and social system.

Professor TAX.—We shall not be able to find a common word

for all non-European cultures, that is, a word for all trees which are not oak-trees, because this is not a legitimate concept.

Dr. J. F. BULSARA.—I think that, in the absence of an unemotive terminology available to social sciences as used by natural sciences, the difficulty of describing the cultural status of ethnic groups is bound to be great. The civilized anthropologists, perhaps unknowingly, made the first mistake of considering the ethnic groups distinct from their own and applied valuational terminology when describing them. This led to the first confusion, and now they are finding it difficult either to sustain their unscientific terminology or to remain scientific if they go on using the unscientific emotive vocabulary. The difficulty could be avoided, as Professor Tax suggested, by recognizing that all known living ethnic groups belong to the genus *Homo sapiens* and that they are different only in the degrees of technological advance. To describe the peoples and their cultures, the names used by the groups or communities themselves should be adopted. To *classify* their degrees of development, factual and current terminology such as "alphabetical" and "unalphabetic" or prescript and postscript may be used.

Moreover, it should not be forgotten that, if we accept the theory and fact of human and psycho-social evolution, the stream of life will have to be treated as one, and we may have to point out the rudimentary traits of a social character which are common to the primates, i.e., *Homo sapiens* and Ape-Man and down to lower mammalian life and birds. If that be so, even the so-called "primitive" man may show the rudiments of culture which would effloresce in the continuous stream of development, which at a certain stage would be taken to mark off *"Homo sapiens."*

REFERENCES CITED

Brain (C. K.) 1958. The Transvaal Ape-Man-Bearing Cave Deposits. *Transvaal Museum Memoir*, no. 11., Pretoria.

Broom (Robert) and Schepers (G. W. H.) 1946. The South African Fossil Ape-Men: The Australopithecinae. *Transvaal Museum Memoir* no. 2, Pretoria.

Broom (Robert), Robinson (J. T.), Schepers (G. W. H.) 1950. Sterkfontein Ape-Man, Pleisianthropus. *Transvaal Museum Memoir*, no. 4, Pretoria.

Broom (Robert), Robinson (J. T.) 1952. Swartkrans Ape-Man, Paranthropus crassidens. *Transvaal Museum Memoir*, no. 6, Pretoria.

Clark (J. Desmond) 1960. Human ecology during Pleistocene and later times in Africa south of the Sahara. *Current Anthropol.*, 1 (4), 307–324.

Dart (R. A.) 1925. Australopithecus africanus: The man-ape of South Africa. *Nature*, CXV, 195–199.

Dart (R. A.) 1948. The Makapansgat protohuman Australopithecus prometheus. *Am. J. Phys. Anthropol.*, 6 (3), 259–283.

Dart (R. A.) 1949. Innominate fragments of Australopithecus prometheus. *A. J. Phys. Anthropol.*, 7 (3), 301–332.

Dart (R. A.) 1949. A second adult palate of Australopithecus prometheus. *Am. J. Phys. Anthropol.*, 7 (3), 335–338.

Dart (R. A.) 1959. Further light on Australopithecine humeral and femoral weapons. *Am. J. Phys. Anthropol.*, n. s. 17, 87–93.

Howell (F. Clark) 1951. Pleistocene glacial ecology and the evolution of classic Neandertal Man. *Southwest. J. Anthropol.*, 8, 377–410.

Howell (F. Clark) 1960. The Old Stone Age in *Book of Popular Science*. Grolier Society Publications, New York.

Howells (W. W.) 1946. Mankind So Far. Doubleday & Co., New York.

Leakey (L. S. B.) 1959. The newly discovered skull from Oldoway: first photographs of the complete skull. *Illustrated Lond. News*, CCXXXV, 288–289.

Le Gros Clark (W. E.) 1052. Hominid characters of the Australopithecine dentition. *J. Roy. Anthropol. Inst.*, LXXX, 37–54.

Lowie (Robert) 1930. Primitive Society. Liveright, New York.

McBurney (C. M. B.) 1950. The geographical study of the older Pleistocene stages in Europe. *Proc. Prehist. Scty.*, N. S. 16, 163–183.

Mednick (L. W.) 1955. The evolution of the human ilium. *Am. J. Phys. Anthropol.*, n. s. 13, 203–216.

Movius (H. L. Jr.) 1944. Early Man and Pleistocene stratigraphy in southern and eastern Asia. (Papers of the Peabody Museum of American Archeology and Ethnology, XIX.) Harvard University Press, Cambridge, Mass.

Movius (H. L. Jr.) 1948. The Lower Paleolithic cultures of Southern and Eastern Asia. *Trans. Am. Philos. Soc.,* n.s., XXXVIII, 329–420.

Murdock (G. P.) 1934. *Our Primitive Contemporaries.* Macmillan, New York.

Oakley (K. P.) 1954. Dating the Australopithecinae of Africa. *Am J. Phys. Anthropol.,* n. s. 12, 9–28.

Oakley (K. P.) 1957. Tools Maketh Man. *Antiquity,* XXXI, 199–209.

Robinson (J. T.) 1954. Prehominid dentition and hominid evolution. *Evolution,* VIII, 324–334.

Service (Elman R.) 1958. *A Profile of Primitive Cultures.* Harper & Row, New York.

Spuhler (J. N.) 1959. Somatic Paths to Culture. In *The Evolution of Man's Capacity for Culture,* J. N. Spuhler (ed.). Wayne State University Press, Detroit, Mich.

Washburn (S. L.) 1950. The analysis of primate evolution with particular reference to the origin of man. *Cold Spring Harbor Symposium on Quantitative Biology,* vol. 15.

Washburn (S. L.) 1959. Speculations on the interrelations of the history of tools and biological evolution. *Hum. Biol.,* 31, 21–31.

STANLEY DIAMOND

The Search for
the Primitive

As soon as a man appears who brings something out of the primitive along with him, so that he doesn't say, "you must take the world as you find it," but rather "let the world be what it likes, I take my stand on a primitiveness which I have no intention of changing to meet with the approval of the world," at that moment, as these words are heard, a metamorphosis takes place in the whole of nature. Just as in a fairy story, when the right word is pronounced, the castle that has been lying under a spell for a hundred years opens and everything comes to life, in the same way existence becomes all attention. The angels have something to do, and watch curiously to see what will come of it, because that is their business. On the other side, dark, uncanny demons, who have been sitting around doing nothing and chewing at their nails for a long time,

jump up and stretch their limbs, because, they say, here is some-
things for use, and so on.   —Kierkegaard

This thing we call "civilization"—all these physical and moral
comforts, all these conveniences, all these shelters, . . . constitute
a repertory or system of securities which man made for himself like
a raft in the initial shipwreck which living always is—all these
securities are insecure securities which in the twinkling of an eye,
at the least carelessness, escape from man's hands and vanish like
phantoms. History tells us of innumerable retrogressions, . . . But
nothing tells us that there is no possibility of much more basic retrogressions than any so far known, including the most basic of them
all: the total disappearance of man as man and his silent return to
the animal scale, to complete and definitive absorption in the other.

No small part of the anguish which is today tormenting the
soul of the West derives from the fact that during the past century—
and perhaps for the first time in history—man reached the point of
believing himself secure. Because the truth is that the one and only
thing he succeeded in doing was to feel and create the pharma-
ceutical *Monsieur* Homais, the net result of progressivism! The
progressivist idea consists in affirming not only that humanity—an
abstract, irresponsible, nonexistent entity invented for the occasion—
that humanity progresses, which is certain, but furthermore that it
progresses necessarily. The idea anaesthetized the European and the
American to that basic feeling of risk which is the substance of
man. . . . Human history thus loses all the sinew of drama and is
reduced to a peaceful tourist trip, organized by some transcendent
"Cook's". . . . This security is what we are now paying for.
                                                —Ortega y Gasset

THE PANDORA'S BOX which I propose to reopen is
vast, complex, and many-chambered. The problems it contains
range from the historiographical to the theological and technological, but I am going to state the case as simply and strongly,
indeed as naively, as I can.

It may seem surprising that anthropologists cannot agree on
a definition of "primitive." After all, we have more or less systematically studied peoples characterized in that way for at least

Reprinted by permission of International Universities Press from Man's
Image in Medicine and Anthropology (edited by Iago Galdston), 1963, pp.
62–115

a century. A few anthropologists even deny the existence of special emphases in native cultures which might, in turn, justify the concept *primitive*. This should not put us off; it is a common fashion in our hyperanalytic age. Physicists, for example, are not at all certain about the attributes of atoms, not to mention the lesser particles, which no human eye has ever observed directly; they seem infinitely divisible and complex, they appear in a variety of states, and it is hard to determine where they begin or end. Yet the atom continues to exist as a conceptual model, as a shorthand way of organizing confusing and inaccessible data. The concept is operative, even if a few very positivistic physicists would deny its descriptive validity. With appropriate modifications, we might similarly describe the relationship of biologist to cells, and geneticist to genes.

The point is that these ambiguities are not the result of too little information or not enough quantifiable science. They arise, rather, from a fashionable mode of looking at the world, a way we have of disorganizing, or disintegrating, our data. One is reminded of the tale told of the aging physicist, who could not walk across a room for fear of falling through the enormous distances that he knew existed between the microcosmic particles that composed his environment—if, I should add, particles they were. This hyperanalytic attitude would seem to be, more than anything else, a reflection of the minute division of labor demanded by our contemporary industrial society, of certain cultural assumptions, and of the equation of science to the machine. It is the very opposite of the primitive view, which is synthetic, or holistic—but I shall deal with this more fully below.

Here, it is enough to suggest that our hestitation in defining "primitive" is paralleled in most other disciplines with reference to their major subject matters. It is not a function of ignorance, but of a scientific *style*, which has grown unreasonably opposed to the idea of fundamental assumptions, of synthesis and of conceptual models, important as such skepticism, from time to time, may be. Still, any human discipline, or any science, that shrinks from epistemology and metaphysics reduces itself, finally, to mere mindless technique.

THE CRITICAL TERM

Primitive is, I believe, the critical term in anthropology, the word around which the field revolves, yet it remains elusive, connoting, but never quite denoting, a series of related social, political, economic, psychological, and psychiatric meanings. That is, *primitive* implies a certain level of history, and a certain mode of cultural being, which, in this paper, I shall make a further attempt to formulate (11).

This mode of cultural being is continuously obliterated or attenuated by the processes of civilization, and more radically so than we are usually able or willing to acknowledge; as a result, the image of an identifiable, cross-cultural, pre-civilized, and, yes, a priori human nature has practically disappeared from our conceptual lexicon. Unyielding cultural relativism, cultural determinism, and social scientism are, in part, and each in its own way, rationalizations of a civilization that has forgotten what questions to ask of itself. These attitudes have helped blunt the sense of universal human need, conflict and fulfillment which has been most adequately expressed, in the past, through art and religion. It is, I believe, a singular task of anthropology, no matter what its practitioners call themselves, to assist in the reformulation of pertinent life-preserving questions.

The search for the primitive is the attempt to define a *primary* human nature. Without such a model, or, since we are dealing with men and not things, without such a vision, it becomes increasingly difficult to evaluate, or even to understand, our contemporary pathology and possibilities. More pertinently, without an anthropology bent on rediscovering the nature of human nature, the science of medicine may survive, but the art of healing will wither away. For healing flows from insight into primary, "pre-civilized" human processes, into a comparative and individualized sense of human needs; that is, it presumes a knowledge of the primitive, a sense of the minimally human, that is, of what is essential to the condition of being human.

Human consciousness is historical; in order to understand ourselves, to heal ourselves, in this age of abstract horror, we must regain the sense of the totality and the immediacy of human experience. In order to determine where we are, we must learn, syllable by syllable, where we have been. The sense of history is, for society in crisis, what relentless self-searching, psycho-analytic or otherwise, is for the individual in crisis, that is, it can be releasing and enriching, cathartic and creative; it may be the only thing that can save our lives. History implies exhortation, because it is confession, failure and triumph. It is the measure of our capacity, the link between man and man, the key to ourselves. The lack of the sense of history, or the mechanization of history, that is, the view of its processes as immutable and inevitable, is the death of man. The only inevitable, literally unavoidable, events are, in the cultural sphere, accidents, and certain categories of natural phenomena, which, from the human perspective, have the fatality of accidents.

Yet, the "post-historic" creature, necessarily congealed in a bureau and reduced to a function, is a common enough plotting of the future (52). This image of the human termites of tomorrow, each exuding its specialized bit of culture to what is conceived as an infinitely rich and almost palpable social whole, used to be one of Kroeber's favorite predictions, based, as it was, on Wheeler's work with insects, and attitudes toward men (58). All those who assimilate human history to natural history, or mechanize it, help dull the sense of history and prevent men from confronting themselves. The penalty we pay for blunting the historical sense is dissociation, both social and individual; the tripping of the fuse on the bomb, will, under such conditions, become only the ultimate incident in the course of a chronic cultural illness—something abstract, that we nevertheless do.

"When we contemplate the past, that is, history," Hegel said, "the first thing we see is nothing but—ruins." Out of these ruins of civilization, we must win through to a whole, but concrete, vision of man. Every thinker of consequence from the beginning of the industrial revolution, to the present has, in one way or another, warned us of this necessity. Darwin, Freud, Marx, Einstein, L. H. Morgan, Tylor, Henry Adams, Paul Tillich,

Boas, Kierkegaard, Sartre (We read these names like Moslem beads, but do we understand them?), have, while concentrating on particular problems, urged us to a vision of the unity and autonomy of man. Modern anthropology itself, as Lévi-Strauss (35) has, in effect, argued, probably germinated in a search for the historical contrast to our own intolerable condition, in a search, that is, for the primitive; it was, no doubt, as he also implies, an expression of remorse for the ideological and technical conquest of the planet by western Europeans, themselves restive in a culture they had learned to wield as a weapon. It follows that the anthropologist has been the disengaged man par excellence, dissatisfied at home, questing abroad. He is a scout sent out by a civilization in turmoil to find a resting place, and learn the lay of the land. He is, if true to his origins, a type of Ulysses, though, I am sure, more Joycean than Homeric.

Modern anthropology is the search for man in history, undertaken by a society threatened with automatism. In broader perspective, anthropology may be said to begin with civilization, certainly with the Greeks, and perhaps with the Babylonians, the Egyptians, the ancient East Indians, or the Chinese. It would be instructive to study the records of the latter four non-western civilizations in order to determine how far anthropology had advanced among them and what forms it took. Wherever civilization arises, the primitive in Man is subordinated; it withers away, grows attenuated or is replaced. Thus the puzzled search for what is diminished, the search for different ways of being human, for the primitive, which is anthropology, begins. Even Plato, who was probably the most beneficently civilized man in history, pays tribute, in the beginning of *The Republic,* to the satisfactions of his bucolic version of primitive life, which he feels plausibly constrained to replace by his towering and totally civilized Utopia. Plato understood that, in civilization, we cannot know what has been gained, until we learn what has been lost.

Later, when brought down to earth in *The Laws,* the last of the Dialogues, the Heavenly city turns into a rather ominous polity. Plato spent his life trying to define and create a model of civilized man in civilized society. All of his work is a kind of anthropology of civilization, a vast exploration of political society, and it should interest us that it ends on a note of despair. For *The Laws* is no longer Plato struggling to grasp, *to create*, civilization as part of an expanding human consciousness; his final social statement is frankly repressive and pragmatic, and prophecy becomes mere prediction. In *The Laws*, human nature has become the enemy, and we recognize civilization. Freud, had he permitted himself the luxury of philosophizing, would have analyzed the Plato of *The Laws* perfectly, just as Plato, had he acknowledged the primal necessity of *poiesis*, of ritual, would have been able to penetrate more deeply into the nature of that "primitive," actually rustic, life which he nostalgically abandons in favor of the ideal state. Yet in *The Republic*, in contrast to *The Laws*, whether we like it or not, we are caught by a vision of man finding himself in civilization, although in ways that are hardly viable since they exclude, rather than incorporate, the primitive.

If Plato concerned himself with the problems of civilization, ranging from the aesthetic to the technical and legal, at a time when civilization in Greece had become an insoluble problem, other philosophers, writers, travelers, and historians have been more deeply concerned with uncivilized people. Their descriptions vary immensely, and many are clearly projective, or otherwise distorted, but what runs through them all, whether drawn by Herodotus or Tacitus, Ovid, Seneca, or Horace, Columbus or Camöens, Montaigne or Gide, Rousseau or Monboddo, de Bougainville, or Melville or Conrad, is the sense of contrast.[1] Civilized men are here confronting what they presume to be primordial; they are saying, "this is the way we were before we became what we are, *this is the other side of our humanity*." That is the anthropological statement, and it will always remain the anthropological question.

1. It is hardly necessary to note that this problem of contrast is an explicit, major theme in the work of many modern students of society, e.g., Redfield, Radin, Sapir, Tylor, Boas, Maine, Maitland, Morgan, Marx, Engels, Tönnies, Freud, Fromm, Weber, Durkheim, Mauss—and a minor theme in Kroeber, Linton, Benedict, Fortes, and a host of others.

Paradoxically, as civilization increases in depth and scope, anthropology proliferates, but it becomes increasingly professionalized. The urgency of the central question is lost sight of, it is even denied. This question of our humanity is repressed *because* of its awful urgency, and the risks we must undergo in attempting to answer it. The very circumstances, then, that lead to the deepening need of the anthropological search, that is, the expansion of civilization, also convert anthropology into a mere discipline with narrowing borders, more mechanical techniques, and more trivial goals. It may even come to pass that the central question, the question of what part of our humanity we have lost, and how and why we have lost it, and how and in what form we may regain it, will soon cease to be a concern of anthropology. Perhaps significant statements about man will no longer be made by anthropologists, just as most sociologists no longer say anything very compelling about society, or political scientists about politics, economists about economics, and so on, precisely because these fields, reflecting the larger division of labor in our culture, and increasingly analytic attitudes, have grown further and further apart. But man cannot be subdivided endlessly; moreover, the most critical tissues escape the scalpel; it is the entire organism which must be studied. Correlatively, history cannot be quantified; we must win back the courage to evaluate.

In the beginning, bureaucracies counted—people, goods, land—in order to muster, levy, and control (9), *to record those facts* which became the basis for civil imposition. It follows that in the logic of history, a bureaucratized discipline is, first and foremost, a quantifying one. Later, quantification becomes an end in itself, not just, as it always is in the human sciences, a problematic and limited means. The principle of evaluation is absorbed into, or subordinated by, this numbers game—an abstract ploy of counters that avoids policy, principle and meaning by presuming to rise above them. The new pedantry is the pedantry of the machine.

The danger that anthropology faces, then, is literally this: it is becoming too civilized, too abstract, too bureaucratized. It is being transformed into just another specialized exercise, a symptom of our civilization, congruent with, rather than antithetical to it. The latter is its true patrimony, and it should be a vocation of anthropologists to make this truth known.

My contention, then, is that the term *primitive* has content in anthropology; that it cannot be evaded; and that the attempt to explore its implications remains our central task, precisely because we are so civilized, and so in need of a deeper vision of man. It is in this way that anthropology can remain one of the most instrumental and useful, though it may often seem the most remote and eccentric, of disciplines.

THE WORD ITSELF [2]

It is generally agreed, that the English word primitive is a direct adaptation of the medieval-modern French form *primitive,* which is the feminine of *primitif.* The only change, apart from the shift in accent from the last to the first syllable, is the shortening of the final *i* in English. Indeed, the first documented appearance of the word in English is in a Middle English tract on surgery, circa 1400, where it is spelled prymytiff, and has the meaning "primary" or "original" (causes prymytiff), a denotation which it has retained through its history. Another very early usage appears in a statement of Henry VII at York, circa 1486, containing the phrase "primative patrone." Here primative implies "earliest," "original," and "primary," not only in time, but in rank. The *a* in primative may reflect a dialectic variation, or, what is more likely, it may be derived from the old French *primat,* which meant a leading dignitary in the Church. It is of some interest to note that the dual meaning of contemporary word primate, that is, "a ruling ecclesiastical figure" and a "biological order comprising lemurs, tarsiers, monkeys, apes, and men," has

2. I wish to acknowledge the kind assistance of R. J. Schork, Chairman, Classics Department, Georgetown University, in tracing the etymology of "primitive." All standard etymological dictionaries were used.

its origin in the feedback between two lines of descent from the original Latin term, *primus,* one denoting rank, the other, temporal order.

The first modern spelling of the word (the adoption of the French feminine form), seems to have appeared in the title of a book published in 1581—*Positions wherein those Primitive Circumstances be Examined which are Necessarie for the Training up of Children.* As an anthropologist, I find this a particularly congenial context. Here primitive has the sense of "primary," with the added nuance of "basic."

The French *primitif* is derived from the medieval Latin *primitivus* (primus = first + ivus, a later adjectival ending), meaning earliest or oldest. *Primitivus* was originally used in postclassical Latin as a grammatical term to indicate archaic words (*verba primitiva*). It was not until the medieval period that *primitivus* gradually came to mean "primary," "earliest," or "oldest." Actually, it does not appear in English and Irish Church texts until the twelfth century, when it began to supplant *Pristinus* and *Priscus.*

Primitivus can be ultimately traced back to classical Latin *primus,* through the derivative adverb *primitus* (in the first place), and the cognate adjective *primituus. Primus,* of course, means "first" or "earliest," and is the superlative corresponding to the Latin comparative *prior* (earlier). *Primus* is, moreover, related to *pristinus,* meaning "existing in, or as if in its first state," and *priscus,* "synonymous with *pristinus* except that the thing represented no longer exists"; both words were eventually replaced by primitive, as indicated. Their denotations were purely temporal, reflecting Cicero's use of *cascus* (old or ancient), a cognate of *priscus,* when referring to time past. Lucretius, it may be noted, is even more diffident; in *De Rerum Natura,* he simply adopts such constructions as *tunc* (then), and *nunc* (now).

The classical Latin forms are probably based on the Homeric adverb and Attic preposition and conjunction *prin,* which means "before." This, in turn, derives from the presumptive proto-Indo-European root *pri,* which also has the sense of "before." In Latin, therefore, the prefixes *prim, prin,* and *pris* are extensions of the Indo-European *pri.* A cognate prefix *pra* exists in Sanskrit (in Doric Greek also); in the former language the words *prakkalina* and *prathamakalina* mean "belonging to an earlier time," which is very close to the etymological "primitive."

All major European languages, except Greek, seem to have adopted the word primitive from a medieval (Church) Latin source; whether the word was mediated through the medieval-modern French, where it first appeared in the 14th century, is, except in the instance of English, difficult to determine. In Spanish, Italian, and Portuguese *primitivo* is the current form; in Romanian (which may have borrowed it directly from post-classical Latin), German, Dutch, Flemish, Danish, Norwegian, Swedish, and Hungarian *primitiv* is used; in Latvian—*primitius;* and so on. There is a parallel word in Greek—*protogonos,* meaning "first born," that is, "earliest" or "oldest."

In none of these languages does the term primitive have an etymologically pejorative significance. Although all languages associated with civilized polities do seem to have words, that etymologically imply the inferiority of other groups, such as the Sanskrit *mlechha,* the Greek *barbaros* and the English *uncivilized,* the word primitive lacks this structural implication. Even *savage* does not suggest anything more, in its derivation, than "living in the woods," that is, "close to nature" (from Latin *siluaticus,* an adjective of Latin *silva*). And the word pagan is ultimately derived from Latin *pagus,* meaning "village," but originally signifying "a boundary post stuck into the ground." More precisely, the Latin *paganus* descends from *pagus,* and means, successively in time, "villager," "peasant," "civilian," and finally, "heathen." Thus the evolution of Rome from "a boundary post stuck into the ground," that is, a compact between villages, to the emergence of the Church is symbolized in the history of the word pagan. But for most of Roman history, before Constantine, a "pagan" was a villager, a peasant, and, perhaps, by literal implication, a man of peace (*pax*), in contrast to the civil-military representatives of the state.

Primitive, pagan, and savage are, then, three perfectly respectable words. But primitive is the most widely disseminated, in the most recognizable forms, in major languages, and has, even today, the least pejorative associations, signifying, as it does, merely a prior state of affairs, a relative sense of origins. Therefore, I see no reason for abandoning the word, as is periodically suggested, hedging it with quotes, prefacing it with the inexplicit irony of "so-called" or replacing it with limited, and misleading expressions such as "pre-literate." [3] The task is, rather, to define further, and help construct a consensus on what primitive means.

PRIMITIVE IN TIME AND SPACE

How are we to locate primitive peoples in time and space? In attempting to answer this question, I shall tentatively adopt the following scheme, based on four very broad phases of development. The *first phase* extends from the initial appearance of culture in the Lower Paleolithic, some half-million years ago, to approximately 10,000 B.C., roughly the Paleolithic-Neolithic period of transition. This tremendous span, despite its diversity, comprises, from the standpoint of succeeding phases, the phase

3. The presence or absence of writing as a criterion of primitiveness is inadequate. The complex, advanced horticultural societies of the Guinea Coast and South America lacked writing, yet they were, as we shall see, archaic *civilizations*. Another difficulty involved in the use of the literate–pre-literate criterion (apart from the prediction inherent in *pre*) is the differential distribution of the trait of literacy within societies that have been classified as literate and therefore nonprimitive. The overwhelming majority of Chinese, for example, have been unable to read and write throughout Chinese history. This is also true of extensive peasant areas in Europe. In contrast, Japan with a peasant society base still largely operative prior to World War II is said to have attained the highest literacy rate in the world.

There is no doubt, that beyond a certain socio-economic level, literacy is a necessary development in any society; it is essential to the acceleration, accumulation, and increasingly complex fiscal-military controls associated with civilization. The mere existence of writing, among a tiny fraction of the populace, as in China before World War II, makes literacy an ambiguous measure. It is, then, the use to which literacy is put, its correlation with society in depth, that converts it into a proper historical diagnostic. The point is that literacy is a secondary, not a primary, tool and symptom of civilization.

of *cultural origins*. Whatever information is available rests on rather slender archeological evidence; we know next to nothing concerning the origins or then extant forms of language, social organization, religion, and so forth; i.e., most of the formative, nonmaterial aspects of culture remain inaccessible to us. The study of contemporary "primitive" peoples sheds no clear light on these matters: Such inquiries give us no insight into the "dawn of human consciousness," for we make suppositions based on material—including, aesthetic—artifacts, assuming always that our knowledge of contemporary pre-civilized groups is applicable, and then, of course, the argument becomes a tautology. What I mean to say, and this will grow more evident later, is that the anthropological "primitive" applies, or should apply, to the condition of man *prior* to the emergence of civilization, and *following* those earliest periods of cultural growth culminating in the Upper Paleolithic. However, the typical institutions of primitive peoples, which I shall discuss below, have long established histories; so far as I am aware, we have never witnessed, nor have we a record of, the ultimate origins of these institutions.

The *second phase* begins about 9,000 B.C., and lasts until the inception of an archaic form of state organization, or civilization, emerging circa 5,000 B.C., in the Middle East, but varying, in time, widely around the world; for example, marginal peoples of the High Nigerian Plateau, or interior New Guinea, are only now becoming involved in political society. This phase, from the Paleolithic-Neolithic transition to one or another early form of the state, is the germinating period of cultural forms that can be called "primitive," and is reasonably accessible to anthropological scrutiny and reconstruction. This is the location in time which Claude Lévi-Strauss (35), considers "primitive," and, as Lovejoy (36) indicates, it is the settled condition which Rousseau sensibly attempted to outline in the *Discourse on the Origins of Inequality*. Be that as it may, it is at this juncture, reached at different times at different places, that the historical and contemporary dimensions of the concept *primitive* coincide in a scientifically acceptable way.

The search for origins cannot effectively be pushed back beyond the Paleolithic-Neolithic transition; even the most peripheral peoples—the Bushmen, Eskimos, and probably the Australians—share basic features with so many other native groups that they can hardly be considered representative of an earlier phase of development, and, if somehow they are, the differences are, for the present purpose, not pertinent. "Primitive," then, refers to widely distributed, well-organized institutions that had already existed just prior to the rise of ancient civilization; it does not imply historically an inchoate time of cultural origins, nor psychiatrically the period when supposed "primary processes" were directly expressed.

But these well-established primitive institutional patterns do not disappear with the emergence of archaic civilizations, the *third phase* in this provisional scheme, encompassing political societies in the Mediterranean Basin, the Further Middle East, the Near East, and the New World.

These archaic [4] societies embrace people who are primitive, in transition from primitive to peasant status, or who have been converted into full-fledged peasants, culturally influenced by and economically dependent upon market centers; they are marked by "pre-industrial" towns whose citizens and slaves discharge commercial, ceremonial, administrative and military functions. Probably, most of the world's population still lives in this archaic, apparently exhausted social environment. Certainly the majority of people studied by anthropologists are found within one or another variety of archaic political structure, whether or not that structure has maintained its integrity. In certain cases, the centralizing mechanisms may even have disappeared, but local groups survive and continue to resonate their previous asso-

---

4. I should note that I am here avoiding the vexing category *feudal*. In Europe, and probably in Japan, feudalism, which is primarily a type of political society, followed the dissolution of archaic state systems. In parts of East Africa, e.g., Ankole (47), feudal conditions were apparently generated by the subordination of primitive cultivators to warrior herdsmen; this pre-state feudalism is evident in the varying forms of clientage and land tenure that developed.

ciations, as among Meso-American and Hausa peasants, and, in a historic instance, as Medieval Normandy after the disintegration of the Carolingian Empire (2).

I should re-emphasize that this *third cultural phase* can develop either prior to, or in the total absence of, agriculture and writing. Advanced horticulturists in West Africa, for example, produced a considerable surplus, which supported a type of organization that included: (a) a complicated system of taxation and conscription; (b) a developing class system; (c) a rudimentary bureaucracy whose primary function was fiscal-military administration of fairly well-defined territories; (d) pragmatically conceived civil laws which arose, at first, to expedite taxation and conscription; (e) chiefs or kings who began to wield secular power within an infant political structure, which maintained many of the forms, while changing the substance, of the previous primitive institutions. At the same time, these advanced horticultural societies rest on, indeed can only survive by, drawing their strength from a base (9) which remains genuinely primitive, according to criteria that I shall attempt to indicate below.

The *fourth cultural phase* is the modern state, that is, contemporary civilization, coincident with the maximal politicization of society. This process began with the mercantile and scientific, and continued through the industrial revolutions in Western Europe; it is now, of course, diffusing rapidly, in a variety of forms, throughout the world. As maximal political societies advance, primitive and archaic traits crumble within their borders and on their frontiers. Put another way, the primitive characteristics which managed to survive under the surface, or in the formal ideological patterns of archaic civilizations, and among the most isolated peoples, became casualties to the total revolution stimulated by the extension of modern civilization.[5] Authentically primitive and maximally civilized traits are, I believe, as antithetical as it is possible for cultural attributes to become within the limits of an established human condition. This is,

5. As in the instance of reincarnation, which can reasonably be considered a formal, archaic elaboration on ritual death and rebirth among primitives.

however, the present fact of history and it constitutes the problem of this paper, for the sickness of civilization consists, I believe, in its failure to incorporate (and only then to move beyond the limits of) the primitive.

"PRIMITIVE"–A POSITIVE DEFINITION

It follows from the foregoing that there are two direct field opportunities for studying primitive groups. One can either pursue the few remaining peripheral peoples, those uninvolved in any archaic superstructure, and reached by only the most superficial of modern civilizing influences; or, alternatively, one can study the more remote local groups associated with still existent archaic civilizations, always attempting to distinguish, of course, between primitive and peasant traits.[6] It is this correlation of the two directly available categories of primitive with archeological, including documentary, evidence that results in a generalized conception of primitive life, fusing historical and contemporary information.

6. I have been fortunate in having been able to undertake field work among a quite marginal group of simple cultivators, the Anaguta of the Nigerian Middle Belt, and in an archaic society—mountain Arabs on the Israeli-Jordan border. I have also studied a modern, in a certain sense, a hyper-civilized, community, the Israeli Kibbutz. The point is that the average anthropologist probably investigates no more than two or three different societies in the course of his career; reflection and reading fill out his training. Thus, the basis of his generalizations is always empirically limited. Moreover, our most important generalizations are interpretive, as they must be in any historical discipline concerned with the problem of meaning, and not merely with the surface of social facts.

There is no ultimate, contemporary authority in these matters, and it is even doubtful whether further information is necessary. The problem is one of integration and synthesis; yet, as Kierkegaard (29) was perhaps the first to indicate, no total or totally objective system is scientifically possible, because man in history is never complete. When all is said and done, we can only express considered opinions on the most significant matters in anthropology or related fields; their relative wisdom will depend upon the depth and imagination of the observer, and on the reality of his commitment; confirmation depends upon what men decide to do in history, and even then may be objectively ambiguous, or, what is worse, merely academic. At any rate, it is at least clear that the profounder facts *do not* speak for themselves.

This is not to deny the uniqueness or societal individuality of one primitive group vis-à-vis another; indeed, the possibility of differential cultural emphasis seems to be greater, even if subtler, among relatively discrete and self-sustaining primitive societies than among civilized groups. One society may emphasize property displays, another the manufacture of baskets of all shapes and sizes, and so on; each emphasis being the hyper-accentuation of diffused or generic, social, economic, or psychological tendencies, which often have the idiosyncratic character of sports or play. But in contrast with civilization, these distinctions fade as the basic similarities are illuminated, for the variations that do occur are elaborations of those fundamental themes that are the very definition of the primitive; they happen within certain limits, and do not threaten the integrity of the society. Moreover, historical contrasts between primitive societies and maximal civilizations are far more fundamental than: (a) "horizontal" variation among primitive societies employing similar subsistence techniques; and (b) primitive societies employing different subsistence techniques, e.g., hunters and gatherers as opposed to simple horticulturalists. The distinctions between the most marginal hunters and a local group in an advanced horticultural society are, of course, significant in many respects, but I am interested here in the substantial similarities that exist, even in such cases.

I will not linger on negative definitions of *primitive*, i.e., on what is *not* primitive in language, religion, magic, art, psychological function, and so on. All these categories are involved, but I prefer to state the cast positively and, since space is limited, while qualifications can go on forever, with minimal circumlocution and explanation. The historical model I hope to induce is just that, a model, a construct, which limits and helps define the range of variations on a level of organization termed *primitive*. Although specific instances and usages are cited, this does not imply their universality insofar as form is concerned, but the functional equivalents of the formal modes specified certainly seem to exist everywhere in the primitive world; and certain fundamental attributions of meaning also seem universal among primitives.

But first I wish to repeat that all primitive peoples are marginal to the mainstream of modern history, primarily because of "accidents" of habitat, that is, removal from the developing centers of civilization. In the sense already noted, contemporary primitives can be roughly conceived as our contemporary, precivilized ancestors. Their organically interrelated characteristics may be outlined as follows:

1. *Primitive societies rest on a communalistic economic base.* This is not to say that everything in such societies is owned in common, which is clearly not the case, but rather that those material means essential to the survival of the individual or the group are either actively held in common, or what is equivalent, constitute readily accessible economic goods. The group can be defined as the customary, cooperative work unit, ranging in size from one or more nuclear families, as among the Eskimo, through the various extensions to the clan or group of clans; or it can be a locality, a village, part-village, or village cluster; in any event, the work unit may shift according to season, purpose and need.

Exceptions to this communal condition dissolve under close scrutiny. For example, it is claimed that members of Hottentot joint families "own" particular cows in the family herd, but we find that they cannot privately dispose of them. It is similarly assumed that individuals "own" particular watering places, but we discover that access is never denied to other people in need of it (23).

On the other hand, true private property does exist among primitives, in the form of tools made by the individual, breechclouts, back scratchers and similar "extensions of the personality." However, private property of this type does not constitute "primitive capitalism"; the latter does not exist, at least among primitives. The private property that can be identified is either not essential for group survival, is readily duplicated by any individual in the society, and therefore need not be owned communally, or is of so personal a nature that it cannot be owned communally.

If primitive capitalism is an illusion, the critical question of primitive property has, unfortunately, been obscured by both the partisans, and the antagonists, of the concept of primitive communism. The partisans too often seemed to be stating that everything in primitive societies is owned in common, including, at one stage, wives and children, thus conjuring up a false image of an absolute, monolithic, social, economic, and psychological collectivism (13). But their antagonists just as often misconstrued the nature and function of the private or personal property that does exist among primitives. Individuals were said, for example, to "own" incorporeal property—songs, magic spells, curing rituals and so on. This may be true, but it is irrelevant to the economic base of primitive communal society. Moreover, such prerogatives tend to be widely distributed; even where certain of them are concentrated in the hands of shamans or medicine men, they remain readily available to other people, in exchange for goods or services that are by no means scarce. Knowledge of esoteric lore is also widely distributed; any elder is likely to know the details of a particular medicine rite, although its exclusive administration may be the profession and prerogative of certain individuals. But even this preference can be waived in the absence, illness, or death of sanctioned persons. In authentically primitive communities, esoteric lore seems to be more publicly known than we have usually supposed.

There are other ways in which attitudes and social behavior have been confused with basic economic functioning, thus further obscuring the issue of primitive property. For example, primitive societies frequently emphasize competitive games, ceremonies, property displays, property giveaways and so on, but such competition, whether assuming an economic form, as in the Kwakiutl potlatch, or an aesthetic form, as in the wonderfully spontaneous and satirical Eskimo sings, does not endanger, and is irrelevant to, the communal functioning of the economic base. Indeed, this type of competition, even when subserving other functions, should be seen, primarily, in a socio-psychiatric context; the Eskimo sings, for example, are creative and socially bounded ways of discharging hostility; they do not lead us to characterize Eskimo society as competitive in the fundamental socio-economic sense.

Even in the proto-states of East and West Africa, the underlying social units, the joint families or clans, work cooperatively and hold land in common, although a certain portion of the surplus they produce is siphoned off for the support of the rudimentary civil power.

The general point, then, is that primitive societies uniformly possess a communal economic base, or, put in a corollary form, economic exploitation of man by man, as we know it in archaic and modern civilizations, is absent. Even where a degree of exploitation develops, as in the proto-states—usually through the payment of tribute or labor service—it rarely results in the economic ruination of one group or individual by another. Thus, we find that in primitive society, in the ordinary course of events, no man need go hungry while another eats; production is for use or pleasure, rather than for individual profit; just as primitive society is not competitive in a basic structural sense, it lacks a genuinely acquisitive socio-economic character. Laurens van der Post spoke to this point as follows: "An old hunter in Africa, the simplest and wisest man I ever knew, once said to me, 'The difference between the white man and the black man in Africa is that the white man 'has' and the black man 'is' " (56).

Correlatively, there are no economic classes, in the sense that any paramount group may be said to own the means of production, although a chief may, in his person, symbolize the property rights of a particular unit. It follows that primitive economies are natural economies; they lack true money. I mean by this that the three related, and defining, attributes of civilized money—that is, money as an abstract, intrinsically valueless medium for appropriating surplus, storing value, and deferring payment or delaying exchange—do not adhere to primitive money. The latter serves as a counter or symbol of value, as in native Dahomey, where cowries were used to represent tribute that was actually collected, in kind, by the king's agents (9).

Even this role of primitive money is marginal. Exchange among primitives is usually effected by barter or gift. These converge toward being, literally, donations, akin to sacrifices (43), that is, not merely a giving of goods, but a giving of oneself. While civilized money tends to alienate man from his labor by transforming that essential function of his humanity into an abstract commodity, by detaching it from him, by transferring considerations of "worth" and "value" from a human to a marketing context, primitive exchange has the contrary effect: Social value and social effort are always directly expressed and understood; they strengthen the sense of community. Indeed, the major emphasis in most forms of primitive exchange seems to be on *giving*, and this may be accompanied by attitudes ranging from the hostile to the generous. The primitive gift may serve an "economic" purpose, within a reciprocal system, but like most significant activities in primitive society, it is multi-functional, a focus for the expression of a wide range of emotions and purposes.

We can conclude, then, that in primitive society, there is no morbid individual anxiety about the fundamental right, or opportunity, to work as a peer among peers; this is simply not at issue. The expectations of food, clothing, shelter, and work are not juridical because they are unexceptionable. The rights and duties involved are completely customary. The basic economic structure functions rationally.

2. *In primitive societies, the major functions and roles of leadership are communal and traditional, not political or secular.* The chief of a clan, or the patriarch of a family, are respected as the embodiments of clan, family or tribal heritage. In many societies, a clan chief is simply the oldest member of the group. Obeisance toward these figures is symbolic, a sign of respect for one's tradition, and thus of self-respect. It is not the result of coercion or an institutionally manipulative social act.

Leadership may be, also, situational, and/or based on skill. Primitive societies abound in "chiefs." In any one tribe, e.g., the Anaguta, there may be hunting, work, dance, women's, age grade, and fishing chiefs. These leaders function only in specific contexts and for limited periods of time; usually, their primacy is based on capacity in the particular activity. It does not carry over into the round of daily life; and, almost everyone in the society is, at one time or another, in a "chiefly" position. W. H. Rivers (50) makes this point as follows:

When studying the warfare of the people of the Western Solomon Islands, I was unable to discover any evidence of definite leadership. When a boat reached the scene of a headhunting foray, there was no regulation as to who should lead the way. It seemed as if the first man who got out of the boat or chose to lead the way was followed without question. Again, in the councils of such people, there is no voting or other means of taking the opinion of the body. Those who have lived among savage or barbarous peoples in several parts of the world have related how they have attended native councils where matters in which they were interested were being discussed. When, after a time, the English observer found that the people were discussing some wholly different topic, and inquired when they were going to decide the question in which he was interested, he was told that it had already been decided and that they had passed on to other business. . . . The members of the council had become aware, at a certain point, that they were in agreement, and it was not necessary to bring the agreement explicitly to notice (50).

Leadership may be, further, a function of generalized rank and status, which automatically accrues to every normal member of the group through the mere fact of his having attained a certain age or undergone certain experiences. In the latter case, a qualification is necessary. Every normal man will have the opportunity to achieve status via certain experiences, but not all men will be equally successful. Statuses may be hierarchically organized in primitive society, but they are not scarce, and their formal distribution and function is part of a historically selective, if "unplanned," rational paradigm.

These factors, along with other social mechanisms, to be considered, are clearly ego syntonic. Moreover, the association of major, traditional, with shifting, situational, and "automatic" types of status leadership, reduces the occasions for what can be termed "broad spectrum" social hostility, while diminishing the alienation that develops in response to arbitrary, remotely exercised, and impersonal authority. In these respects, and others, primitive systems do not squander their substance by inequities woven into the social fabric. In a profound psychological sense, primitive societies are democratic, though they are not reductively "equalitarian." Equality is not construed as identity in primitive life. Leadership is reasonably distributed and exercised.

3. *It is a logical corollary and a historical truth, that in primitive societies, laws, as we know them, do not exist.* Society operates through custom, and by well-understood informal sanctions, not by means of a legal apparatus administered from above in the interest of this or that group, i.e., not by codified laws. There are no special legal functionaries; there is no specific and exclusively legal apparatus. The multitudinous occasions for law that we are familiar with in civilization, e.g., commercial rights, governmental levy, and bureaucratic function, simply do not occur in primitive society. As Tylor put it, "one of the most essential things that we can learn from the life of rude tribes is how society can function without the policemen to keep order" (55). There are certain obvious exceptions to this generalization, for example, the Plains Indian buffalo police, but they are the exceptions that prove the rule, explicable as the result of particular circumstances; they are neither permanent formal groups, nor manifestations of an over-arching legal order (37).

In the proto-states, of course, specialized laws, courts, and judges had begun to develop, but at the primitive base of these complex societies, the traditional, customary machinery continued to operate (45).

Among primitives, then, there is no body of law, and no permanent supportive militia standing apart from, and above, the people at large. Thus, that curious aspect of alienation that arises in all political societies, the division between "we" and "they," the citizen versus constituted public authority (44), does not develop. The people and the militia, the people and the tradition are for all practical purposes indistinguishable. Among primitives, the public authority is representative in fact; there is no constitutional theory. In civilization, the theory of public authority adhering to one or another form of government is paramount, but representation, in fact, becomes problematical.

4. *Primitive societies tend to be conservative; they change slowly compared with more technologically advanced cultures;* [7] *consequently, they do not manifest the internal turbulence endemic in archaic or contemporary civilizations.* The fact that sanctions are customary is not the only reason for the relative conservatism of primitive life. A more significant factor is that primitive societies tend to be systems in equilibrium; they are not disrupted by institutional conflicts, although they contain well-structured, often cyclical conflicts among institutions; and, of course, personal conflicts do exist. The former is exemplified in the limited struggles among sodalities, and in certain types of institutionalized deviancy; the latter in the ordinary play of personalities, which may intensify to witchcraft. Indeed, the built-in social mechanisms for the expression of hostility which these structured conflicts partly are, help strengthen the social fabric; the society so to speak, recognizes and provides for a wide range of human expression.

Despite, or rather, because of this, society to the primitive is apprehended as a part of the natural order, as the backdrop against which the drama of the individual life unfolds. It is sanctified by myth, revealed in ritual, and buttressed by tradition. The social network is perceived as a more or less permanent arrangement of human beings vis-à-vis each other. Since the basic needs for food, clothing, shelter and, as we shall see, personal participation are satisfied in all primitive cultures in a socially nonexploitative manner, revolutionary activity is, insofar as I am aware, unknown. It is probably safe to say that there has

7. Technical development alone may seem, at first glance, a perfectly objective measure of progress, as many social scientists still contend. But in the perspective of a primitive society, the culturally defined needs of which are being adequately met by the available techniques, it might seem otherwise. A prologue to a theory of progress is perhaps implicit in the argument I am presenting, but does not seem worth pursuing, since it is already part and parcel of Twentieth Century disenchantment with "perfectly objective" measures of human affairs.

never been a revolution in a primitive society; revolutions are peculiar to political societies. Indeed, the Messianic and nativistic movements that have periodically swept primitive cultures under the threat of external destruction, indicate the relative state of institutional grace in which they ordinarily function.

The primitive, then, is a conservative; his society changes its essential form only under the impact of external circumstances, or in response to drastic changes in the natural environment. Institutional disharmonies never reach the point of social destruction, or, correlatively, of chronic, widespread individual disorganization.

5. *It follows that, in primitive societies, there is a very high degree of integration among the various major modalities of culture.* Between religion and social structure, social structure and economic organization, economic organization and technology, the magical and the pragmatic, there are intricate and harmonious correlations. These correlations have two major effects: (*a*) they tend toward the optimal practical efficiency of the system; and (*b*) they integrate a whole series of emotions and attitudes around a given activity, rather than isolating or abstracting the activity from its human context. An obvious example of the first effect is the maximal use of technology by primitive economic systems; so far as I know, no primitive economic system is dysfunctional with the available technology. Neither does it utilize technology in a wasteful or inefficient way, no matter what "bizarre" means are brought into play to dispose of surplus beyond the point where the subsistence needs of the group are met, or to stimulate exchange. The second effect is exemplified in the validation of practical activities by magico-religious means, as in the classic case of the expert Trobriand canoe maker, who confirms the step-by-step construction of his craft with spell and incantation.

A rough and simplified model of functional integration in primitive society is provided by a type of joint family structure widely distributed throughout Africa, although parallels are found in other major ethnographic areas. The nucleus of such a (predominantly) unilateral, unilocal family may consist of (if it is patrilineal and patrilocal) the patriarch, one or more younger brothers, and his and their sons and unmarried daughters; around the nucleus circulate the wives of the male members. The culture in which this residential unit is the critical, but not the sole, social group can be analyzed as functioning on three primary, interrelated levels:

The dominant ideological activity = ancestor worship.
The dominant social unit = joint family.
The dominant economic activity = shifting horticulture.

These three particular forms or usages, representing the major, reciprocating levels of the society, constitute the core of the culture. They are, so to speak, the culture in essential cross-section. Obviously, they do not comprise the entire culture, but each is critical on its level, and is functionally correlated with the critical forms and usages on the other levels. When we say that such a culture changes, we mean, in effect, that the core processes have changed, and they always change in a demonstrable relation to each other.

In this system, extensive areas must be regularly cleared, cultivated with hoes, and periodically abandoned; this requires a cooperative labor unit, which happens to be efficiently achieved by a group of nuclear families residing together and related generationally, as, in this example, through the male line—a joint family—in a structure sanctified by ancestor worship.

I am not implying here that shifting hoe cultivation, joint family structure, and ancestor worship are inevitably linked traits. Ancestor worship functions in systems that are not predicated on shifting horticulture. Joint families exist in the absence of any kind of horticulture. And shifting horticulture is associated with ideological and social complexes which cannot be precisely defined as ancestor worship or joint family organization. The linkage of forms, in the model outlined above, is historically and functionally, not inevitably determined. Moreover, I am not suggesting that religion is merely epiphenomenal to a socio-economic base—even though ancestor worship, for example, persists so long as the joint family-horticultural system maintains its integrity; the native religion, will indeed, absorb Christian elements when under missionary assault, if the social economy remains relatively unshaken, but it disintegrates rapidly when the society to which it is immediately relevant crumbles. In this sense, the socio-economic base may be considered an independent, the religion, a dependent variable. But this applies only to a particular *form* of religion, not to religion as such. Even the specific forms of religion must be viewed as social inventions, and not as automatic projections of a particular social economy, just as a social form viable to a particular technology is, also, an invention and not a logically inevitable development.

That is, religion, *qua* religion, is a fundamental mode of cultural behavior, correlated with other modes, but not *caused* by them. It is, I believe, as absurd to assume that religion germinates in economic and social factors as it would be to claim the opposite—that the roots of economic (or social) activity lie in religion. They are equal, and equally ancient, needs, capacities and propensities of human nature, related, in their generality, in ways that are incredibly complex, and far from evident. Moreover, when the form of a major ideology, such as ancestor worship, its substructure undermined, collapses its insights and postulates do not vanish from the consciousness of men; they become part of a universal inheritance.

Returning now to the specific joint family structure under consideration, the land cannot be alienated or sold because the primitive living within the system views the earth as the dwelling place of his ancestors; it is *terra sancta*. Thus, we can trace a functional connection between religion and land tenure, an economic factor.

The patriarch is the family priest, the living link to the ancestors and thus the embodiment of family tradition. Yet he serves also as coordinator—though not necessarily field chief—of the cooperative labor unit, and as the channel for the distribution of the social goods produced. The family itself is not only a labor force, but a ceremonial group; it is, so to speak, its own congregation. Thus, connections between socio-economic and ideological factors are readily identified.

The patriarch functions also as the arbiter of disputes within the family and, in many instances, among families. He, therefore, discharges a social task having political and juridical aspects.

When the family grows beyond the size at which it can efficiently operate, given its ecological circumstances, a new joint family buds off from it into free clan or village lands. The new patriarch, who may be a younger brother or an older son in his compound of origin, sets up a new establishment; and this is considered a culturally heroic act. He may be regarded, literally, as a culture hero—and ecological necessity thus becomes permeated with a moral purpose, which to the primitive, moving within the system, is not segregated from other purposes, and may indeed be said to be primary.

In short, within the typical joint family structure, there develop complex correlations among economic, social (including political, legal), and ideological factors, or alternatively stated, particular persons function in a multiplicity of ways, and specific activities bind a wide range of responses. These correlations do not unite *all* economic, social and ideological activities; only the major ones on each level are involved, the sum of which are essential to the survival of the group. The others, whether economic, social or ideological, are subsidiary, as, for example, fishing is among cultivators.

To the primitive acting within the society, the major elements interpenetrate in a circular manner: All aspects of behavior converge in a system that strives toward maximum equilibrium. We, of course, can and do, analyze out the component parts of the system; *we* can demonstrate that changes in technology, in the mode of making a living, or land tenure, introduced by Europeans, shatter the joint family structure and with it, eventually, ancestor worship—but the primitive person moves within this system as an integrated man. His society is neither compartmentalized nor fragmented, and none of its parts is in fatal conflict with the others. Thus the primitive does not perceive himself as divided into *"Homo economicus," "Homo religiosus," "Homo politicus,"* and so forth. He stands at the center of a synthetic, holistic universe of concrete activities, disinterested in the causal nexus between them, for only consistent crises stimulate interest in the causal anlysis of society. It is the pathological disharmony of social parts that compels us minutely to isolate one from another, and inquire into their reciprocal effects. And it is at least likely that Malinowski's (39) functionalism is the reflection of the primitive view from within the system, raised to the level of theory, and converted into a tool for analyzing all societies, even where inappropriate.

As Sapir (51) implied, this primitive holism is in startling and significant contrast to our own conflict filled, isolating, and abstract—our increasingly civilized—experience of society.

6. *A fundamental reason for this contrast is that the ordinary member of primitive society participates in a much greater segment of his social economy than do individuals in archaic, and in technically sophisticated, modern civilizations.* For example, the average Hottentot male is an expert hunter, a keen observer of nature, a craftsman who can make a kit bag of tools and weapons, a herder who knows the habits and needs of cattle, a direct participant in a variety of tribal rituals and ceremonies, and he is likely to be well versed in the legends, tales, and proverbs of his people (and a similar list could be drawn up for the Hottentot female). The average primitive, relative to his social environment, and the level of science and technology achieved, is more accomplished, in the literal sense of that term, than are most civilized individuals. He participates more fully and directly in the cultural possibilities open to him, not as a consumer, and not vicariously, but as an actively engaged, complete man.

A major reason for this functional integrity is in his control of the processes of production; that is, the primitive, in creating a tool, creates it from beginning to end, uses it with skill, and controls it. He has no schizoid sense of it controlling him, and he has direct access to the fruits of his labor, subject to the reciprocal claims of his kinsmen. He stands, in the face of nature, much less elaborately equipped than ourselves, with his whole being and all of his faculties and activities geared for the survival and perpetuation of his family, clan, village, or tribe. In Kenyatta's words:

Before the advent of the white man the institution of serfdom and wage-workers was unknown to the Gikuyu people. The tribal customary law recognised the freedom and independence of every member of the tribe. At the same time all were bound up together socially, politically, economically, and religiously by a system of . . . mutual help, extending from the family group to the tribe (28, p. 168).

In contrast, glance again at the frequently drawn portrait of the fractionated worker, emerging in modern civilization (not to mention the serf or slave who occupied the stage before him), compelled to sell his labor power as a marketable commodity. Indeed the worker who appeared after the industrial revolution began to regard *himself* as a commodity, as a tool, or an extension of a tool—the very opposite of the primitive view of the tool as an extension of the personality. The modern worker, and to varying degrees his predecessor in archaic civilization, became alienated, specialized, and morally estranged in the process of production. Correlatively, the power of the "owners," or chief executives, became an inhuman power; [8] their freedom is pseudo-freedom for it is based on the coercion of subordinate groups; they are bound to those whom they exploit. Their social ties grow manipulative; their privileges—irresponsible. Nor do the managers, tech-

8. Goldenweiser (17, pp. 108–109) gives an interesting linguistic illustration of this: "When the executive speaks, words emerge from his lips not unlike mechanical tools which, having established contact with those spoken to, make them go through their paces. Such words are brief, as precise as possible, and thoroughly impersonal."

He continues by drawing a contrast with the example of a more primitive function of speech: "But we also speak to reveal content, inviting the one spoken to to participate in our ego. . . . Here personality comes to the fore, time flows easily, what counts is the enhancement of the moment through psychic interplay. . . . Such was the conversation of primitive folk . . . here folk-lore thrived and mythology took form. Such also is the conversation of peasants, with its proverbs, allusions, metaphors, its pithy descriptions and composed narratives."

nicians, bureaucrats and clerks escape this fate. It is the present agony and peril of all classes and grades in civilized society. If civilized production has helped disorganize modern man, and deprive him of his moral center, primitive production helped to integrate primitive man.

7. *A fundamental reason for the holistic and moral, but not moralistic, character of primitive society is that it is organized on a kin or tribal, not on a political basis.* All significant economic, social and ideological functions are discharged within and among kin or quasi-kin groupings, whether these are nuclear families, joint families, clans, clusters of clans, or the various types of sodalities. Society thus functions on a personal, corporate and traditional, rather than on an impersonal, civil, and individualized basis. The words of a Pomo Indian are pertinent:

In the white way of doing things, the family is not so important. The police and soldiers take care of protecting you, the courts give you justice, the Post Office carries messages for you, the school teaches you. Everything is taken care of, even your children, if you should die, but with us the family must do all that. Without the family, we are nothing, and in the old days before white people came, the family was given first consideration by anyone who was about to do anything at all. That is why we got along. With us the family was everything. Now it is nothing. We are getting like the white people, and it is bad for the old people. We had no old people's home like you. The old people were important. They were wise. Your old people must be fools (21).

Kin units, then, together with the technically non-kin institutions patterned after their image (age grades, specialized friendships, cooperative work groups, male or female clubs, etc.) *comprise* primitive society. Although the immediate biological family is everywhere evident (38), it is usually found merged within a larger unit. The important point is that all meaningful social, economic, and ideological relations have a kin or transfigured kin character. Even within the most extensive clan organizations, where hundreds of people may be said to descend from a common ancestor, and the actual blood relationships may either be entirely attenuated or completely fictitious, people still behave toward each other as if they were kin.

This *personalism*, splendidly illustrated by Hallowell (19), is the most historically significant feature of primitive life, and extends from the family outward, to the society at large, and ultimately to nature itself. It seems to underlie all other distinctive qualities of primitive thought and behavior. Primitive people live in a personal, corporate world, a world that tends to be a "thou" to the subjective "I," rather than an "it" impinging upon an objectively separate, and divided, self. Consciousness for the primitive is the most common condition in the universe, a perception that is also found, in more civilized and abstract forms, in the work of Whitehead, Haldane, and Teilhard de Chardin.

Negative traits of primitive society, such as witchcraft, represent the dark side of this personalism. Yet primitive witchcraft seems significantly distinct from the civilized species of witchcraft, which implies the arbitrary attribution to, or assumption of destructive and occult power by, civilized individuals, and is apparently the result of rigidly repressed instinctual urges and projected feelings of guilt. Among primitives, witchcraft seems to arise rather from the intensity of personal life, which produces unusual sophistication and subtlety about people, and in certain areas, a dangerous sensitivity. Yet, the belief that people can make other people sick contains its obvious truth; it need not be based on chronic insecurity in human relations and is not only the result of scientific ignorance. Indeed, further studies of the types of people who are considered witches, within a given primitive society and cross-culturally, should be illuminating in terms, for example, of the conception of the witch as an inordinately narcissistic person, a bad mother, or unfulfilled woman.[9] As the Gikuyu say, "To live with others is to share

9. Among the Anaguta, a witch (*ukiri*—the most obscene word in the language) was identified after a social consensus was reached through dreams experienced by many people, in which one particular person appeared constantly as a threatening or destructive agent. Anybody could, in theory, become a witch, but the actual incidence was quite rare, and usually resulted in the suicide of the person concerned. Even in such cases, being a witch was considered an unfortunate attribute, for which the person was not, in his very "essence," condemned. The individual who was acting as a witch (this is more accurate than simply calling the person a witch) was never accused directly, but ultimately in subtle, yet well-structured ways, the message struck home.

and to have mercy for one another," and, "It is witch-doctors who live and eat alone" (28, p. 172).

At its most positive, however, primitive personalism is the "one touch of nature that makes the whole world kin"; it suggests the quality of "co-naissance," of universal relatedness, of being born together, which, interestingly enough, the French Catholic Existentialist Paul Claudel, reaching deeply into his own consciousness, has illuminated in his art.

8. This brings me to the observation that *primitive modes of thinking are substantially concrete, existential, and nominalistic, within a personalistic context.*[10] This does not suggest a lack of abstract capacity (*all* language, *all* culture and convention flow from this phylogenetic human endowment), but it does indicate an emphasis functional with the kinship structure of primitive society, and a lack of concern with the specific type of abstraction that may be called, in the Western civilized world, Platonic.

Boas wrote:

Primitive man, when conversing with his fellow man, is not in the habit of discussing abstract ideas. . . . Discourses on qualities without connection with the object to which the qualities belong, or of activities or states disconnected from the idea of the actor or the subject being in a certain state, will hardly occur in primitive speech. Thus the Indian will not speak of goodness as such, although he may very well speak of the goodness of a person. He will not speak of a state of bliss apart from the person who is in such a state. He will not refer to the power of seeing without designating an individual who has such power. Thus it happens that in languages in which the idea of possession is expressed by elements subordinated to nouns, all abstract terms appear always with possessive elements. It is, however, perfectly conceivable that an Indian trained in philosophic thought would proceed to free the underlying nominal forms from the possessive elements, and thus reach abstract forms strictly corresponding to the abstract forms of our modern languages (3).

10. Here, I am adopting terms that have grown within a civilized philosophic tradition. But this is not to imply that primitives are technically or self-consciously existentialist, nominalist, and so on. *We* can, however, approximately, so classify their modes of thinking. Perhaps it would be more suitable to refer to *existentializing* and *nominalizing* tendencies, but this is a quibble, since the nominal forms of such labels cannot be used precisely to identify even the appropriate civilized systems of thought.

And further:

If we want to form a correct judgment we ought to bear in mind that our European languages, as found at the present time, have been moulded to a great extent by the abstract thought of philosophers. Terms like "essence, substance, existence, idea, reality," many of which are now commonly used, are by origin artificial devices for expressing the results of abstract thought. In this way they would resemble the artificial, unidiomatic abstract terms that may be formed in primitive languages (3).

I can only add that my own experience with primitive modes of thinking bears this out completely. For example, the Anaguta, of the High Nigerian Plateau, never count in the abstract, but count only with reference to concrete things or people; the numerals change form according to the classes of objects being counted, but are not grammatically concordant with them. Yet the Anaguta are fully capable of grasping number unrelated to particular objects. But they do not deify or reify number; there is no occasion for doing so in their society, and the idea seems meaningless to them.

Similarly, in explaining the meaning of a proverb, a concrete context is always presented, for the abstract idea is regarded as inconclusive. Context and existence rather than essence constitute the established aspects of thought. So, for example, the Anaguta say: "Demean the man's character, but never the man himself." This means that a man must be judged on what he *does*, for what he *is* is not only inaccessible, but can lead to many contradictory actions. That is, one can never reach a final judgment on his manhood, only on this or that aspect of his behavior.

Here it is worth noting that Dorothy Lee (34), in classifying Trobriand thought as essentialist, uses "essence" in an ambiguous manner. She does not adopt the Platonic definition, i.e., an ideal or universal form, imperfectly and variously reflected in earthy particulars—but claims, in effect, that each concrete particular (e.g., tubers, in varying conditions or stages of growth) is distinctly named and conceived to have its own being, or "essence." But this is, actually, a nominalist as opposed to a conceptual realist position; the particulars do not refer back to an abstract universal; the individual thing is the ultimate reality. Lee's pure Trobriand essences are, I believe, better described as singular existents; the category "essential" confuses the issue.

However, what F. S. C. Northrop (46) has called a "naive" form of realism is commonly expressed among primitives, emanating, it is evident, from their personalism. But this realism is not of a conceptual character, and may be assimilated to the existentializing tendency. Spirits, for example, are individuated; they concretely exist. As Paul Radin beautifully put it:

> It is, I believe, a fact that future investigations will thoroughly confirm, that the Indian does not make the separation into personal as contrasted with impersonal, corporeal with impersonal, in our sense at all. What he seems to be interested in is the question of existence, of reality; and everything that is perceived by the sense, thought of, felt and dreamt of, exists (48).

The existentialist, rather than the technically essentialist, mode of Trobriand thought is further indicated, even if inadvertently, by Lee when she states: "The magician does not *cause* certain things to be, he does them. . . . It follows that the Trobriander performs acts because of the activity itself. . . ."

I would, also, restate Lee's insistence on the irrelevance of "causality" to Trobrianders as a reflection of the typical primitive holistic and synthetic view, outlined above; the lack of concern with causality can thus be understood as the absence of an analytic, specialized, "scientific" approach to nature and society. But this unconcern, it must be emphasized, is with the elaboration of objective theories of causality; it does not obstruct the sequence of empirical efforts involved in any given task.

Finally, it seems that Lee contradicts herself in claiming that, although the position of a thing or event in a pattern is of paramount importance to Trobrianders, this does not reflect a concern with relationships. Obviously, I take the contrary view, that is, the intricate arrangements of people vis-à-vis each other, the kin nature of primitive culture, is mirrored in the concern with pattern and order in things and events.

9. *In primitive society, the ritual drama is a culturally comprehensive vehicle for group and individual expression at critical junctures in the social round or personal life cycle, as these crises are enjoined by the natural environment or defined by culture.* In such ceremonies, art, religion, and daily life fuse, and cultural meanings are renewed and re-created on a stage as wide as society itself.

In a sequence from archaic to modern civilization, we can trace the process through which religion, drama and daily life split apart. The drama, the primary form of art, retreats to the theater, and religion escapes into the church. The sacraments, those formalized remnants of the primitive crisis rites, and the "theater, the play," develop into carefully cultivated and narrowly bounded conventions.[11] Civilized participation in culture becomes increasingly passive, as culture becomes increasingly secularized.

Among primitives, rituals, are cathartic and creative. They are cathartic in that they serve as occasions for open, if culturally molded expressions of ambivalent feelings about sacred tradition, constituted authority, animal and human nature, and nature at large.

A good example of the cathartic expression of *ambivalence toward the sacred* occurs in the Wintun's Hesi ceremony, "the acme of Wintun ceremonialism." The clown directs his comic assaults at the leader:

When the captain of the host village was singing as he marched slowly about the inside of the dance house, one of the clowns staged himself

11. During 1959 and 1960, several letters and articles appeared in the Soviet press decrying the lack of ritual, of sacramental elements in daily Soviet life (*Izvestia* [25]). Marriage, in particular, was described as being too civil, too casual, in a word, not *holy* enough (*Komsomol-Skaia Pravda* [31]). And it was assumed that institutions such as the Palace of Marriage in Leningrad would help ameliorate this situation (*Izvestia* [26]). However, the sacred and dramatic possibilities of existence are generated by culture as a whole, by the setting of culture in nature, and of human nature in culture—bureaus and monuments are more symptomatic than remedial, as several of the contributors indicated. The Soviet problem, now apparently under discussion, is that the society is, literally, too civilized.

before the captain and marched slowly backwards in step with him, while
delivering joking remarks concerning the leader's ability to sing and the
particular song he was voicing. This did not seem in the least to dis-
concert the singer who continued to sing in his gravest manner; but his
song was not received with the usual seriousness (1).

Ritual expression of *ambivalence toward constituted author-*
ity is illustrated among the Anaguta. Men who are being initiated
into the status of elders had the right publicly to challenge elders
of long standing, who were still physically vigorous, to a combat
with clubs. This took place within a circle of young, newly
initiated men dancing slowly to the beat of drums and the sound
of horns. No man could be struck above the trunk, and the
challenge need not be given or accepted. But for those who de-
sired to do so, this final phase of the men's initiation ceremony
afforded the opportunity to work off hostility against particular
elders who might have abused their authority. Painful injuries
occasionally resulted. Physical cowardice or bluster were exposed,
but did not brand a man beyond the situation, and, as noted,
there was no obligation to participate, although it was honorable
to do so. Nor did the ceremony threaten the general respect in
which the elders were held; on the contrary, the institutionalized
expression of ambivalence helped buttress the social structure
generally.

These rituals are also creative in the dramatic revelation of
symbols, and the anticipation and elaboration of new roles for
individuals; they make meanings explicit and renew the vitality
of the group.

The Hottentot role—transition rites are indicative. At puberty, childbirth, the death of a spouse, and on the contraction
of certain diseases, the slaying of an enemy in war, the killing
of a large game animal, and similar occasions, the individual
is said to be in a condition called !nau (i.e., in an unclean, labile,
or dangerous state). During these periods, he is suspended between two statuses, and is considered to be dangerous to himself
and to others; he is *of* the tribe but not *in* it. Therefore, he is
isolated, and placed in the care of an immune guardian, who

has passed through the *!nau* period for the identical event. In order to be restored to normality, a person must undergo a ritual cleansing, participate in a common meal with people who have emerged from the same situation, and then be reintroduced into the life of the tribe by his guardian, at a ceremonial dance. The person is, in short, conceived to be reborn (22).

Put another way, the primitive rituals are creative in the reduction and cultural use of anxiety arising out of a variety of existential situations. Birth, death, puberty,[12] marriage, divorce, illness—generally speaking, the assumption of new roles, responsibilities, and psychological states, as these are socially defined and naturally induced—serve as the occasions for the ritual drama. Naturally, the formal ritual structure varies from culture to culture, but the functions are mutually assimilable.

Such rituals are, I believe, primarily *expressive*,[13] as opposed to the predominantly binding, compulsive, "ritualistic" behavior encountered as neurotic phenomena among civilized individuals.

The primitive ritual also differs from ritualized *group* occasions in civilized society; the latter strive toward repression of ambivalence rather than recognition and consequent cultural

---

12. Puberty may be, as Radin (49) believed, the primary, pivotal rite of mankind—fusing as it does economic and sexual maturation, while polarizing male and female, and projecting the polarity onto nature at large.

13. An Eskimo game bordering on ritual, reported by Peter Freuchen (15) is illustrative: "There was also the rather popular game of 'doused lights.' The rules were simple. Many people gathered in a house, all of them completely nude. Then the lights were extinguished, and darkness reigned. Nobody was allowed to say anything, and all changed places continually. At a certain signal, each man grabbed the nearest woman. After a while, the lights were put on again, and now innumerable jokes could be made over the theme: 'I knew all the time who you were because—.'

"Several old stories deal with this popular amusement. It should be said that—crude as it may seem to us—it often served a very practical purpose. Let us, for instance, say that bad weather conditions are keeping a flock of Eskimos confined to a house or an igloo. The bleakness and utter loneliness of the Arctic when it shows its bad side can get on the nerves of even those people who know it and love it the most. Eskimos could go out of their minds, because bad weather always means uncertain fates. Then suddenly someone douses the light, and everybody runs around in the dark and ends up with a partner. Later the lamp is lit again, the whole party is joking and in high spirits. *A psychological explosion—with possible bloodshed—has been averted.*" (Italics added.)

use. One can hardly imagine a "burlesque of the sacred" (54), taking place at, let us say, a patriotic ceremony; in this sense all state structures tend toward the totalitarian. But, among primitives, sacred events are, as noted, frequently and publicly caricatured, even as they occur. In primitive rituals, the fundamental paradoxes of human life—*love and hate, the comic and the tragic, dedication and denial,* and their derivatives—are given free, sometimes uninhibited, even murderous, "play," in quite the sense that Huizinga (24) uses that word.[14] But let us remember, to adopt an extreme example, that even ritualized cannibalism or the torture of self or others, recognize and directly confront the concrete humanity of the subject. The purpose of ritual cannibalism is the humiliation of the enemy, but also the absorption of his heroic human qualities. In a way that is repugnant to civilized sensibilities, cannibalism was a bloody sacrament, perhaps the first sacrament. Torture, whether inflicted on self or others, is, of course, sadistic, and masochistic, but it was frequently a test of endurance, of manhood, and of the capacity for spirituality.

Yet the sanguine and terrifying aspects of primitive life, which civilized individuals could hardly sustain, precisely because of the immediate personal contexts in which they occur, do not begin to compete with the mass, impersonal, rationalized slaughter that increases in scope as civilization spreads and deepens.

In this connection, how can I ever forget the shock and horror expressed by an Anaguta informant of mine, whom I had persuaded to attend an American (war) movie in a nearby town. This man spent several hours acting out, in my presence, the indiscriminate and casual, unceremonious killing which he had witnessed on the screen. It was almost impossible for him to be-

14. "The concept of play," writes Huizinga, "merges quite naturally with that of holiness . . . any line of tragedy proves it. By considering the whole sphere of so-called primitive culture as a play-sphere we pave the way to a more direct and more general understanding . . . than any meticulous psychological or sociological analysis would allow.

"Primitive . . . ritual is thus sacred play, indispensable for the well-being of the community, fecund of cosmic insight and social development. . . ."

lieve that human beings could behave in this way toward each other, and he decided that it must be a special attribute of white men—superhuman, and at the same time, subhuman. He finally sublimated the experience to the character of a legend. It was his first movie.

The point is that the wars and rituals of primitive society (and the former usually had the style of the latter), are quantitatively and qualitatively distinct from the mechanized wars of civilization. The contrast is not merely in the exponential factor of technology multiplying a constant, homicidal human impulse; in primitive society, taking a life was an *occasion;* in our phase of civilization it has become an abstract, ideological compulsion. The character of this contrast is implicit in the words of George Bird Grinnell (18):

Among the plains tribes with which I am well acquainted—and the same is true of all the others of which I know anything at all—coming in actual personal contact with the enemy by touching him with something held in the hand or with a part of the person was the bravest act that could be performed.

". . . the bravest act that could be performed was to count coup on—to touch or strike—a living unhurt man and to leave him alive, and this was frequently done. . . .

"*It was regarded as an evidence of bravery for a man to go into battle carrying no weapon that would do any harm at a distance.* It was more creditable to carry a lance than a bow and arrows; more creditable to carry a hatchet or war club than a lance; and the bravest thing of all was to go into a fight with nothing more than a whip, or a long twig—sometimes called a coup stick. I have never heard a stone-headed war club called coup stick." [*Italics added.*]

Such a war is a kind of play. No matter what the occasion for hostility, it is particularized, personalized, ritualized. Conversely, civilization represses hostility in the particular, fails to use or structure it, even denies it. And it explodes with a redoubled, formless bestiality, while we, so to speak, look the other way, refined and not responsible; we wage increasingly impersonal wars, and, unlike the Crow, kill at increasing psychic distance from our victims. Civilization blames its crimes on its leaders, more sophisticatedly on abstract, historical forces, and, finally, abandoning these culprits, despairs utterly of man. Dissociation culminates in depression.

But such unbalanced despair is not reflected, so far as I am aware, in the oral traditions of primitive peoples. Certain ritual dramas or aspects of them acknowledge, express, and symbolize the most destructive, ambivalent, and demoniacal aspects of human nature; in so doing, they are left limited and finite; that is, they become self-limiting. For this, as yet, we have no civilized parallel, no functional equivalent.[15] Even the primitivistic drama of Christianity, with its civilized insistence on the vicarious experience of pain, and joy, has become refined and collectivized to the vanishing point.

10. *If the fulfillment and delineation of the human person within a social, natural, and supernatural (self-transcendent) setting is a universally valid measure for the evaluation of culture, primitive societies are our primitive superiors.* This is not meant as a play on words. What I mean is that in the basic and essential respects which are the concern of this paper, primitive societies illuminate, by contrast, the dark side of a world civilization which is in chronic crisis.

The primitive realization of the person can be termed *individuation*, and it is the antithesis of ideological "individualism."

15. Meyer Fortes expresses a parallel idea: "I do not mean to imply that everybody is always happy, contented, and free of care in a primitive society. On the contrary, there is plenty of evidence that among them, as with us, affability may conceal hatred and jealousy, friendliness and devotion enjoined by law and morals may mask enmity, exemplary citizenship may be a way of compensating for frustration and fears. The important thing is that in primitive societies there are customary methods of dealing with these common human problems of emotional adjustment by which they are externalized, publicly accepted, and given treatment in terms of ritual beliefs; society takes over the burden which, with us, falls entirely on the individual. Restored to the esteem of his fellows he is able to take up with ease the routine of existence which was thrown temporarily off its course by an emotional upheaval. Behavior that would be the maddest of fantasies in the individual, or even the worst of vices, becomes tolerable and sane, in his society, if it is transformed into custom and woven into the outward and visible fabric of a community's social life. This is easy in primitive societies where the boundary between the inner world of the self and the outer world of the community marks their line of fusion rather than of separation" (14).

Ideological individualism is a reflection of what Redfield calls *individualization;* the latter is a symptom of civilization—and denotes the increasingly mechanical separation of persons from each other, as a result of the shrinkage and replacement of primitive, organic ties by civil, collective connections. The pathological loneliness, the schizoid character that Sullivan identified as a prevailing pattern in American life, and as the substratum of psychoses is the corollary of civilized "individualism." Indeed, the recognition and confrontation of this sense of personal isolation has been a major, if not *the* major, theme in the work of the most important contemporary artists and philosophers.

Here is the paradox: Rationalized, mechanized, and secularized civilization tends to produce standard and modal, rather than natural varieties of persons.[16] The individual is always in danger of dissolving into the function or the status. This is, for example, apparently Erving Goffman's thesis in *The Presentation of Self in Everyday Life* (16), and in his studies of total institutions, but such ultimate role playing or infinite masking of the self is not universal, as he would have us believe. It may be dramaturgical or theatrical, as Goffman describes the process, but it is not dramatic. The latter has its roots in the catastrophies and paradoxes, the meanings of ordinary existence, first celebrated and given form in the primitive ritual drama. Mere dramaturgy has as much relation to the living, historical heart of drama as religion has to religiosity. Indeed, such conventional play acting is the anthithesis of the drama. Yet it is instructive that a civilized sociologist should, while accurately describing the intricacies of collective role playing, mistake the construction of a *persona* for the development of the self.

16. Goldenweiser (17, pp. 130–131) expressed it this way: "The factories flooded society with machine-made commodities, all cut to pattern, disindividualized and standardized. From pins to houses, . . . from IQs to Ph.Ds, mechanical uniformity settled upon industrial lands.

"The material base thus transformed tends to affect other aspects of life and thought. Power, speed, efficiency (results), organization, centralization, size, quantity—tend to become universal standards. Society, material and spiritual, begins to move in the direction of a socialized Super-Robot, built after the pattern of a machine."

In the name of individualism, civilization manufactures stereotypes: Dumb Doras, organization men, or Joe Magaracs, whose prototype, in the popular tale, is transformed into the very steel that he helps produce. Such stereotyping usually leads to a culturally formed stupidity, a stupidity of the job itself, which grows to encompass the person, feeding on itself as both a defense against experience and the result of being deprived of it. But the psychologically isolated individual, dulled by the division of labor, and threatened by leisure, yet somehow treasuring the idea that, in his name, society functions and battles are fought, is unknown in primitive society. To be "detached," "unattached," or "objective," that is object-oriented, becomes, as civilization advances, both the symptom of a social condition and the expression of an intellectual attitude. Yet it is precisely this kind of "individualism" that inhibits the growth of the indivisible person, that inner union of contraries. To paraphrase Erich Kahler (27, p. 8), the history of civilization could very well be written as a history of the alienation of man.

Conversely, in primitive society, authentic individuation is more likely to occur, because the pre-conditions for personal growth, which I shall shortly attempt to summarize, are present. Paul Radin, who enjoyed one of the most intense and consistent experiences of a primitive people (the Winnebago) that any anthropologist has ever had, wrote:

Free scope is allowed for every conceivable kind of personality outlet or expression in primitive society. No moral judgment is passed on any aspect of human personality as such. Human nature is what it is, and each act, emotion, belief, unexpressed or expressed, must be allowed to make or mar a man. . . . Limitations to this expression naturally exist— but these flow directly from an intense and clear-cut appreciation of the realities of life and from an acute sensitivity to group reaction (49).

Radin sums up his viewpoint as follows: "Express yourself completely but know yourself completely and accept the consequences of your own personality and actions" (49).

Jomo Kenyatta attempts a similar assessment: "The African is conditioned, by the cultural and social institutions of cen-

turies, to a freedom of which Europe has little conception, . . ."
(28, p. 306). And Christopher Dawson, referring to the tribal
background of the Celts, agrees:

Nevertheless, though the tribe is a relatively primitive form of social
organisation, it possesses virtues which many more advanced types of
society may envy. It is consistent with a high ideal of personal freedom
and self-respect and evokes an intense spirit of loyalty and devotion on
the part of the individual tribesman towards the community and its
chief (8).

I believe these statements to be substantially true, which is
to say that they accord with my experience. The point is that
primitive man is not a mere reflex of the group. On the contrary,
the group is "embedded, indeed embodied, in the very individuality of the individual" (27, p. 43). Anyone who has ever
witnessed a ceremonial African dance will certainly agree that
the individual's sense of personal power and worth is immeas-
urably heightened by the communal nature of the event. It is
as if the person is expressing an energy beyond his own. Yet
the bodily movements, the facial expressions, often the steps,
vary from person to person—the individual style comes through.
Such an organic group is the converse of the mob, that is, a collectivity of detached individuals losing themselves in some
furious activity, seeking an anonymous union; the mob is a civilized not a primitive phenomenon; it is the collective in frenzy,
the repressed emotions explode outward without restraint or
form, balance or responsibility. The image of the mob is part
of our image of the city, and the city is the carrier of the best
and the worst of civilization.

But the primitive society is a *community*, springing from
common origins, composed of reciprocating persons, and growing from within. It is not a collective (10, 11); collectives emerge
in civilization; they are functional to specialized ends and they
generate a sense of being imposed from without. They are objectively perceived, objectifying, and estrainging structures.
Leopold Senghör spoke to this point as follows: "Above all, we
have developed cooperation, not collectivist, but communal. For

cooperation—of family, village, tribe—has always been honored in Black Africa; once again, not in collectivist form, not as an aggregate of individuals, but in communal form, as mutual agreement" (53).

A collective has the form of a community but lacks the substance; it is involved with the concept "public," which is not at all the same as the idea of the social. The fully functioning, highly individuated member of society is the antithesis of the public man. "A public," wrote Kierkegaard, "is neither a nation, nor a generation, nor a community, nor a society, nor these particular men, for all these are only what they are through the concrete. . . . The public will be less than a single real man, however unimportant" (30). That is a dreadful statement, but can we, in conscience, deny it?

SUMMARY

I wish, in summary, briefly to review, extend, and present for further exploration some of the most critical aspects of the primitive features already outlined. Among primitives, we customarily encounter, within the web of kinship:

1. Good nurturance. The infant's psychophysiological contact with a "mothering one" is both extensive and intensive. Whatever childhood disciplines are imposed, and they vary widely from society to society, in time of imposition, mode and content, function within a dynamic affective field.[17]

17. Throughout the High Nigerian Plateau, for example, children are customarily force-fed water by hand during infancy. The infant may scream, become furious, and even momentarily lose consciousness. But this amuses, rather than disturbs the mother, for she knows well enough that she is not committing a hostile act. She remains firm, but persistent during the brief conflict. Afterwards, the infant quiets down very quickly and is rewrapped into his secure position on the mother's hip or back. It is this unfailing association with the mother, and mother surrogates, that makes the infant receptive to the customary disciplines, and renders them nontraumatic. The "instinctual" life is neither feared by adults, nor harshly repressed in children.

2. Many-sided, engaging personal relationships through all phases of the individual's life cycle, further developing and strengthening the sense of self, and others, for these are reciprocal processes.

I would, further, hypothesize, that the socialization process among primitives results in a high modal capacity to relate things and events, that is, to think "conceptually." This most striking, indeed this defining, component in human intelligence would seem to be a function of the "quality and nature of concrete affective relationships" at critical points in the life cycle. The conceptual or "abstract" capacity is, of course, the ability and desire to make connections and not, necessarily, to deal with abstractions in the Western philosophic sense. Just as the primitive people I have known give an over-all impression of alertness and intelligence, so people who have become specialized in civilized political economies frequently impress one with the automatism of their responses, and their boredom. Boredom is a highly civilized, not a primitive characteristic; but these probable relationships between social-historical character and intelligence have hardly begun to be explored (10).

3. Various forms of institutionalized deviancy. These have the effect of accommodating idiosyncratic individuals to the group, while permitting unconventional behavior. In such cases the deviant may be both privileged and penalized, but he does not become a social derelict.

4. The celebration, and fusion, of the sacred and the natural, the individual and society, in ritual; through ritual, life culminates in the form of drama; social and existential anxieties are creatively used.

5. Direct engagement with nature and natural physiological functions. Thus the sense of reality is heightened to the point where it sometimes seems to "blaze." It is at this point that the experiences of primitive and mystic converge, for mysticism is no more than reality, perceived at its ultimate subjective pitch. Merely filthy or nasty attitudes about natural functions are rare —although broad, even wild (trickster) humor—is commonplace.

6. Active and manifold participation in culture. This, together with (5), contributes to feelings of individual worth, dignity, and competence.

7. As Leach (33), Boas (4), Weltfish (57), and others have emphasized, an ordinary man-made, and a natural environment more aesthetically perceived than is commonly the case in civilization. Artisanship is highly prized, and widespread among primitives; the continuous contact with finely, and individually made everyday objects helps to personalize, and charge with meaning, primitive surroundings. "Among primitive people," concludes Boas, "goodness and beauty are the same" (4).

8. Socio-economic support as a natural inheritance; or conversely stated, socio-economic risk is equitably distributed throughout society. Therefore, no crippling anxieties, or doubts about personal worth derive from that fundamental source. This, in addition to all preceding points, explains the minimal occurrence, or absence, of civilized types of "crime" in primitive society.

These prominent features of primitive society should lead us to anticipate an exceedingly low incidence of the chronic characterological, or psychoneurotic phenomena that seem to be growing with civilization, as Meyer Fortes (14), among others, has indicated. This reflects my own experience; I would add only that the disciplined expressiveness of primitive societies, together wth traditional social and economic supports, results, also, in a greater tolerance of psychotic manifestations, no matter what the actual rate of psychoses may be, relative to civilized cultures.

CONCLUSION

The individuation, personalism, nominalism and existentialism so markedly apparent in primitive society continuously reinforce each other, and as we have seen, they are fully consonant with the social structure. Similarly, it is interesting to note that Heidegger (20) believes that the break in the Western tradition between the Pre-Socratics and Plato, that is, between what I would roughly identify as precivilized and civilized conceptions, is symptomatic. Each inter-related mode may be summarized as follows:

Primitive (precivilized, prealienation) existentialism is evident in: (1) The ritual expression of the primary needs of the person in nature and society; meanings are questioned and resolved; a literal "being born with others," "Co-naissance" (Claudel [7]), "the free abandon of communion" (Marcel [40, 41]) occurs; or, as Boas (4) puts it, "The readiness to abandon one's self to the exultation induced by art is probably greater [than among ourselves] because the conventional restraint of our times does not exist in the same form in their lives"; (2) the emphasis on existence rather than essence; (3) the responsibility of the individual to self and society; and (4) the lack of concern with analytic modes of thought.

Primitive Personalism is revealed in: (1) The web of kinship; (2) the organic community; and (3) the apprehension of consciousness throughout society and nature.

Primitive Nominalism is focused in: (1) The emphasis on concrete particulars and contexts; (2) the naming of *existents* in nature and society, in dream and reality, and (3) in the fact that ideas, as such, are not, typically, hypostatized or reified.

Primitive Individuation is nurtured by: (1) The full and manifold participation of individuals in nature and society; (2) the intensely personal socialization process through which individual qualities are delineated; and (3) the expression of society in the person and the person in society.

The four dominant qualities, or modes of thinking, or psychological perspectives, or ways of behaving—they are all of these simultaneously—find their antithesis in the prevailing modes of conduct and thought that arose and steadily intensified with the growth of civilization.

In each of these critical areas—critical because it is within their parameters that the crisis of civilization is expressed—civilized behavior may be characterized as increasingly: A. *Essentialist;* quantification becomes etherealized, which is, as we have seen, a political, philosophic and, finally, a scientific process. Western science is conceived in Galileo, but Plato is the Godfather (5, 6, 32); B. *abstract and analytic;* C. *impersonal and mechanical, in short,* D. *collectivized,* that is, involved with aggregates of individuals, in pursuit of specialized activities that tend to transform their human associations into technical, or even merely spatial, arrangements. *Personae* are substituted for persons.

Our pathology, then, consists in our dedication to abstractions, in our collectivism, pseudo-individualism, and lack of institutional means for the expression and transcendence of human ambivalence. But the pathology of primitive society has quite another source: It arises from ignorance, the rudimentary state of science, and a consequent relative unconcern with abstract analytic procedures; thus the negative aspects of primitive personalism find their own subjective balance, but cannot be objectively checked.

Our illness springs from the very center of civilization, not from too much knowledge, but from too little wisdom. What primitives possess—the immediate and ramifying sense of the person, and all that I have tried to show that that entails—we have largely lost. If we have the means, the tools, the forms, the rational imagination to transform the face of the earth and the contemporary human condition, primitive society at its most positive, exemplifies an essential humanity. That is what civilization must selectively incorporate; we cannot abandon the primitive; we can only outgrow it by letting it grow within us. While civilization instructs and transforms the primitive, let it remain the special duty of anthropologists to learn how, for thousands of years, on a prior level of cultural development, man deeply defined his nature; and let us propagate the lesson. It is the least that we, and our brothers, the poets, can do.

REFERENCES

1. Barret, S. A. The Wintun Hesi Ceremony. *Amer. Archaeol. Ethnol.,* 14:437–488, 1919.
2. Bloch, Marc. *Feudal Society.* Chicago: University of Chicago Press, 1961, p. 445.
3. Boas, Franz. *The Mind of Primitive Man.* New York: Macmillan, 1938, pp. 216–219.
4. ———. *Primitive Art.* New York: Dover, 1955, p. 356.
5. Burtt, E. A. *The Metaphysical Foundations of Modern Physical Science.* New York: Harcourt, Brace, 1925.
6. Cassirer, Ernst. Galileo's Platonism. In *Studies and Essays in the History of Science and Learning, offered in homage to George Sarton,* Ed. M.F. Ashley Montagu, New York: Schuman, 1944, pp. 279–297.
7. Claudel, Paul. *Art Poétique: Connaissance du Temps. Traité de la Co-naissance au Monde et de soi-même.* Paris: Mercure, 1929.
8. Dawson, Christopher. *The Making of Europe.* Cleveland: World, 1961, p. 75.
9. Diamond, Stanley. *Dahomey: A Proto-state in West Africa.* Ann Arbor: University of Michigan Microfilms, 1951, pp. 32–76.
10. ———. Kibbutz and Shtetl: The History of an Idea. *Social Problems,* 5:68–100, 1957.
11. ———. Plato and the Definition of the Primitive. In *Culture in History,* Stanley Diamond, Ed. New York: Columbia University Press, 1960, pp. 118–141.
12. ———. The Kibbutz: Utopia in Crisis. *Voices of Dissent.* New York: Grove, 1960, pp. 283–290.
13. Engels, Frederick. *The Origin of the Family, Private Property and the State.* Chicago: Kerr, 1902.
14. Fortes, Meyer. Mind. In *The Institutions of Primitive Society,* E. E. Evans-Pritchard, Ed. New York: Free Press, 1956, pp. 90–94.
15. Freuchen, Peter. *Book of the Eskimos.* Cleveland: World, 1961, p. 92.
16. Goffman, Erving. *The Presentation of Self in Everyday Life.* Edinburgh: University of Edinburgh, Social Sciences Research Center, 1956, p. 47.
17. Goldenweiser, Alexander. *Robots or Gods.* New York: Knopf, 1931.
18. Grinnell, George Bird. Coup and Scalp Among the Plain Indians. *Amer. Anthropologist,* 12:296–297, 1910.

19. Hallowell, A. Irving. Ojibwa Ontology, Behavior, and World View.
In *Culture in History*, Stanley Diamond, Ed. New York:
Columbia University Press, 1960, pp. 19–52.
20. Heidegger, Martin. *Platos Lehre von der Wahrheit, Mit einem Brief
über den "Humanismus."* Berne: A. Francke, 1947.
21. Hoebel, E. Adamson. *Man in the Primitive World.* New York:
McGraw-Hill, 1958, pp. 355–356.
22. Hoernle, A. W. *Certain Rites of Transition and the Conception
of !nau among the Hottentots (Harvard Africa Studies, Vol.
2).* Cambridge: Harvard University Press, 1918, pp. 65–82.
23. ———. The Expression of the Social Value of Water among the
Naman of South-West Africa. Johannesburg: *South African
J. of Sci.*, 20:514–526, 1923.
24. Huizinga, Johan. *Homo Ludens, A Study of the Play-Element in
Culture.* Boston: Beacon, 1955, pp. 1–27.
25. *Izvestia.* March 29, 1959, Moscow.
26. ———. February 14, 1960, Moscow.
27. Kahler, Erich. *The Tower and the Abyss.* New York: Braziller,
1957.
28. Kenyatta, Jomo. *Facing Mt. Kenya.* New York: Vintage, 1962.
29. Kierkegaard, Søren. *Concluding Unscientific Postscript to the Philosophical Fragments.* Walter Lowrie, Ed. Princeton: Princeton University Press and American-Scandinavian Foundation, 1941.
30. ———. The Present Age; A Literary Review. In *A Kierkegaard
Anthology.* Bretall, Ed. Princeton: Princeton University
Press, 1946, pp. 266–267.
31. *Komsomol-Skaia Pravda:* August 20, 1959, Moscow.
32. Koyré, Alexandre. Galileo and Plato. *J. Hist. Ideas,* 4:400–428, 1943.
33. Leach, E. R. Aesthetics. In *The Institutions of Primitive Society.*
E. E. Evans-Pritchard, Ed. New York: Free Press, 1956,
pp. 25–38.
34. Lee, Dorothy. Being and Value in Primitive Culture. *J. of Philosophy,* 46:401–415.
35. Lévi-Strauss, Claude. Tristes Tropiques, From an Anthropologist's
Memoirs (III). London: *Encounter,* April, 1961, pp. 28–41.
36. Lovejoy, Arthur O. *Essays in the History of Ideas.* New York: Put-
nam's (a Capricorn book), 1960, pp. 29–37.
37. Lowie, Robert H. *The Crow Indians.* New York: Rinehart, 1956,
p. 5 ff.
38. ———. *Social Organization.* New York: Rinehart, 1956, p. 217.
39. Malinowski, Bronislaw. *Argonauts of the Western Pacific.* New
York: Dutton, 1932, pp. 509–518.
40. Marcel, Gabriel. *Metaphysical Journal.* Bernard Wall, Trans. Chi-

cago: Regnery, 1952 (*Journal Métaphysique*. Paris: Gallimard, 1927).

41. ———. *Being and Having*. Katherine Farrer, Trans. London: Dacre Press, 1949 (*Etre et Avoir*. Paris: Ferdinand Aubier, Editions Montaigne, 1935).
42. Mauss, Marcel. *The Gift*. New York: Free Press, 1954.
43. Moody, Ernest A. Galileo and Avempace: Dynamics of the Leaning Tower Experiment. In *Roots of Scientific Thought*. Philip P. Wiener and Aaron Noland, Eds. New York: Basic Books, 1957, pp. 176–206.
44. Moore, Stanley: Marxian Theories of Law in Primitive Society. In *Culture in History*. Stanley Diamond, Ed. New York: Columbia University Press, 1960, pp. 642–662.
45. Nadel, S. F. *A Black Byzantium*. London: Oxford University Press, 1942, p. 68.
46. Northrop, F. S. C. In personal conversation at Arden House, Harriman, New York, November 18, 1961.
47. Oberg, K. The Kingdom of Ankole in Uganda. In *African Political Systems*. M. Fortes and E. E. Evans-Pritchard, Eds. London: Oxford University Press, 1955, pp. 121–162.
48. Radin, Paul. Religion of the North American Indians. *J. Amer. Folklore*, 27:335–373, 1914.
49. ———. *The World of Primitive Man*. New York: Schuman, 1953, p. 152.
50. Rivers, W. H. *Instinct and the Unconscious*. Cambridge, England: Cambridge University Press, 1924, p. 95 ff.
51. Sapir Edward. Culture, Genuine and Spurious. In *Selected Writings of Edward Sapir in Language, Culture and Personality*. David G. Mandelbaum, Ed. Berkeley and Los Angeles: University of California Press, 1951, pp. 308–331.
52. Seidenberg, Roderick. *Posthistoric Man*. Boston: Beacon, 1957.
53. Senghor, Leopold Sedar. Teilhard de Chardin and African Policy. *West African Pilot*. Lagos: December 12, 1961, p. 5.
54. Steward, J. H. *The Ceremonial Buffoon of the American Indian*. Papers of the Michigan Academy of Science, Arts and Letters, 14:187–207, 1931.
55. Tylor, Edward B. *Anthropology: An Introduction to the Study of Man and Civilization*. London: Watts, 1946, Vol. 2, p. 134.
56. van der Post, Laurens. *The Dark Eye in Africa*. New York: Morrow, 1955, p. 115.
57. Weltfish, Gene. *The Origins of Art*. Indianapolis: Bobbs-Merrill, 1953.
58. Wheeler, William Morton. *Emergent Evolution and the Development of Societies*. New York: Norton, 1928, p. 44.

ASHLEY MONTAGU

The Concept of
"Primitive" and Related
Anthropological Terms

A Study in the Systematics of Confusion

When *I* use a word, Humpty Dumpty said in a rather scornful tone, it means just what I choose it to mean—neither more nor less.
—Lewis Carroll, *Through the Looking Glass*

Mann kann wohl sagen, dass alle Absuditäten und Ungeheurlichkeiten, auf die wir in der Philosophie-, Religions-, und Wissenschaftsgeschichte treffen, darauf berhuhen, dass eine an einem bestimmten Wirklichkeitsbereich ausgebildete Denkform als die einzige richtige und der ganzen Wirklichkeit voll entsprechende ausgegeben wird.

—Leisgang, *Denkformen,* 1928, 442

To know requires exertion, it is intellectually easiest to shirk effort altogether by accepting phrases which cloak the unknown in the undefinable.

—Karl Pearson, *The Grammar of Science,* 1899

ONE OF the most important of all the activities of man is language. Language constitutes the process of communication of meanings in order to produce some form of action upon those capable of understanding the meanings employed. Whether the action be an overt act or the generation of an idea, whether it be negative or positive action, the end is always the same; namely, some vital response on the part of those who receive the communication. When words produce acts, they do so through the agency of the meanings they possess for the actors upon whom they act. All words, even when they are not understood in the dictionary sense, possess some active power. The active or activating power may be very little, as when some utterly strange word is offered to our ears. In such case the word acts upon us not merely as a group of sensations which has been experienced or passively received, but as a stimulus which irritates us into the struggle to endow it with some sort of meaning, however weak the stimulus, however weak the irritation, and however weak the struggle.

The meaning of a word lies in the action it produces.

Meaning represents an attempt to understand a thing, the emergent of a struggle between the thing and the whole body of meanings which control us or we control. Whether we fail or succeed or are only indifferently successful in emerging with a meaning which describes the thing or referent will depend upon the standards of judgment against which success or failure in such matters is measured. Since these judgments are them-

Reprinted from the American Anthropologist, *vol. 47, No. 1, January–March 1945, 119–133. Revised.*

selves systems of meanings, they may be wholly or partially erroneous, and thus lead to the perpetuation of further additional erroneous meanings. Such erroneous meanings can only be discovered by continuous critical analysis. Their exposure renders the development of more accurate meanings possible, and represents one of the most important tasks of critical analysis.

Many scientists are, unfortunately, unaware of the important role that words play in regulating and conditioning their observations, their inferences, and their conclusions. Some fall into the use of terms the meaning of which has never been clearly defined, and which they use in a vague and loose manner, sometimes meaning one thing and sometimes another; sometimes thinking one thing yet writing another, in Housman's phrase "calling in ambiguity of language to promote confusion of thought." [1] From the scientific viewpoint terms possessing such unanalysed versatility are worse than useless, they are confusing, and should not be used until they have received a definition which agrees with the facts so far as it is possible to determine them.[2] In this connection it is well to recall that the word fact, *facere*, originally meant a thing made. We still make our own facts but fail to realise how much of ourselves we put into them.

In the field of physical anthropology which deals with the phylogeny, ancestry, and classification of man such loose terms are particularly abundant, and perennially confusing. Some of these terms, and others suffering from similar defects, occur also in the field of cultural anthropology. In both fields many of these terms are nothing more than pseudological rationalizations based on unanalyzed concepts. In the present paper I propose to examine critically the most hard-worked of these terms, discuss the senses in which they have been used, show how they have contributed to confused thinking, and see what can be done about rescuing some of them for use with a clear conscience and

1. A. E. Housman, *The Name and Nature of Poetry* (Cambridge: The University Press, 1933), p. 31.
2. "Definitions are not truly meaningful at the beginning of an inquiry, but only at the end." Bertram Morris, *The Aesthetic Process* (Evanston, Northwestern University, 1943), p. 1.

a steady meaning. Unclear terms are the bane of a science and can do more to befog thinking upon important issues than any other single thing. In anthropology there are quite a few such "fuzzy" terms. It may serve a useful purpose to take an objective and critical look at them.

In the criticisms which follow I should like it to be clearly understood that I have myself, at one time or another, used the terms mentioned in precisely those ways which I now find so unsatisfactory. Were I to cite examples I need not go further for them than my own past writings. It is because I have found these terms so difficult to use clearly and unequivocally that I felt bound to examine them, and this paper simply represents my own attempt at clarification of the meaning of these slippery terms. I have not cited examples from specific authors because the usages I have here referred to are practically universal; readers of this paper will, in most cases, be sufficiently acquainted with those usages to render the citation of specific examples superfluous.

PRIMITIVE

One of the most frequently used terms in anthropology is the word "primitive." The sense in which it is most commonly used is that of "early" or "undeveloped" or in the combination of both meanings. Generally a culture is judged "primitive" when by comparison with the standards of our own it is in almost all respects very appreciably less "advanced." From the physical standpoint some group of mankind, living or extinct, is said to be "primitive" when, in comparison with ourselves, its members display characters which are believed to be of an "earlier" type or less "developed."

Whether the term is used in the cultural or morphological sense, there are always two elements present in it: One is a conception of time, and the other is a conception of progress or development. This is clearly illustrated by the meaning of the term which is usually opposed to "primitive," namely "advanced." By "advanced" we usually understand the accomplishment of progress or development upon an earlier stage, the going forward or upward from an earlier or lower stage. When we use the word "advanced" we assume an earlier less developed stage, and it is this earlier less developed stage that we call "primitive." Thus, "primitive," as generally used means earlier in time and less complex in progress or development. This is more or less implied in its original lexical meaning as pertaining to the beginning or origin. Thus, anything that is primitive is nearer the origin than that which is advanced, nearer the origin both in time and stage of development.

Since the publication of Darwin's *Origin of Species* in 1859, evolutionary or phylogenetic diagrams have taught us to look for the earliest forms in the lower sections of the diagram, sections generally corresponding to the position of the earlier geological strata or ages. Thus "lower" has come to have an equivalent meaning to "early" or "earlier" and thus directly to "primitive," since "earliness" is implied in the term "primitive." The notion of "lowness" in the evolutionary "scale" of development is then extended to mean "lowness" in the intellectual and moral as well as the physical character of the individual or group defined as primitive. Thus, for example, the general picture of "primitive man" which physical anthropologists perpetrated upon an innocent world, was that of a bestial-looking creature, who could not stand erect, but shuffled about with knock-knees and bow legs, possessed a bull neck, ape-like lips, claw-like hands, mentally resembling a low-grade moron, and possessing the morals of an officer of the Gestapo, a wretched cannibalistic creature who bludgeoned his females into stupidity and dragged them around by the hair of their heads!

So strongly was this view entrenched in the minds of some anthropologists in the first quarter of the twentieth century that when they came to make their reconstructions of the remains of fossil man they made them not according to the morphological facts but as they thought those facts ought to be represented. Boule's famous reconstruction of the Chappelle-aux-Saints skeleton is a case in point. Boule incorrectly interpreted the structure of the cervical vertebrae and gave the best preserved specimen of Neanderthal man a bull neck like the gorilla. He similarly misinterpreted the morphology of the thigh bones and the knee joints, and endowed Neanderthal man with knock, bent, bowed knees, and a stoop.[3] Similarly, when the official report of Rhodesian man was published the latter was likewise endowed with lower extremities such as it is perfectly certain he could not and did not possess during life. Most illuminating of all are the reconstructions of the physiognomy and expression—of which we can know absolutely nothing—of "primitive" man as represented by Neanderthal man, and "advanced" man as represented by Cro-Magnon man. In the former case the physiognomy and expression is made to appear very bestial, while in the latter the spirit of nobility, high intellect, and humanity radiates from every reconstructed idealized line in the face. In other words, "primitive" man was a "low" creature, nearer the beasts than Cro-Magnon man, the true member of our own "highly advanced" species, *Homo sapiens*.

It is in the field of physical anthropology that "primitive" and "early" are most often "equated"; and here we are afforded an illuminating example of the manner in which this type of equation regulates the thinking of its makers. If "early" is equivalent to "primitive," then everything "early" is *ipso facto* primitive. Therefore, when skeletal remains are found in an early horizon they must be primitive. From this it follows that if the remains are not primitive they could not have been found in a genuinely early horizon, or if they were found in such an early horizon then they must be intrusive, that is to say, washed-in or a burial. This type of argument is perfectly legitimate when used as a methodological device, and in the case of the famous Galley Hill skeleton it was fully vindicated ultimately by a

3. W. L. Straus, Jr., and A. J. E. Cave, *Pathology and Posture of Neanderthal Man* (Quarterly Review of Biology, Vol. 32, 1957), pp. 348–363.

reinvestigation both of the site and of the skeleton.[4] But when it is too rigorously applied it may shut off the possibility of admitting alternative fruitful hypotheses. Such an hypothesis, for example, as that which is based on the Middle Pleistocene Swanscombe skull, and the pre-Mousterian Fontéchevade skulls. Upon the basis of these finds, all of which are fragmentary, but with the exception of the Swanscombe skull, sufficiently well-preserved in the critical frontal area in the Fontéchevade remains, it is not unreasonable to infer that man of *sapiens* type appeared much earlier in the evolution of man than would ever be allowable on the "early-primitive" conception of hominid evolution. In short, it is suggested not that the "early-primitive" equation be abandoned, but that it be used with caution and without prejudice.

The terms "low" and "high" are generally equated with "inferior" and "superior." Thus, culturally and physically Neanderthal man was, and the Australian aboriginal is, regarded as "inferior" to Caucasoid man. Indeed, since Caucasoid man is the classifying agent he is "superior" and all others who do not closely resemble him are "inferior." These terms, "low," "high," "inferior," and "superior," are heavily weighted with strong value judgments. Anything qualified by these terms is endowed with an active qualitative interest determining the mode of conduct which shall be adopted towards the designated object. Each time these words are used they condition thought along certain definite intellectual and emotional lines. This is so whether it be the man on the street or the cultural anthropologist who is using the term; although it may at once be said that no one has done nearly as much for the better understanding of these matters, and no one is more free of the tyranny of such value judgments, than the cultural anthropologist. This has not been so in the case of the physical anthropologist who, as we shall have occasion to see, has done much to obfuscate thought in these connections. The

4. M. F. Ashley Montagu and K. P. Oakley, *The Antiquity of Galley Hill Man* (American Journal of Physical Anthropology, n.s. Vol. 7, 1949), pp. 363–384.

cultural anthropologist himself, however, has not been altogether free of the confusing effects of these terms. While such terms as "inferior" and "superior" and the concepts for which they stand have been virtually completely eliminated from the vocabulary of the cultural anthropologists, such terms as "higher" and "lower" civilizations or hunters are still occasionally to be met with in the writings of some cultural anthropologists. The usage of such qualifying terms is, of course, of more than merely academic interest since they serve to influence the behavior of every one of the millions of persons who use them; not alone of the man on the street, but the behavior of men of distinguished mind and considerable humanity. Thus, for example, Karl Pearson could write at the beginning of the present century:

"It is a false view of human solidarity, a weak humanitarianism, not a true humanism, which regrets that a capable and stalwart race of white men should replace a dark-skinned tribe which can neither utilize its land for the full benefit of mankind, nor contribute its quota to the common stock of human knowledge." And in a footnote to this Pearson adds "This sentence must not be taken to justify a brutalizing destruction of human life. The anti-social effects of such a mode of accelerating the survival of the fittest may go far to destroy the preponderating fitness of the survivor. At the same time, there is cause for human satisfaction in the replacement of the aborigines throughout America and Australia by white races of far higher civilization." [5]

These statements occur in a book which did more for the clarification of the thought of two generations of men of science than perhaps any other single volume. But Pearson, who was closely familiar with the ethnological literature of his time, was so much influenced by the prevailing pattern of anthropological thought, that he accepted the division of mankind and its cultures into "lower" and "higher" types. That division being accepted it was a simple step to take, in the direction determined

5. Karl Pearson, *The Grammar of Science*, London, Second Edition, 1900. Revised reprint, Everyman Library, New York, Dutton & Co., 1937, p. 310.

by the Darwinian concept of "the struggle for existence" or "the survival of the fittest" to the notion that the "lower" races must inevitably be supplanted by the "higher" races to the ultimate advantage and good of mankind as a whole. The further implication being that the "lower" races of mankind are not really full members of the family of mankind at all, and that the good of "mankind" is best served by the replacement of the "lower" by the "higher" races of mankind. Today in the South, and elsewhere, this view amounts to the explicit belief that such peoples do not belong within the framework of human brotherhood.[6] This is, unfortunately, still a widespread belief, and is to be found among certain anthropologists and biologists who are committed to the philosophy of judging mankind in terms of "superiority" and "inferiority." We find Professor S. J. Holmes, for example, practically repeating Pearson's words. "It may be urged with much reason," he writes, "that the birth rate of superior peoples should be kept high in order that they may conquer and supplant inferior types." [7] Such views are, of course, part and parcel of the modern conception of "race." [8] Views to which the physical anthropologists have made the principal contribution by their practice of speaking of "from monkey to man" and then arranging the various groups of primates upon a phylogenetic tree in which the white man is shown to be the latest and highest form while the members of various other divisions of man are shown coming off earlier and lower from the trunk of the phylogenetic tree.

Such amiable post-prandial exercises have done considerable

6. "Why was southern conduct, then, [in the year 1942–43] so contrary to all preaching and principles which, without a peradventure of doubt, were sincere? Why didn't the tenets of fellowship and Christian religion hold here? The only answer was that the Negro did not come within the framework of human brotherhood." Howard W. Odum, *Race and Rumors of Race* (Chapel Hill, N.C., 1943), p. 23.

7. S. J. Holmes, *The Trend of the Race* (New York, 1921), p. 123.

8. See Ashley Montagu (Editor), *The Concept of Race* (New York, The Free Press, 1964; and Ashley Montagu, *Man's Most Dangerous Myth: The Fallacy of Race*, 4th ed., Cleveland and New York, World Publishing Co., 1964.

harm, in that they have for the most part been responsible for giving a spurious scientific support to prejudices for which there can be no justification. As I have elsewhere written:

> The average person in our society observes that certain other persons belonging to different ethnic groups possess physical and mental traits which differ from his own. He concludes that these physical and mental traits are somehow linked together, that these traits are inborn, and that they are immutable. Vague notions about a unilinear evolution assist him to believe that such "races" are "lower" in the "scale" of evolution than is the group to which he belongs. From such a starting point as "prehistoric man" he envisages a continuous progression upwards culminating in the development of his own "race" or group.[9]

The concept of orthogenetic evolution, of evolution in a straight line, a progression forwards or upwards in which an immediately ancestral "inferior" form gives rise to a "superior" form, characterizes much of the thinking of writers on evolutionary subjects. This, in fact, is what evolution is taken by many to be. But in actual fact evolution does not occur by the budding-off, as it were, of "superior" forms from "inferior" forms, but by changes within a group which serve to differentiate it from the ancestral group. Those changes may actually render the new group less complex than it was before, or they may render it more complex. The new group does not necessarily become "superior" by virtue of the change it has undergone but merely *different*. Under certain conditions such changes may prove of advantage to their possessors so that they eventually come to be the dominant traits in that particular group. But under other conditions those very same traits might prove a handicap to their possessors and would cause them to die out. Clearly there can be no question then of terming such traits either "superior" or "inferior" in the kind of absolutist sense in which those terms are commonly applied. The possession of a black skin is a great advantage in regions of intense sunlight, it is of no advantage, perhaps even disadvantageous, in areas of low sunlight intensity. In the former region a white skin is at a disadvantage, in the latter at

9. *Man's Most Dangerous Myth: The Fallacy of Race*, p. 106.

an advantage. Thus, it is the conditions in which it functions not the trait itself which, if anything, determines the value of a trait, a value which always refers to specific conditions and not to conditions in general or to traits in general. Hence, it may readily be seen that any description of the characters of living peoples as either "superior" or "inferior" to one another is erroneous and confusing.

We shall touch upon these matters again later. Meanwhile we may pause to take stock of the manifold meanings which are implicit in the term "primitive." From what has already been said with regard to it, it will be seen that the term is a confusing one, for it embraces a large number of different ideas or concepts. Some of these concepts are "early," "lower," "inferior," "undeveloped," "retarded," "nonprogressive," "nonevolved," and "simple." The value-judgments associated with these various ideas when the word "primitive" is customarily used lean heavily towards the depreciative side. It will scarcely be denied that the belief is very strongly entrenched that "primitive" cultures and "primitive" people are not as "good" as we are. The "good" in this context usually carries with it a moral as well as a biological judgment. The man in the street has not the least doubt that in the scale of human values he is a far better man than the "savage." Cultural anthropologists, as a rule, do not suffer from any such delusions, though it is obvious that they have not wholly succeeded in making it clear that they do not.

As Ruth Benedict has said:

> Early anthropologists tried to arrange all traits of different cultures in an evolutionary sequence from the earliest forms to their final development in Western civilization. But there is no reason to suppose that by discussing Australian religion rather than our own we are uncovering primordial religion, or that by discussing Iroquoian social organization we are returning to the mating habits of man's early ancestors.
>
> Since we are forced to believe that the race of man is one species, it follows that man everywhere has an equally long history behind him. Some primitive tribes may have held relatively closer to primordial forms of behavior than civilized man, but this can only be relative and our guesses are as likely to be wrong as right. There is no justification for

identifying some one contemporary primitive custom with the original type of human behavior.[10]

These admirable *obiter dicta* have not, however, prevented many anthropologists from continuing to speak of "primitive religion," "primitive culture," "primitive economics," and "primitive law." It may be suggested that such a usage represents not only an error of conceptualization but implies the existence of a fundamental misunderstanding having serious methodological consequences. The error of conceptualization is to regard any form of activity qualified as "primitive" as nearer the primordial state of things than that which is not "primitive." The methodological effect of such a view is to create an artificial evolutionary cultural framework from which to view the development of culture from the primitive to the advanced, from the simple to the complex. In point of fact most so-called primitive cultures are far from primitive and far from simple. In quite a number of respects such cultures are very much more complex than is any western culture. The classificatory system of relationships and all that that implies is a good example of the great complexity of certain aspects of so-called "primitive culture." But much more impressive even than this are so-called "primitive languages." Of these it may, in general, be said that they are vastly more complex, and in many ways both more supple and more subtle than any western language. And yet these are the languages of peoples who have found no use for writing and have therefore failed to develop it. For the same reason these isolated peoples have not developed all those other traits of culture which are to be found among the cultures of the West. There has simply been no necessity, and in the absence of necessity—the mother of invention—has essentially been due to the isolation of most of these peoples from the fertilizing effects which result from contact with peoples of very different cultures. These isolated cultures are in many ways not as highly complicated as ours, but that does not mean that they are themselves not complex or that they are primitive or simple.

10. Ruth Benedict, *Patterns of Culture* (Boston, 1934), p. 18.

The attempt to escape from the consequences of the term "primitive" by the substitution of the term "simpler" was bound to meet with failure for the reason that the members of such cultural isolates are not really as simple as the comparative term suggests. The term "simple" is only a little less objectionable than the term "primitive." It suggests "simple-mindedness," and simpleness where simpleness does not exist, as in the religious, linguistic, and social organization of the people. The German *Naturmenschen* is equally objectionable because the peoples whom the term is intended to describe are far from being "Nature folk," and the term carries too many implications about being nearer to Nature than other peoples. It may be suggested that a more accurate term than any of these would be "isolate or isolated peoples." Such a term would suggest that such peoples have been more or less culturally isolated from others for substantial periods of time, and would imply that such differences as might culturally distinguish them from other peoples would, to an appreciable extent, be due to this cause. The term "isolate" might still serve to define more or less culturally isolated groups in other populations.

When a term possesses confusing qualities and is lacking in definiteness it ought either to be redefined or if that is impossible, eliminated altogether from the vocabulary of the scientist. I believe that the term "primitive" falls into the latter category.

ADVANCED–SPECIALIZED

By "advanced," it has already been pointed out, we usually understand the accomplishment of progress or development upon an earlier stage, the going forward or upward from an earlier or lower stage. The term "advanced" is usually contrasted with its antonym "primitive." Other antonyms of "advanced" are "backward," "retrogressive," "arrested," and "retarded." All these terms have on different occasions been used by both cultural and physical anthropologists. It is obvious that such terms, if they are to be used at all, must be used with the greatest caution. "Backward" implies an inherent quality of deficiency, as a "backward child" is one who despite the best of opportunities is incapable of developing beyond a certain point. In such a sense there are no "backward peoples." It seems to me, therefore, that this term should never be used.

"Retrogressive" in the sense of "backsliding" or reversion to an earlier condition is a permissible term in cultural but not in physical anthropology. The same may be said of "arrested" in the sense of "a stoppage at a certain stage," and of "retarded" in the sense of a slowing down of development by an occasional stoppage or other means.

By the measure of certain standards certain cultures are, either as a whole or in particular respects, more advanced than other cultures, and similarly by the measure of certain standards, so are certain physical types of men or certain of their physical characters more advanced than others. "Advanced" is a comparative term, its use will always be perfectly legitimate if the standard by which the comparison is to be made is always clearly defined. The objection to the use of the term arises when its use becomes indiscriminate owing to the nondefinition of the standard to which reference is being made. Nowhere is the confusion greater with respect to the use of this term than in physical anthropology.

It is, for example, commonly said that Neanderthal man is not as advanced a physical type as is *Homo sapiens*. By this is generally meant that taken as a whole Neanderthal man more closely resembles the putative ancestral stock of the Hominidae than does *Homo sapiens*. The latter has developed further away from this stock than has Neanderthal man, hence *Homo sapiens* is more advanced than the latter. The idea of development further away from is associated with a reference in time, for the further away one is from the ancestral stock the longer is the lapse of time taken to be which has occurred since the original departure from that stock. This is how the notion arises that "primitive" is associated with "early," and "advanced" with "late." But there is no necessary relationship between these diverse factors; the common assumption that there is is erroneous and has led to much confused thinking. It is possible that *Homo sapiens* represents a physical type which appeared earlier than the Neanderthal type. Now, in what respects may Neanderthal man be said to be closer to the ancestral stock of the Hominidae than *Homo sapiens?* If he is not so in time, what of his physical characters?

In order to answer this question it would first be necessary to know something about the morphology of the ancestral stock of the Hominidae to which these forms are usually referred, or supposed to be referred, for comparison. But the fact is that with the exception of a few teeth and portions of the upper and lower jaws we know nothing of the morphology of the putative ancestral stock of the Hominidae. This stock is generally assumed to be represented by the Miocene fossil genera of apes, *Dryopithecus* and *Sivapithecus.* Teeth and fragments of the jaws are all that we know these creatures by. Reconstructions of the form of the jaws and palate with the teeth placed therein have been made from such remains, and such reconstructions are probably reasonably accurate, but beyond such limited reconstructions it is not possible to go, except in a very general rather vague sort of way. Studies of the actual fossil teeth and jaws in relation to the problem of the origin of man have thrown an invaluable light upon that problem, but only in so far as the evolution of the teeth and jaws are concerned. Inferences as to any other part of the skeleton can at best only be speculative.

Now, how do the teeth of Neanderthal man and *Homo sapiens* compare with the *Dryopithecus-Sivapithecus* teeth and jaws? The answer to this question is that the teeth of Neanderthal man are further removed from the type of teeth found in the *Dryopithecus-Sivapithecus* stock than are the teeth of *Homo sapiens.* This is particularly true with respect to the form of the pulp-cavity, the "taurodontism" which is more frequently found in Neanderthal man than in *Homo sapiens,* but in the form of the symphyseal region of the jaw Neanderthal man with his

receding or undeveloped chin more closely approaches the condition found in the supposed ancestral stock than does *Homo
sapiens.* The fact is that the chin region of the Neanderthal jaw
very much more closely resembles that of *Homo sapiens* than it
does any of the Miocene apes.

In view of such facts it is obviously a meaningless question
to ask which is more advanced, Neanderthal man or *Homo
sapiens?* Yet that is the way in which the question is usually
asked. The only correct way in which the question can be asked
is: In what respects have Neanderthal man and *Homo sapiens*
become differentiated from the *Dryopithecus-Sivapithecus* stock,
and how, in these respects do the two former compare with one
another? We should ask the latter part of this question not because we wish to determine which form stands "higher" or
"lower" than the other in the "scale of evolution" but because we
desire to discover exactly what changes have occurred. Up to the
present moment, however, it has been the custom of most anthropologists, as well as other scientists, to think of evolution in terms
of a straight line vertically oriented, so that every variety of an
order must be conceived to stand either above or below some
other variety in the line or scale of evolution. This persisting
error of thought is responsible for the habit of anthropologists of
making comparisons between types as if one must be either inferior or superior to the other, and the task of the anthropologist
is to discover into which categories they are "naturally" supposed
to fall. Thus systematically do anthropologists confuse themselves, forcing on nature the limitations of their own minds and
identifying their view of reality with reality itself. The physical
characters of many types of extinct and probably of all living
varieties of man represent variations which have occurred in
different groups all originating at the same time from the same
common ancestral stock. There has been, one would say, parallel
differentiation in somewhat different directions as a result of
mutation, mutations which have proven adaptively useful. In this
sense then, there has been an adaptive radiation of types, not a
straight line development of one into the other.

When these facts are understood it becomes clear that we can only deal with the question of the variability of man in terms of variation and little else. *Homo erectus* and *Homo sapiens* were very probably contemporaries in one phase of their development, but it is highly improbable that they both originated at the same time from the same stock. *Homo erectus* undoubtedly originated earlier, *Homo sapiens* later. Actually we do not know, but it would seem reasonable to regard some type like *Homo erectus* as one which led to the subsequent appearance, by hybridization and mutation, of *Homo sapiens*. Recently extinct and existing types of men did not come into being at one stroke as it were. There has been evolution, and more "primitive" (= early) types have given rise to more "advanced" (= later) types, but this is quite a different thing from saying that all the fossil types we know today stand in a linear relationship to one another, and that the "primitive" types are in all or most respects more "primitive" (= less differentiated) than the more "advanced" (= more differentiated) types.

Indeed, it is frequently claimed that *Homo sapiens* preserves a very large number of primitive characters, and that he is far less "specialized" an animal than the gorilla or chimpanzee. The suggestion is even made that man has deviated less from the ancestral stock than have the two African apes. If *Homo sapiens* is less "specialized" than these two animals, this should mean that *Homo sapiens* is less "advanced" than the gorilla and chimpanzee. But in the next breath the same writers will claim that man stands not only at the head of the primates but also at the head of the whole animal kingdom as its most highly developed and most advanced representative! Now, while the reader may be an adherent of the belief that the principle of excluded middle belongs to the Middle Ages, and that a thing can be both A and not-A at one and the same time, he will doubtless perceive that all the statements contained in the above sentences cannot be true, and that there is evidently some confusion somewhere.

The error principally responsible for this confusion lies in the practice of taking the part for the whole. It is a fact that man's brain is functionally more complex than that of any other animal. The peculiar character of man's brain has yielded him a supremacy over his environment such as no other animal is capable of attaining. In this respect there can be no question that man *is* the most advanced member of the whole animal kingdom. Everyone would agree to this, but then, in their unguarded moments most writers will proceed to argue as if man were the most "advanced" animal in every other respect; and then when it suits the direction of their argument they will write as if he were the one primate who had managed to retain an unusually large number of primitive characters. Interestingly enough this latter attribute is generally used to demonstrate the superiority of man above the other primates, for this retention of primitive characters is used to support the view that man has thereby been rendered more plastic, more malleable, more adaptable to the various environments which, during his long history, he has encountered. The great apes have become over-specialized, the argument usually runs, very much like the dinosaurs, they have developed great canine teeth, have become too large and heavy, and as a consequence of their narrow specialization are doomed to eventual extinction.[11] Man, it is generally held, has not gone in for such specialization, and has therefore remained unspecialized and extraordinarily adaptable.

When, however, the facts are considered, facts which are explicitly denotable as opposed to this type of implicit language usage,[12] there is more than a doubt that such views can be seri-

11. At least one writer, Gerrit S. Miller, Jr., includes man in common with the great apes in this judgment, in his paper *Man's Biological Outlook* (Science, Vol. 94, 1941), pp. 163–164. See also Ashley Montagu's reply, *Man's Biological Outlook* (Psychiatry, Vol. 6, 1943), pp. 359–360.

12. "Anything to which the human organism can react serially point for point is referred to as *explicitly denotable*. That which we know as 'finger,' or 'penny,' or 'stone,' is such an object. 'Fascism,' or 'democracy,' or 'nation,' to which an individual cannot react in this way, may be referred to as *implicit language usage*." Raymond Rhine, *Explicit Denotation in Language: A Psychological Contribution to Methods in the Social Sciences* (The Journal of Social Psychology, Vol. 18, 1943), pp. 331–363. See also F. H. Allport, *Motive as a Concept in Natural Science* (Psychological Review, Vol. 37, 1930), pp. 169–173.

ously maintained. "Specialization" is another of those fuzzy terms which may be loosely used in a variety of ways, and which may therefore serve the purposes of a writer who will use it in both contradictory and contrary ways. An animal is said to be specialized when in one or more of its characters it has developed to such an extent that it is apparently committed to a definite course of present life and future development. It cannot reverse the evolutionary trend determined by its specializations. This phenomenon is embraced by Dollo's so-called "Law of Irreversibility of Evolution." This "law," to which there are many exceptions cannot be discussed here, but in the light of modern genetic knowledge there is some doubt as to its validity. The canine tooth of the gorilla, for example, is said to be a highly specialized or over-specialized tooth. It has become tusk-like. None of the fossil anthropoids was characterized by the possession of such a markedly developed tooth. In man, on the other hand, this tooth has undergone an appreciable reduction in size. It is difficult to see why reduction in size cannot be regarded as much a specialization as increase in size. The foot of the orang is regarded as a highly specialized grasping organ. But there seems no good reason to regard the human foot as anything but a highly specialized supporting organ adapted to the erect posture, bipedal locomotion, and a wholly terrestrial existence. Furthermore, the human pelvic girdle is very much more specialized in all its features than is that of any other primate. So is the human face. In fact, man is in many unique ways quite as specialized a creature as is any primate. The specializations which occur among the rest of the primates have simply proceeded in different directions, precisely as one would expect in an Order characterized by such remarkable powers of variability.

Hence, it seems fairly clear that if the term "specialization" is to be used at all, it must be used, as must the term "advanced," to refer to specific characters and not to the status of the animal as a whole, nor should the term be restricted to increase in size as opposed to decrease in size. In other words, specialization may assume different and contrary forms, and no arbitrary selection may be made from among these forms.

ATAVISM

The concept of "atavism" reached its greatest heights of popularity during the second half of the nineteenth century, but it still occasionally makes its appearance in the writings of biologists [13] and some anthropologists. In point of fact, however, this term has always belonged to the world of the imagination rather than to that of reality, and it should therefore be completely dropped from the vocabulary of the scientist.

"Atavism," from the Latin *atavus,* an ancestor, is the term used to describe the supposed reappearance of an ancestral character in a descendant member of a group in which the character has been lost and does not normally appear. One of the most frequently cited examples of the supposed reappearance of lost ancestral structures in man is the gill-pouches of fishes, which are alleged to make their appearance in the early human embryo [14] and which may persist in the adult to form an open fistula on the side of the neck. The persistence of such a cleft has, of course, no connection whatever with the reappearance of a character which man has lost, for man has not lost this particular character. It is present in the early embryo in the form of branchial arches separated from one another by grooves, and the persistence of such a groove in an occasional adult is simply due to an abnormal process of development or to an arrest in development. The condition is neither degenerative nor reversionary but, as I have said, simply due to a disturbance in development.

The occasional occurrence of a "tail" in man or of an azygous lobe of the right lung, microcephaly, large canine teeth, the fourth molar, the divided malar bone, the "third trochanter" of the femur, the entepicondylar foramen of the humerus, supernumerary mammae, and many other characters have been, and still are, cited as examples of "atavism." Yet in every case it can

13. For the erroneous use of this concept see I. Cornman, *A Basis for Ostensible Reversal of Evolution* (American Naturalist, Vol. 77, 1943), pp. 80–93.

14. Neither in birds, nor in mammals are functional gills ever present at any stage of development. The so-called gill-pouches of man are more correctly spoken of as branchial arches. A complex cleft is not present between the arches as in fishes.

be conclusively shown that such characters are not upon any view to be regarded as reversions to an ancestral condition. Changes in development and in developmental rates resulting in persistence, suppression, reduction, hypertrophy, duplication or multiplication of structures and normal variability, are processes quite adequate to account for the so-called "atavisms" which are commonly cited.

Not every character, however, which has been described as an "atavism" can be explained in this way. Most of the Lombrosian school's "atavistic" characters, and such suggestions as von Luschan's that Beethoven possibly represented a reversion to the Neanderthal type, and that his musical genius may have been "atavistic," [15] may be dismissed as sheer nonsense. The fact is that modern genetic knowledge renders it quite certain that the alleged phenomenon of "atavism" is quite impossible, for it is quite clear that only such characters can develop as lie within the potentialities of the genetic systems of the mating organisms. Hence, as a concept to account for the appearance of certain physical characters or forms of behavior "atavism" belongs in the Academy of Discarded Curiosities.

15. See F. H. Hankins, "Atavism," in *Encyclopedia of the Social Sciences,* New York, Vol. 2, 1932, pp. 290–291; and M. F. Ashley Montagu, *The Concept of Atavism* (Science, Vol. 87, 1938), pp. 462–463.

ASHLEY MONTAGU

"Primitive" Art

Is "PRIMITIVE ART" primitive? The question is a spurious one for the term "primitive" begs the question. Indeed, the indiscriminate application of the term to the art of different peoples of different ethnic origins, of different histories, of different cultures, of different times, and of different places, arbitrarily serves as a universal criterion by which to describe and classify the art of such peoples. If a people is "primitive" its art must be primitive. The number of questions begged in that statement are many. The fact is that none of the peoples called primitive are so except for their technological development and economic organization. Every nonliterate society has had as long a history as every civilized society; the environmental challenges to which they have been constrained to respond have been different in each case, and if some are in some respects less developed than others, it is not because their members have been less intelligent or less well-endowed than the members of more developed societies, but simply for the reason that the challenges with which they have been confronted have required no more than the appropriate responses. Where there is no increase in the complexity of the challenges there is no development in the character of the responses. In art the complexity of the challenges are always present no matter what the degree of technological development. The challenges are to the imagination, the emotions, technique and skill, and these have been operative from the earliest times, and the earliest artists responded magnificently to them.

The basic error committed by those who speak of "primitive art" is the generalization from one or another aspect of the culture, such as technology, transportation, and economics, which may be comparatively undeveloped, to the assumption that every other aspect of the culture must be equally undeveloped. This is almost equivalent to the fallacy of *post hoc,* the fallacy of assuming that because some variables are associated therefore they must be causally related. Perhaps the fallacy committed by those who adhere to the belief in "primitive art" should be called *the fallacy of unwarranted extension,* for it is an unwarranted procedure to extend to all traits of a culture a quality which may characterize some other of its traits. The truth is that when we compare such traits, in nonliterate cultures, as language, religion, mythology, the kinship system, novelizing, balladry, tracking abilities, mechanical abilities, and the like, the members of nonliterate cultures not only compare favorably with the members of civilized societies, but often excel them.

Implicit in the concept of "primitive" for many who employ the term is the idea of inferiority. The inherent idea is that nonliterate peoples are "primitive" because they are essentially inferior, because, in short, they have not developed the qualities necessary for the development of civilization. It is from such an elevated viewpoint that all the cultural traits of "primitive" peoples were judged, and still continue to be judged, by many people.

When an Australian aboriginal sketched the head of a man without a mouth, this was put down to his unsophistication, to his naïveté. That the aboriginal preferred to draw that way, that his art was highly stylized, and that when he wished to he could draw as well in the style of the "civilized" world as any skilled artist of the western world somehow failed to be recognized.[1]

When the beautiful Ifé bronzes of Nigeria were discovered, it was argued by some that they could not possibly have been the work of Negroes. Various authorities argued that either Roman, Greek, Egyptian, Renaissance Italian, and even Portuguese Jesuits were most probably responsible for these masterpieces. It was far simpler to suppose, it was argued, that a master artist of some such origin had wandered down from North Africa into Nigeria, than to credit a "primitive" people like the Nigerians with such creative genius. Indeed, how could one credit any "primitive" people, people without writing or the ability to read, with a primitive technology, in short, with a "primitive" culture, with such a variety of styles and so sophisticated an imagination as is displayed in such art?

Arguing thus the only possible explanation was the introduction of a *deus ex machina* who was not a member of a "primitive" people, but a "racially" acceptable Caucasoid from North Africa, even though he might have been a Mediterranean. This is what happened when the first cave art was discovered. The learned world refused to accept the notion that such accomplished paintings could have been the work of prehistoric man. They must have been the work of a modern artist who occupied his idle hours imitating the example of Michelangelo in the Sistine Chapel. It took repeated discoveries of cave art throughout Europe and many years of debate before the theory of the itinerant modern artist was abandoned, and the grudging admission wrung from the skeptics that, difficult as it was to believe, these extraordinary works were, indeed, the product of prehistoric men. Both the refusal to admit and the final reluctant admission constituted

1. Miller, Mary D., *Child Artists of the Australian Bush*. London: Harrap, 1952.

testimony to the fact that though this art might be the work of prehistoric man it was not primitive.

The literature on the art of prehistoric and of "primitive" man is now considerable. Hardly a year elapses without its shelf of books on the subject. Artists and critics admire, and collectors and museums pay substantial prices for works of art that are no longer condescendingly considered as the quaint productions of naïve minds. Such works are today appreciated for their unique qualities as works of art, works of art which may be compared on their own merits with those of other peoples of any time and place. All this has had the effect for many of entirely destroying the myth that the art of nonliterate peoples is "primitive." Nevertheless the notion rather more than lingers, and since it contributes to its perpetuation it would constitute a contribution to clearer thinking and to a just estimate of these works if the term "primitive art" were to be dropped altogether.

Prehistoric art, at any rate, the prehistoric art that we know, may be prehistoric, but it is not "primitive." Like the art of nonliterate peoples it represents a highly advanced expression of the life of its prehistoric creators.

A number of writers, sensitive to the defects of the term "primitive art" have suggested various substitutes for it. "Ethnic," "ethnological," "preliterate," "pre-urban," "precivilized," "traditional," "tribal," and "folk," have been suggested as adjectives, and they are all as unsatisfactory as the term they are designed to replace.

It would be far more sensible and vastly more useful to employ the specific adjective which particularizes the art of a particular people. Yoruba art or Igorot art or Pitjendara art tells us at once what we want to know, namely, that this is the art of these particular peoples. The context in which the art is described will give the geographic location of the people, the African Yoruba, the Philippine Igorots, and the Australian Pitjendara. Whether such more general broader categories as "African art," "Philippine art," and "Australian art," are categories that can be usefully employed would depend upon the care with which such terms were employed. In general it would be more useful to speak of the art of the specific group which it characterizes, or even better, whenever possible, of the particular artist who produced the work, his locality and his social position.

As Compton has written,

The term "primitive" was adopted to describe a certain type of culture complex at a time when anthropological attitudes were considerably different from those generally prevailing now. The term was quite frankly intended to describe cultures which were different from and, as the anthropologists believed, "inferior" to the historic and contemporary culture of the Western world plus those cultures, historic and contemporary, of Africa and Asia which were deemed to be comparable, however different in detail, to the Western cultures. At that time the term "primitive" was easily definable; it meant any culture which did not "measure up" to the Western norm. Most anthropologists have abandoned this naive attitude, and so the term "primitive" is either ambiguous or meaningless.[2]

Davis writes,

Since the arts, like language, are part of a total communication spectrum which makes up culture, we might model the precision and some of the tactics of our approach on that of the linguists. As an example, no one today speaks of primitive language or ethnological or ethnic language. Instead, modifiers are introduced which give either the where and when of the language in question or some neutral term of group identification—Turkic, West African, Uto-Aztecan, etc. "North American Indian languages" cues a reader as to expectable range of language types and geographical loci. The qualifier "primitive" is left out, since no language is primitive. Neither is art, although there is a greater range of skill and practice among its users. . . . There is palaeolithic mural painting, Florentine sculpture, and nineteenth-century Maori skin-carving, but there is no "primitive art." It's a rubbery, shapeless, inappropriate term.[3]

Gerbrands believes that "further study of the so-called primitive arts undoubtedly will lead to a final evaporation of the term."[4]

2. Compton, Carl B., "The Concept of Primitive Applied to Art." *Current Anthropology,* vol. 6, 1965, p. 432.
3. Davis, Emma L., *op. cit.,* p. 433.
4. Gerbrands, Adrian A., *op. cit.,* p. 435.

Klausen writes, "nothing in the literature on this subject known to me reveals any fundamental difference between 'primitive art' and European art, neither with regard to technique, form, symbolic content, nor social function. . . . Thus my conclusion is that we do not need a special term 'primitive art,' any more than we need a term 'primitive kinship.' " [5]

Finally, let us conclude with the words of Claude Roy, "It is only to the degree that we share the illusion of 'savagery' that any art can be called 'savage.' It is only by forgetting our profound kinship with everyone who has ever exemplified in signs or images our common human problems of life and thought, that any art can be called 'primitive.' Although it first occurred to anthropologists to give the lovely name, The Museum of Man, to their own museum in the city of Paris, actually this is the one title that perfectly fits every museum the world over. A single immense Museum of Man dominates the infinite variety of mankind, and in it a Dan mask is not *more beautiful* than Corot's *Woman in Blue*, a bronze statuette from Sardinia made a thousand years before Christ is not *more beautiful* than a Rodin statue. The quality of human life is not measurable quantitatively, not by instruments and not in numbers. When the work of art is the only one of the works of man that lasts, then it is the one that realizes for us an art of living created by men otherwise unknown." [6]

5. Klausen, Arne M., *op. cit.*, p. 435.
6. Roy, Claude, *The Art of the Savages*. New York, Essential Encyclopedia Arts, Inc., 1958, p. 14.

KATHERINE GEORGE

The Civilized West

Looks at Primitive Africa: 1400–1800

A Study in Ethnocentrism

To BE born into a culture has generally implied being supported by it, being upheld, as it were, on a pedestal, from which one might look down with varying degrees of disinterest or antagonism upon other, alien cultures. Hence, the observer of alien cultures has tended to be prejudiced, in the simple sense that he has preferred his own to all other existent cultures and

Reprinted from ISIS Volume 49, Part I, Number 155, March 1958, pp. 62–72.

[175]

has viewed the strange as a malformed deviant from the familiar. The ego-flattering naiveté of the Aristotelian division of the world's population into Greeks and barbarians, or freemen by nature and slaves by nature, has formed the usual pattern into which men have fitted their observation of human differences.

The category of barbarism is for Aristotle notably inclusive, and without distinction as to region, people, or custom; but in the writings of most commentators upon human affairs variations in the extent of cultural difference have been associated with variations in the kinds of observational judgments made. The greater the extent of cultural difference, the greater is the amount of antagonism or scorn expressed. Primitive cultures, as described by the civilized observer, have suffered in particular, therefore, from the fashion of disparaging the alien; and the commandment, "Thou shalt not bear false witness," has proven particularly difficult of observance in this area of cultural description.

It is the purpose of this paper to analyze in one segment of the literature about primitive cultures something of the precise nature of the prejudices involved and the extent to which they were obstructive of adequate and truthful description. First, as to the total literature susceptible of this type of investigation, a geographical limitation has been set: This paper is concerned only with the literature of European contacts with primitive Africa, particularly with Negro Africa. There is also a temporal limitation: Intensive reading has been done only in literature written from the fifteenth through the eighteenth centuries. To provide background and comparison, however, the principal classical and medieval sources have also been considered. As an analysis of the total sum of writings existent even within these limitations, this study does not presume to be exhaustive. Nevertheless, the well over a hundred reports of African travel or relevant geographical treatises which have been consulted constitute a sufficient sampling of the whole literature to enable sound generalizations as to content.[1]

1. Two bibliographies are of particular service in regard to this literature: first, Edward Godfrey Cox, *A Reference Guide to the Literature of Travel*

Classical accounts of the primitive inhabitants of Africa are in general scattered and brief, and tend consistently to emphasize the strange, the shocking, and the degrading qualities of the peoples and cultures they deal with, and thus to emphasize the gulf between the civilized and the primitive worlds. Something of the nature of such accounts is due, of course, to the extreme inadequacy of the information on which they were based, for effective classical knowledge of Africa was limited to the Mediterranean littoral, principally to the two recognized civilizations which flourished there, the Egyptian and the Carthaginian. But more than a mere scantiness of data limits these accounts of the African primitive; they are characterized, too, by a selection of data on the basis of an attitude of superiority and disapproval, and by the reporter's increasing propensity, as he moves farther from the sections of the continent relatively familiar to him at first or second hand, to substitute antagonistic fantasy for fact. Thus, even that most noted of classical geographers, Herodotus, in describing the native peoples of the Great Sahara, comes at last to the hazy realms of far western Libya, where "the huge serpents are found, and the lions . . . and the creatures without heads whom the Libyans declare to have their eyes in their breasts, and also the wild men, and the wild women. . . ." [2] And Diodorus makes the following statement in introducing a discussion of certain Ethiopian primitives:

The majority of them . . . are black in colour and have flat noses and woolly hair. As for their spirit, they are entirely savage and display the nature of a wild beast . . . and are as far removed as possible from

---

(Seattle, 1935), vol. I, *The Old World*, section XIII, "Africa," pp. 354–401; and second, Monroe N. Work, *A Bibliography of the Negro in Africa and America* (New York, 1928), part I, "The Negro in Africa," section I, "Discovery and Exploration in Africa from Ancient Times to 1800," pp. 1–17. Though their coverage in period and area is different from that of this paper, two book-length treatments of similar travel material ought to be mentioned here: Geoffroy Atkinson, *Les Relations de Voyages du XVIIᵉ Siècle et l'Evolution des Idées* (Paris, 1924); and Roy H. Pearce, *The Savages of America: A Study of the Indian and the Idea of Civilization* (Baltimore, 1953).

2. Herodotus, *The History*. Translated and edited by George Rawlinson (London, 1910), I, p. 362. (Book II, Ch. 191.)

human kindness to one another; and speaking as they do with a shrill voice and cultivating none of the practices of civilized life as these are found among the rest of mankind, they present a striking contrast when considered in the light of our own customs.[3]

This statement adequately conveys the tone of the descriptions which succeed, for the long list of primitive groups whom Diodorus here considers (most of whom were presumably situated in the area between the Nile and the Red Sea) are generally said to be strange and miserable folk who barely exist in continual hunger and fear, ruthlessly kill their aged and their sick, and practice sexual promiscuity.

The classical consensus, then, is that these peoples in the hidden interior and on the farthest shores of Africa not only lack civilization but any worthy ethic of social organization or conduct as well. Anarchic, promiscuous, and cruel, they live the life of beasts rather than that of men. The most remote, in addition, are often denied the possession of a truly human form. The dominant attitude in these accounts conceived of civilization—Graeco-Roman civilization in particular—as an essential discipline imposed upon the irregularities of nature; as nature—blind nature—without restraint and guidance, runs to monstrosities, so culture without civilization runs to disorder and excess. There was established thus early the pattern of thought which for many future centuries formed a basis for approach to the primitives of Africa, and which defined them primarily not in terms of what they were and what they had, but in terms of what they presumably were not and had not —in terms, that is, of their inhumanity, their wildness, and their lack of proper law.

In the fifteenth century direct and consistent European contact with the Africa beyond the Mediterranean littoral is initiated, and the travel reports with which this study is principally

3. Diodorus Siculus [Works], trans. by C. H. Oldfather (London, 1935), II, pp. 103–105. (Book III, Ch. 8.) Ethiopia proper has been viewed since antiquity as a civilized land, and reports of its inhabitants and their culture will therefore not be considered in this study.

concerned begin to be written.[4] From the fifteenth century itself come only a handful of such accounts, all either of Portuguese or Italian authorship.

The great physical extension of European contact with Africa inevitably produces an increase of knowledge about the area, an increase of knowledge chiefly about African geography, but about African peoples and cultures to some extent as well. The end of the century sees an outline map of the continent closely approximate to the present form, and the monsters of classical imaginings have largely disappeared from the more distant shores and even from the as yet unpenetrated interior. But the pressures of an aggressive civilization, even then embarking upon a more ambitious program of exploiting the alien and primitive than any previously known, are still at work shaping what the observer sees and what he reports. The problem of ethnocentrism is still present.

Ethnocentrism exerts its influence in these reports in a variety of ways. First and most importantly, it makes for that negative prejudice toward the primitive and his culture whose power for distortion has already been discussed. Second, it makes for indifference toward the primitive and his culture, so that little time or care is given to the reportage of such matters, and for every item which is described many other items easily within reach of the observer are ignored. Such sins of omission are inherent in the very nature of this early modern travel literature; they are perhaps more significant, indeed, than the sins of commission which are more easily cited. Third, the ethnocentric bias induces a too ready and too complete identification with the familiar cultural background of anything in the new cultural situation found to be sufficiently similar. This identification,

4. Because of limitations in space, medieval accounts, whether Arabic or Christian, will not be considered here. Arabic reports of North African places and peoples beyond the confines of old and well known centers of civilizations are based for the most part on first-hand knowledge and are therefore greatly superior to both classical and contemporary Christian accounts; but they are products of an intensely militant culture in the heyday of expansion, and even the best of them (Ibn Battuta's *Travels*, for example) are overburdened and limited by the political concerns and religious judgments of the writers.

which does not necessarily imply approval of the trait in question, and most definitely not of its cultural context, is probably ascribable merely to that indifference to the characteristics of an alien culture referred to above. Finally, ethnocentrism, which is itself a tradition and a habit, also encourages the persistence of other traditions or habits of reporting, since it tends to focus the observer's attention not so much on what he sees in an alien culture as on what he has heard about it in his own culture. Thus, particular kinds of prejudice, particular items of description, and even particular turns of phrase become established and persist, often through centuries, and lend the weight of specific instances of statement to the impression of continuity which this literature conveys.

The descriptions of the political institutions of African primitives in the accounts of the fifteenth century contain elements both of change and of persistence, but themselves set up a tradition to be followed in future reports. For the complex political structure of West African Negro societies in particular was too obvious to be ignored by those engaged in mercantile negotiations in the region. In the case of such societies, the classical stereotype of the lawless primitive had to be abandoned, but it has been replaced by only a somewhat lesser distortion, since their political institutions, without regard to differences from tribe to tribe, are identified with those of contemporary Europe. One hears not only of African kings and an African nobility but also of African dukes and counts and knights.[5] On the other hand, the more remote African primitives, in the fifteenth century, the "tawnie Moores" of the Sahara especially, are still reported to be ignorant of all law and order,[6] and between the two po-

5. See Gomes Eannes de Azurara, *The Chronicle of the Discovery and Conquest of Guinea*, trans. by C. Beazley and E. Prestage (London: Hakluyt Society, 1896), I, pp. 48, 281, 284. It should be noted that the placing of each account in its century grouping is based in this study upon the date at which the journey in question was made and/or the account was written, rather than upon the date even of initial publication.

6. *Ibid.*, II, p. 233; also Alvise da Cadamosto, *The Voyages of Cadamosto and Other Documents on Western Africa*, trans. by G. R. Crone (London: Hakluyt Society, 1937), p. 54.

litical extremes little if any ground is given to subtleties of variation.

The charge of bestiality, so much the mark of the primitive among classical geographers, is abundantly encountered in these fifteenth-century accounts. The absence of recognized institutional formalities is in the traditional view an absence of an important adjunct of humanity, hence bestial. The society without law, regulations of sexual conduct, or religion is, in respect to each of these lacks, a bestial society, and several African societies are declared by writers of the century to be without one or another such institutional forms. One traveler asserts that certain Negroes living in a vaguely identified area south of the Sahara "are in carnal acts like the beasts, the father has knowledge of his daughter, the son of his sister." [7] Cannibalism is, in the traditional view, a bestial practice, too, and the same traveler asserts that the same Negroes are "eaters of human flesh." [8] Any peculiarity of dress, diet, or manner which was distressing to European sensibilities could be made to contribute to this image of African bestiality.[9] The following statement well illustrates this: The writer is endeavoring to justify the Portuguese slave trade (this trade depended in its early years upon the slave raid), and he has spoken first of the "happy" situation of the kidnapped Africans, now enslaved, in Portugal:

And so their lot was now quite contrary of what it had been; since before they had lived in perdition of soul and body; of their souls, in that they were yet pagans, without the clearness and the light of holy faith; and of their bodies, in that they lived like beasts, without any custom of reasonable beings—for they had no knowledge of bread or wine, and they were without the covering of clothes, or the lodgment of houses; and worse than all, through the great ignorance that was in them, in that they had no understanding of good, but only knew how to live in a bestial sloth.[10]

7. Antoine Malfante, "The Letter of Antoine Malfante from Tuat, 1447," in Cadamosto, *op. cit.*, p. 89.
8. *Ibid.*
9. For references to certain African customs of eating and dressing as "bestial," see Azurara, *op. cit.*, II, pp. 231–232; and Cadamosto, *op. cit.*, p. 41.
10. Azurara, *op. cit.*, I, pp. 84–85.

This statement presents the issue of Christianity's influence upon the civilized view of the primitive, and upon the problem of the present study, that of ethnocentrism. For the classical dichotomy between Greek and barbarian Christianity did substitute a more generous and more flexible measure by which to divide humanity—the measure of a faith, which its adherents were constantly endeavoring to expand. Nevertheless, no more than does the rigid exclusiveness of the Greek view does this proselytizing character of Christianity provide a basis for a favorable or objective interest in the qualities of man or of man's culture which lie outside the pale. And the judgments which arise from either position fall likewise with special displeasure upon the primitive way of life. Raw nature, "fallen" nature, which for the Greek was disorder, is for the Christian even worse: it is sin. In addition, Christianity did not eliminate older hierarchies based on race, nationality, class or occupational status, but it rather collaborated with such hierarchies and more frequently than not strengthened instead of weakening them— though it did introduce the complicating idea of a possible restatement of human relations in the society of another world. The availability of salvation to all properly indoctrinated souls alike, despite bodily inequalities—we find this gift of Chirstianity in the previously cited passage. But does it lessen the writer's prejudice? To the contrary. It enables him instead to commend actions (the kidnapping of helpless people) as morally virtuous, actions which to classical observers would have seemed merely expedient.

Christianity, or the religious frame of reference in general, also tends to foster the atmosphere of moral judgment which pervades this travel literature. Whatever else may or may not be reported about an African people, some statement regarding their "character" is almost always made. Usually it consists of a listing of vices, though an occasional virtue may also be acknowledged. The vice most consistently noted is thievishness; [11]

11. See Cadamosto, *op. cit.*, p. 19.

the virtue, hospitality.[12] In both judgments an ethnocentric bias is the guiding principle: The reporter considers the Africans, not in terms of how they deal with one another, but in terms of how they deal with Europeans.

The physical attributes of the African primitive are likewise subjected to this parochial appraisal and, typically, are measured against the esthetic standard of the European Caucasoid. The physical traits peculiar to the Negro, his thick lips and his dark skin, are always thought ugly; a Negro is only said to be less ugly as he is less Negroid. The absolute nature of this judgment is striking; it is made without the smallest consciousness of its relativity. Indeed, the esthetic judgment assumes in time the dimensions of a moral judgment too. For when the traditional climatic explanation of Negro skin coloration has been replaced by the genetic, which in these accounts has occurred by the sixteenth century,[13] the rationale is generally provided by the presumed descent of the Negro from Ham, the accursed. The dark skin of the Negro becomes more than esthetically displeasing; it becomes the symbol and the product of a moral taint as well.[14]

One further notable feature of the reporting is the tendency to view the culture of the primitive African as poverty-stricken in material skills and resources, and to make any reference to material culture a basis for invidious comparison with the

12. *Ibid.*, p. 33. The initial reception of the intruding Europeans by African peoples was almost invariably non-hostile. So friendly were the natives at one spot on the southeast coast of Africa where the ships of da Gama's first expedition were anchored for a period that the country was called "Terra da Boã Gente" (land of good people) by the Portuguese. *A Journal of the First Voyage of Vasco da Gama, 1497–1499,* trans. and ed. by E. G. Ravenstein (London: Hakluyt Society, 1897), pp. 17–18.

13. The climatic theory is still found in Malfante, *op. cit.,* p. 86. For the biological theory in the sixteenth century, see Duarte Lopez, *A Report of the Kingdom of Congo and the Surrounding Countries,* trans. by Margarite Hutchinson from the Italian account of Philip Pigafetta (London, 1881), pp. 16–17.

14. See Father Jerom [Girolamo] Merolla da Sorrento, "A Voyage to Congo," in John Pinkerton, *A General Collection of . . . Voyages and Travels. . . .* (London, 1808–1814), XVI, p. 267.

achievements of Western civilization.[15] Fact and prejudice no doubt coincide more nearly in this than in most areas of comparison. But again, the nature of the prejudice prevents adequate observation or adequate description of what is observed, for it brings into primary focus the absence rather than the presence of cultural qualities.

Inevitably, the emphasis of a paper such as this is upon what is "wrong" with the accounts in question, rather than upon what is "right." But to maintain that these early accounts are inadequate from any standpoint is not to deny that they contain a considerable amount, and a steadily growing amount, of accurate information concerning the cultures with which they deal. One must take full cognizance, too, of the sheer physical enormity of the task of making contact with, and coming even superficially to know the peoples of this vast and hitherto inaccessible continent. The difficulties of encountering in relatively rapid succession a large number of new cultures and strange languages should certainly excuse much. Still, such considerations do not entirely serve to explain the fact that whereas by the end of the fifteenth century the outline map of Africa was accurately delineated, no similarly reliable sketch of African primitive cultures existed or was to exist for a very long time to come. In the one field, knowledge kept pace with experience; in the other, aggressive factors were at work to perpetuate ignorance.

The reports of contacts with primitive Africa of the sixteenth century are still few in number. Though still primarily of Italian or Portuguese authorship, they are no longer exclusively so. A spreading interest in African trade has induced other nationalities, notably the English, to make occasional contributions to the accounts.

Much of the spirit and content of these accounts continue as in the century before. The West African political structure is again described in terms of its kings and nobility, and one also hears something of East African Negro potentates, of an em-

15. See Cadamosto, *op. cit.*, p. 31.

peror of Monomotapa, for example, who maintains a ceremonious court, possesses great wealth, and has among the most valiant of his armed supporters a troop of Amazons.[16] Less patently organized primitive Africans are still said to be lawless, to lack religion, to be sexually promiscuous, and to live "like wild beasts." [17] The charge of cannibalism is frequently made, and acquires the colorful details which take it well out of the realm of fact and into the realm of slander. One writer declares that a certain Negro people of the interior, about whom he knows only by hearsay, "have a shambles for human flesh, as we have of animals" and devour the bodies not only of enemies taken in battle, but also those of their "friends, subjects, and even relations," [18] a description which becomes one of the stock tales of African travel. One ideological addition appears in the accounts of the sixteenth century, for by this time the West African coastal Negroes, at least, had experienced considerable exposure to civilizing influences; and the Western writers of reports about these people are therefore able to document their complacency regarding the superiority of their own to a primitive culture by citing instances of improvement in Negro customs brought about by European example.[19]

16. See Duarte Barbosa, *The Book of Duarte Barbosa. An Account of the Countries Bordering on the Indian Ocean and Their Inhabitants,* trans. by M. L. Dames (London: Hakluyt Society, 1918), I, pp. 12–13. The non-existent Amazons of eastern Africa are mentioned several times in accounts of the sixteenth and seventeenth centuries; the female soldiers who actually formed part of the retinue of the rulers of Dahomey are not remarked upon until the eighteenth century.

17. *Ibid.,* p. 16; and Duarte Lopez, *op.cit.,* p. 125.

18. Duarte Lopez, *op. cit.,* pp. 28–29. Cannibalism is or has been practiced by certain peoples of Africa, but it has been almost entirely limited to cere-monial occasions. With a few possible exceptions, human flesh appears never to have been the common article of diet which the early voyagers assumed it to be.

19. *Ibid.,* p. 72; also João de Barros, "Extracts from the 'Decadas da India,'" Cadamosto, *op. cit.,* pp. 107–108. Leo Africanus, a Moroccan-born Arab, in his sixteenth-century account of travel in North Africa, attributes to the extension of Moslem influence such improvement as has occurred in the bestial ways of the primitive Africans who have come within his purview. See Leo Africanus, *History and Description of Africa,* trans. by John Pory (London: Hakluyt Society, 1896), III, p. 820.

The seventeenth century sees a marked increase in the number of accounts of travel to primitive Africa and in the number of nationalities represented by the authors. South Africa becomes in this century the one area of real European colonization on the continent, and two little known peoples, the Bushmen and Hottentots, are thereby exposed to view.

The accounts of the seventeenth century evince a quality of transition between a definite viewpoint of the past (as embodied in fifteenth- and sixteenth-century accounts) and an equally definite, though very different, viewpoint of the future (as embodied in eighteenth-century accounts). But it is the dominance of the past which is first and most forcibly apparent. The negative portrait of African character is more emphatically and fully drawn than before,[20] and the opinion still prevails that the African primitive is improved in character and customs by contact with the European. The tendency to deny to certain primitive African cultures the possession of some one or another of the institutional forms likewise persists. Religion is particularly apt to such eliminating from the tally of African cultural equipment. In one highly antagonistic account of Hottentot culture, this simple people is indeed brought perilously close to the ancient prototype of the altogether brutish primitive. "These lawless barbarians and immoral pagans," the author writes, "practice only those habits to which a blind impulse of nature irresistibly impels them." [21] The boldest forms of such a concept are now found, however, not in accounts directly attributable to specific travelers, but in that more backward form of travel literature, the digest of the accounts of others. In one such treatise on Africa

20. See Jacques Joseph Le Marie, *A Voyage of the Sieur Le Maire to the Canary Islands, Cape Verd, Senegal and Gamby* (London, 1696; translated from the French original), pp. 79–82; and William Bosman, *A New . . . Description of the Coast of Guinea* (London, 1705; translated from the Dutch original), p. 117.

21. Willem ten Rhyne, "A Short Account of the Cape of Good Hope" (translated from the Latin original) in Isaac Schapera, *The Early Cape Hottentots, Described in the Writings of Olfert Dapper (1668), Willem ten Rhyne (1686), and Johannes Gulielmus de Grevenbroek (1695)*, Cape Town, 1933), p. 127.

we are told of "the Caffers, or Libertines, who hold many Athe-
isticall Tenets, live together promiscuously . . . following their
. . . unbridled lust. . . ." [22] And here too we meet again that
first fifteenth-century conception of the two political systems existent among African primitives:

> As for their Governments, some of them know none, neither ever
> scarce heard of any, but live in a confused Ataxy, sway'd on all occasions
> like tumultuous Herds, and at other times like tame Cattel feeding, and
> following their idle pleasures. But the rest are all Monarchical, living
> under Laws, Order, and Princes.[23]

But, despite the fact that cultural parochialism and negative
prejudice are still the major features of the accounts of the seventeenth century, new elements deserve acknowledgment. These
accounts are on the whole considerably more informative than
those of the past; they tend to be longer, fuller, and more concerned with cultural matters. This improvement should be cred-
ited in part to the increase of data about African cultures almost
inevitably consequent upon extension and repetition of contacts
with them. But new ideas and influences are also involved. As
befits a century in which Europe saw a great growth in interest
in voyage literature, there is to some extent an emergence of
a consciousness of contributing to a specific literary genre, of
a certain pride in workmanship, and of a sense of responsibility
to the standards of their task. To be the eyewitness of a fact and
to tell the truth about it—these requirements to which writers
of earlier centuries paid scarcely any heed are seriously invoked
by occasional seventeenth-century travelers as guides to proper
reporting.[24]

Only one account from the century, however, sharply de-
parts from most of the tendencies of the past and breaks a new
pathway of approach to primitive African culture: that written

22. John Ogilby, *Africa* (London, 1670), p. 34. This treatise appears to
be in the main a translation of Olfert Dapper, *Beschreibung von Africa und
den gehörigen Königreichen und Landschaften* (Amsterdam, 1670).
23. *Ibid.*, p. 318.
24. See Bosman, *op. cit.*, Preface.

by Grevenbroek, who became the first champion of the natives
of South Africa before the world. One quotation from his report
(in the form of a long letter to a European friend, and hence
rather disorganized) sufficiently indicates the revolutionary quality of his outlook:

> I am astonished that . . . those half-truths that are spread about our
> Africans should have reached even your ears. I found this people with
> one accord in their . . . daily life living in harmony with nature's law,
> hospitable to every race of men, open, dependable, lovers of truth and
> justice, not utterly unacquainted with the worship of some God, en-
> dowed . . . with a rare nimbleness of mother wit, and having minds
> receptive of instruction . . . it is through the faults of our countrymen
> . . . that the natives have been changed for the worse. . . . From us
> they have learned . . . misdeeds unknown to them before, and, among
> other crimes of deepest die, the accursed lust for gold.[25]

The important fact about this remarkable statement is that
Grevenbroek's report, despite its casual letter form, is certainly
one of the two or three best of the century.

Thus we come to the end of the seventeenth century, with
two new principles beginning to influence writers about African
culture: one, a new insistence on the responsibility of the traveler
to check the accuracy of reports, preferably by eyewitness observation, and the other, the wholly fresh idea of viewing primitive life and customs in terms of their positive values and virtues.

Accounts of African travel in the eighteenth century are
more numerous than in any previous era, and they are also more
various in respect to the nationalities, the interests, the training,
and the professions of the travelers writing them. There are
missionaries, traders, and officials, as in the past, but in addition there are numbers of an entirely different breed, men who,
with a considerable background of education in the philosophical
and scientific thought of the day, came to Africa primarily to
explore and to observe. It is in the reports of such men as these,

25. Johannes Gulielmus de Grevenbroek, "An Elegant and Accurate Account of the . . . Hottentots" (translated from the Latin original), in
Schapera, *op. cit.*, p. 173.

Thunberg, Sparrman, Le Vaillant, Bruce, Mungo Park, and others, that the new spirit, barely indicated in seventeenth-century accounts, achieves its full development. So persuasive and powerful was this new spirit, however, that almost all eighteenth-century reports of travel to primitive Africa show it.

The two components of this spirit, an increased regard for accuracy of reporting, and an unprecedented sympathy for the primitive and his culture, which consistently tend to reinforce one another, cooperate in stimulating active criticism of previous prejudice and error, so commonly found in eighteenth-century accounts. The mistakes of classical geographers had occasionally been indicated by earlier writers, but not until this century does criticism of past inadequacies of reporting become wholesale, consistent, and searching. The superiority in obtaining and conveying sound knowledge on the part of the "new man" on the African scene, the explorer and student of natural history, over the merchant, the conqueror, and the missionary, who had hitherto monopolized the field, the proneness to exaggeration and outright falsehood of the latter, and their excessive dependence upon that enemy of truth, the hearsay report—these ideas appear repeatedly in these accounts.

As the debris of old error is thrust aside, new patterns of description are constructed. The "character" of the African primitive is quite rebuilt. Added to his one traditional virtue, his hospitality, which had stood so long alone amid a sea of vices, are other virtues—his willingness to share, his emphasis on the equality of all members of the group in feast or famine [26]—insights that derive not from the sole concern for relationships between African and European but from an interest in relationships within African society itself. Even the traditional "vice" of the African primtive, his propensity to steal from Europeans, is explained away in terms of the enormous relative wealth of the European traveler, his externality to the rules of the tribal unit, and the consequent strength of temptation to which the

26. See Peter Kolben, *The Present State of the Cape of Good-Hope* (London, 1731; translated from the German original), p. 165.

native is exposed.[27] The charge of cannibalism ceases to be a prominent part of the accounts; the tale of the bloody shambles of human flesh is not repeated.[28] Not that the African primitive is made to seem a saint; he still is assigned his share of vices and foolish ways. But the eighteenth-century traveler typically conceives of his own culture, too, as often vicious and wrong-minded. He can look at himself and say, as does one writer, "that we Christians have as many idle ridiculous Notions and Customs as the Natives of *Guinea* have, if not more." [29]

In this new atmosphere of thought, what happens to the hitherto characteristic modes of description of African institutions? In the first place, with the disappearance of the concept of the bestial African primitive, the lawless promiscuous society peculiarly associated with him also disappears. The universality of regulations of sexual conduct is recognized. An effort is made to describe more accurately the social or political organization, both of the "monarchies" of the West Coast and of the "free republics" or "independent hordes" elsewhere in Africa; and on the whole the weight of preference and interest swings away from the former to the latter. Though in an occasional eighteenth-century account some African group is said to lack religion,[30] the tendency is to be more generous in attributing religious beliefs to African peoples, and far more often than in the past they are asserted to have achieved some sort of faith in a single deity.

The institutions and customs of the African primitive are

27. Mungo Park, "Travels," in Pinkerton, *op. cit.*, XVI, p. 871.
28. Two writers of eighteenth-century accounts declare that all assertions of African cannibalism have been based on hearsay evidence, and categorically deny the existence of such a custom. John Atkins, *A Voyage to Guinea, Brasil and the West Indies* (London, 1735), Preface; and Thomas Winterbottom, *Nachrichten von der Sierraleona-Kuste und ihren Bewohnern*, aus dem Englischen . . . herausgegeben von T. F. Ehrmann (Weimar, 1805), pp. 218–219. (Translation of Winterbottom's *An Account of the Native Africans in the Neighborhood of Sierra Leone* [London, 1803].)
29. William Smith [fl. 1726], *A New Voyage to Guinea* (London, 1744), p. 267.
30. Andrew Sparrman, *A Voyage to the Cape of Good Hope* . . . 1772–1776 (London, 1786; translated from the Swedish original), I, p. 207.

not merely accepted with a new tolerance by the eighteenth-century traveler; they are even fairly often upheld as models to be admired and emulated by the civilized world. For the "noble savage" is indubitably a personage in these accounts. We cannot take time now to explore the nature and history of the ideas behind this image, but at least two ingredients are inherent in it: first, a definite dissatisfaction with the inadequacies and injustices of Western civilization; and second, the citing of some actual primitive group or culture as an instance of a presumed improvement or remedy.[31] The qualities of primitive African character particularly apt to such selection are his hospitality, his love of his fellows and his generous sharing with them, his lack of envy and avarice. The qualities of primitive African society which tend to be similarly exalted are its freedom, its equalitarianism, its responsiveness to the needs and desires of all its members. One also often hears of the absence among primitive Africans of some foolish prohibition or unnatural restriction which in civilized society obstructs the course of life.

On the basis of such an approach to the African primitive one would expect that the charge barely heard in earlier writings, that contact with European civilization corrupts rather than benefits, would become the dominant opinion in eighteenth-century reports. And so it is. The whole European effort in Africa

31. The idea of the "noble savage," which, though it has foreshadowings in scattered references such as those of Tacitus, first appears in developed form in an essay by Montaigne, must be carefully distinguished from the superficially similar concept of the Golden Age. The latter idea also begins, to be sure, in discontent with the restraints and tensions of a given civilization, and also plays with equalitarian and libertarian sentiments; but, instead of encouraging admiration for existent primitive society (more often than not it is linked with a marked scorn for such society) it leads to a yearning contemplation of a never-never land of fancy somewhere in the remote origins of civilization. The gulf that separates the two concepts is nicely illustrated in Shakespeare's play of shipwreck and romantic wilderness, *The Tempest*. Gonzallo, the noble councillor, worn with the wickedness of the world he knew, alludes to the Golden Age when he talks of a society without private property, class distinctions, or authoritarian coercion, a society very like the Stoic state of ideal nature, or the Christian Garden of Eden. But Caliban, the monster, who emerges even from Shakespeare's somewhat pitying treatment as bestial in body and corrupt in soul—here is the actual primitive as Shakespeare and the majority of Shakespeare's time still saw him.

of conquering, trading, and colonizing is for the first time
brought to the bar of judgment for analysis and attack. In all
the major accounts of travel in South Africa from this century
are 'many passages critical of colonial policies. The slave trade
is no longer taken for granted but becomes a subject for debate.
Several writers argue for its abolition, but even those who continue to accept it as necessary are driven to seek a new and more
persuasive rationale.

It must, of course, be acknowledged that the entire complex
of impulses to defend and exalt the primitive which we have
been discussing—particularly the vision of the "noble savage"
—is itself a kind of prejudice, a kind of ethnocentrism even,
which springs from a dynamic operating in the homeland environment of the traveler, and which is essentially extraneous
to the data he observes; it is a romanticism, which in its extremer
forms, at least, can and does distort objectivity.[32] But all the
errors to be chalked up against this new positive prejudice in
favor of the African primitive are as nothing beside the almost
countless errors of commission and omission attributable to the
earlier negative prejudice.

The concept of the "noble savage," it must be further remembered, emerged in the same period and from many of the
same influences as the idea of progress. Its real purport was not
to assert the superiority of primitivism as a whole to civilization
as a whole, nor yet to return civilization to a primitive condition,
but, by an appeal both to new concepts of natural right and
to the concrete facts of primitive life, to remove or reform certain specific abuses—certain social inequalities and political
tyrannies in particular—which, it was thought, had intruded into
civilized society and were interfering with its continued growth.
In terms of these very functions, however, the concept of the
"noble savage" became of necessity a friend rather than an

32. François Le Vaillant, *Travels from the Cape of Good Hope into the
Interior Parts of Africa* (London, 1790; translated from the French original);
and *New Travels into the Interior Parts of Africa* (London, 1796; translated
from the French original).

enemy to the advance of knowledge about the primitive. A bias it might remain, with capacities to distort; but, whereas the older prejudice had obstructed the study of primitive culture, this new prejudice instead introduced a compulsion to go forth and observe.

The accounts of the eighteenth century—even the best of them—when viewed according to the standards of modern anthropological research and writing, still appear limited and crude. Beside a Herskovits or a Schapera, even a Sparrman is clumsy and uninformative in the cultural field. There is, to begin with, a primary preoccupation with botanical, zoological, and geographical data. In so far as observation of really scientific calibre is present in eighteenth-century accounts, it concerns the physical and biological much more than cultural or human material. In regard to cultural data, moreover, there is still too much involvement with issues of moral judgment. Any judgment, whether positive or negative, is ethnocentric in its emphasis, and derogates from the dignity of primitive cultures by refusing to grant their right to exist and to be studied as entities independent of all value systems. The concept of the "noble savage" may have been a door to objectivity; it is not objectivity itself.

If one considers these eighteenth-century accounts, however, in comparison with the earlier literature, one is struck by a crucial change. A decisive expansion of human interests and sympathies has occurred. Real progress in the direction of a fuller understanding of man and his culture has been made. Indeed, I know of no body of data which compels one more forcibly and directly to an admiration for the intellectual and moral magnificence of the eighteenth century.

MARSHALL SAHLINS

Tribesmen in History
and Anthropology

NOT VERY long ago, there was a primitive world and a civilized world. On islands of the South Seas, in the jungles of South America and the grasslands of East Africa, tribal people were still constructing new versions of a cultural order that in Europe was a forgotten era. But to speak today of "the civilized world," implying some primitive outer darkness, is to speak the language of history. Modern civilization knows no borders; those curious peoples beyond the pale have been in the course of Europe's four-century planetary reconnaisance drawn into the main sphere. Once discovered, they were rapidly colonized,

Marshall D. Sahlins, Tribesmen. © *1967. Reprinted by permission of Prentice-Hall, Inc., Englewood Cliffs, New Jersey.*

baptized, and culturally traumatized—"acculturated" is the technical term. . . .

> Collapsed in equatorial acquiescence,
> Agreed to cultural obsolescence,
> Built dada villages of rusted scraps
> Of corrugated iron and busted water taps.

And now, having bit deeply into native custom, civilization allows itself the luxury of an intellectual digestion: The primitives are largely anthropologized. (So anthropology, as one amateur practicitioner of its cynically observed, becomes an inquest into the corpse of one society presided over by members of another.)

THE RISE AND FALL OF TRIBAL CULTURE

If the world today belongs to nation-states to do with what they will, in a similar way several thousand years ago, it had fallen to tribal peoples. The spread of modern civilization has been likened to an evolutionary success story: The rise, spread, and diversification of an advanced type, spelling the displacement of primitive types. But the scenario had been produced before, on a prehistoric stage, during the transition from the Paleolithic to the Neolithic, the advantage then going to tribal culture and displacement the fate of indigenous hunters and gatherers. On the momentum given by neolithic agriculture and animal husbandry, tribal peoples became dominant over much of the earth. The hunting life, man's mainstay for the first two million years, suddenly became a marginal strategy.

History had been decided by economic power. The same happens so regularly as to suggest the rule—or "law" as some are pleased to call it—that cultural dominance goes to technical predominance: The cultural type that develops more power and resources in a given environmental space will spread there at the expense of indigenous and competing cultures. This "Law of Cultural Dominance" explains in a general way the neolithic-tribal success story. Hunting and gathering regimes cannot hold most terrains against farming and herding. In environments that yield to neolithic technology, hunters are not able to generate the manpower or organization to match intrusive cultivators—unless the hunters themselves take up domestication and thereby transcend the paleolithic condition. In the event, once cultivation and husbandry appeared it was not long before roving food collectors were limited to inhospitable margins and interstices of a larger neolithic map. In isolated places, and in geographic extremes such as deserts where food collection yields higher returns than would neolithic techniques, the paleolithic might hold on. But now only as an historic sideshow.

All this had happened quickly—considering it from the total perspective of human history. The earliest farmers on archaeological record occupied hilly forests and valley oases of the Near East, where the neolithic seems to have developed in the period 10,000 B.C. to 7,000 B.C. By 2,000 B.C. neolithic communities had been established the length of Eurasia, from Ireland to Indonesia. In the New World, food domestication began somewhat later than the old. The main staple of the American neolithic, maize, seems to have been first brought under cultivation about 5,000 B.C. in Middle America. After a period of slow gestation, neolithic culture spread widely and rapidly; by the time of Christ it was distributed from Peru to the American Southwest.

To this point, we have allowed ourselves some crude assumptions. Tribal peoples and cultures have been linked with neolithic techniques of production, as if the latter necessarily usher in evolutionary advances beyond the cultural capacities of hunters. One of the tasks of this book must be to refine such evolutionary equations and distinctions; or better, to make students knowledgeable enough to criticize them. Here then is one *caveat*: While it is true that most tribesmen are farmers or herders, thus cultural descendants of the Neolithic, not all are. Moreover, it is doubtful that tribal culture originated with the Neolithic Revolution; it could have emerged before. A complicated development of clans and chiefs, as is beyond the culture of mobile hunters and as we might like to call "tribal," occurred in recent times among Indians of America's Northwest Coast. The Kwakiutl, Nootka, Tsimshian and other tribes of the American Northwest were as highly organized as most Indians north of Mexico. This is just to name one instance where *food collectors,* here blessed with abundant maritime resources, are known to have reached the cultural average of neolithic communities. So where nature is exceptionaly prodigal, hunters and gatherers may surpass the cultural circumstances typical of that economic mode.[1] And the same could easily have happened during the later Paleolithic—here and there. The Neolithic, then, did not necessarily spawn tribal culture. What it did was provide the technology of tribal *dominance.*

Neolithic techniques equip societies to creatively transform their environments. Neolithic communities do not operate under the same natural constraints as hunters: food domestication allows agriculturalists to maintain comparatively high degrees of cultural order in a variety of geographic settings; whereas, hunters can do the same only where nature provides abundant wild food. Thus, while it is possible that a few favorably situated hunting societies of the Paleolithic advanced to tribal levels, a general advance of primitive culture on a planetary scale waited on the Neolithic Revolution. Likewise, most of the tribes with which we shall deal in this book are agriculturists and pastoralists, *food producers,* though some are hunters, fishers, and gatherers.

The Neolithic was the historic day of tribesmen. But even as this day was dawning on the margins of Europe, Asia, and the Americas, the tribal sun was in eclipse in critical core areas. Civilization was coming into being, as early as 3,500 B.C. in the Near East, and neolithic tribes were being superseded just as they had before superseded paleolithic hunters. By 2,500 B.C. civilization had been developed in the Indus River Valley, by

1. See Elman R. Service's book in this series, *The Hunters* (Englewood Cliffs; Prentice-Hall, 1965).

1,500 B.C. in the Yellow River Valley of China, by 500 B.C. in Middle America and Peru. This was a new dominant type, ever creating new varieties as it advanced, and ever opposing and undermining indigenous tribalism. Even before Europe began its ominous mission of giving "new worlds to the world," before, say, the sixteenth century, the distribution of tribal culture had been seriously curtailed. It was confined in the main to North America south of Canada and north of the Valley of Mexico, the Caribbean and Amazonia, portions of Africa south of the Sahara, Inner Asia and Siberia, hinterlands of Southeast Asia, and islands of the Pacific.

These several areas make up the tribal world of modern Cultural Anthropology. Here we have not prehistory but *ethnography*—eyewitness accounts of tribes as going concerns. Indeed anthropologists, except as they become interested in recent cultural changes, rather like to think the natives still exist in their pristine state—or at least talk about them that way. We adopt the convention of the "ethnological present," discussing the Iroquois or the Hawaiians as they were at the time of European discovery, that is, when they were "really" Iroquois and Hawaiian. But of course there is more than antiquarian nostalgia in this convention; for comparative purposes it is necessary to characterize primitive cultures apart from the distortions introduced by Europeans. May the reader then indulge us in this romantic manipulation of history, and join in our contemplation of tribesmen—of the ethnographic present.

TRIBES AND CIVILIZATIONS: THE STATE OF NATURE AND THE NATURE OF THE STATE

Hereby it is manifest, that during the time men live without a common Power to keep them all in awe, they are in that condition which is called Warre; and such a warre, as is of every man, against every man.
　　　　　　　　　　　　　　　　　　　　—Thomas Hobbes, *Leviathan*

Tribes occupy a position in cultural evolution. They took over from simpler hunters; they gave way to the more advanced cultures we call civilizations. But civilization is not an advance over tribal society simply by reason of its dominance power. Civilization is an advance in organization, a qualitative transformation of the culture type.

In its broadest terms the contrast between Tribe and Civilization is between War and Peace. A civilization is a society specially constituted to maintain Law and Order; the social complexity and cultural richness of civilizations depend on institutional guarantees of Peace. Lacking these institutional means and guarantees, tribesmen live in a condition of War, and War limits the scale, complexity and all-round richness of their culture, and accounts for some of their more "curious" customs.

Permit me to explain.

Obviously, I mean something different by "War" and "Peace" than is commonly understood. In fact, we ought to spell it "Warre" as Hobbes usually did, and with him intend by the word not just "battle" but a general disposition and right to fight, if necessary. . . .

For WARRE, consisteth not in Battell only, or the act of fighting; but in a tract of time, wherein the Will to contend by Battell is sufficiently known: and therefore the notion of *Time,* is to be considered in the nature of Warre; as it is in the nature of Weather. . . . So the nature of War, consisteth not in actual fighting; but in the known disposition thereto, during all the time there is no assurance to the contrary. All other time is PEACE.

In the social condition of Warre, force is a resort legitimately available to all men. There need not be violence, but neither is there assurance to the contrary. As a matter of fact, fighting may be at a discount within the tribe—a Hopi Pueblo is as non-belligerent a community as one may find. On the other hand, the everyday violence of the United States of America has few parallels in history or ethnography. But politically the American citizenry differ from the Hopi in this: They have "a common Power to keep them all in awe," a Government, which precludes that anyone take the law in his own hands, thus keeps the peace. Tribes such as the Hopi lack a sovereign political and moral authority; the right to use force and do "Battell," if not the inclination, is instead held by the people in severalty. Technically this is an internal social condition of "Warre." Expressed another way, in the language of older philosophy, the United States is a state, the tribe a state of nature. Or then again, the United States is a *Civilization,* the tribe a *Primitive Society.*

The state differentiates civilization from tribal society. The development of civilization was nothing less than a transformation in quality of the social system. A contrast with tribalism is not usefully made by reference to one or a few simple features. It has proved futile to search for some decisive invention standing at the evolutionary divide. Writing, for instance, does not a civilization make. Primitives are conventionally called "preliterate peoples," but lack of writing does not exclusively distinguish them, as the sophisticated yet illiterate native kingdoms of Peru or West Africa will testify. Nor is urbanity in the literal sense of cities the litmus reaction of civilization. The appeal of such criteria of civilization as writing and cities is mainly to the preanthropological supposition that primitive peoples are essentially yokels.

Another conventional formula, "kinship to territory"—supposing primitive society to be "based on" kinship, civilization on territory—better expresses the evolutionary transformation. But it is overly compressed, and thereby vulnerable to naive criticism. The rankest anthropological novice can point out that many primitive peoples occupy and defend discrete territories; or that the constituent groups of tribal societies, such as lineages and clans, are often centered in territorial estates, and without its land the clan is dead. This criticism is informed enough of primitive society, but insufficiently informed of the meaning of "kingship to territory," which is a kind of evolutionary proverb, the metaphorical condensation of a complex development. At the least, "territory" should be here understood as a dominion, the realm of a Sovereign. Thus the critical development was not the establishment of territoriality in society, but the establishment of society *as* a territory. The state and its subdivisions are organized as territories—territorial entities under sovereign authority—as opposed, for instance, to kinship entities. Sir Henry Maine, who popularized "kinship to territory," once epitomized it this way: The transition to civilization occurred when "The King of Franks" took the title, "The King of *France*."

In a state there is a public government structurally separated from the underlying population and placed above them. This authority is sovereign in the territory of the state: Control of force has precipitated it from society at large to rest exclusively with Government. No one in general has leave to proceed by force; only the government in particular has leave to decree rules of order and to enforce them—thus peace is an internal condition of the system as constituted. More analytically, a state or civilized society is one in which: (1) there is an official public authority, a set of offices of the society at large conferring governance over the society at large; (2) "society at large," the domain of the authority, is territorially defined and subdivided; (3) the ruling authority monopolizes sovereignty—no other person or assembly can rightly command power (or force) except by sovereign delegation, leave or consent; (4) all persons and groups within the territory are *as such*—by virtue of residence in the domain—subject to the sovereign, to its jurisdiction and coercion.

But "civilization," one might reasonably argue, has a much richer connotation. More than a formal political apparatus, it is a large and complex culture. The word conjures images of great cities and monumental architecture, dense populations and a wealth of goods. We think of a social system richly textured, with artisans and merchants, peasants, priests, proletarians, and princes. Fair enough. But the objection may yet confirm our reasoning, the soundness of isolating the state as *the* criterion of civilization. A civilization is a society both massive and divided within itself. The population is large, perhaps ethnically diversified, divided by its labors into specialized occupations and, by unequal interests in the means of power, divided into unequally privileged classes. All the cultural achievements of civilization depend on this magnitude and complexity of organization. Yet a society so large, heterogeneous and internally divided will not stand without special means of control and integration. Consider the situation if everyone were left to protect and advance his own interests as best he could—if everyone might proclaim, "*l'état, c'est moi!*" The system would disintegrate in chaotic factionalism, sedition and civil war. The cultural richness that we call civilization has to be instituted in state form.

Government is to the social organism as the central nervous system is to the biological organism. Just as in biological evolution, only a certain minimum of cultural complexity was possible prior to the development of a central, sovereign mechanism. That which "keeps them all in awe" keeps the differentiated parts of civilization in collaborative order—not, as I say, by abolishing violence but by making it illegitimate. To complete the analogy, a tribe is an animal without a central regulative system. Limits are thereby imposed on tribal scale, complexity and over-all cultural elaboration. Such are the disadvantages of "Warre. . . ."

Whatsover therefore is consequent to a time of Warre, where every man is Enemy to every man; the same is consequent to the time, wherein men live without other security, than what their own strength, and their own invention shall furnish them withall. In such condition, there is no place for Industry; because the fruit thereof is uncertain: and consequently no Culture of the Earth, no Navigation, nor use of the commodities that may be imported by Sea; no commodious Building; no Instruments of moving, and removing such things as require much force; no Knowledge of the face of the Earth; no account of Time; no Arts; no Letters; no Society; and which is worst of all, continuall feare, and danger of violent death; And the life of man, solitary, poore, nasty, brutish, and short.

—Hobbes, *Leviathan.*

We have learned much about primitive peoples since the seventeenth century. At this late date Hobbes reads like parody. This "nasty, brutish, and short" passage is indeed a favorite subject for modern textbook burlesque. But in thus congratulating

ourselves at Hobbes's expense on matters about which we are
better informed—thanks to the investigations of countless people
over three centuries—we tend to overlook the things Hobbes
knows better than we, and thus manage not to learn anything.
The burden of the passage just cited is that where force is held
in severalty, the society is inadequately organized to bear an
elaborate cultural development. Here is a key to the comparative
limitations of tribal society, and to the evolutionary significance
of the state. To use a favored expression of New Guinea pidgin-
English: "Something true here!"

"The war of every man against every man" is also true—
although it has never happened.[2] Individuals and subgroups of
tribal society maintain the certain right and potential inclination
to secure by force their safety, gain and glory. In the event,
Warre exists. But mainly in the form of an underlying circumstance. In *fact*, tribesmen live in kin groupings and communities
within which feuding is usually suppressed, and they have
benefit too of economic, ritual, and social institutions conducive
to good order. To speak of Warre, then, is to uncover by analysis
tendencies ordinarily concealed by powerful impositions of the
cultural system. Primitive anarchy is not the appearance of things.
It is the unconscious of the system. Yet as the outward behavior
of a person may not be intelligible except as the transfiguration
of unconscious desires, so the objective organization of tribal
society may only be understood as the repressive transformation
of an underlying anarchy. Many of the special patterns of tribal
culture became meaningful precisely as defense mechanisms,
as *negations of Warre*.[3]

For in a situation of Warre, where every man is empowered
to proceed against every man, peacemaking cannot be an occa-

2. Hobbes neither insisted nor did he believe that warre was ever a general empirical condition (see *Leviathan*, Part I, Chapter XIII).

3. Perhaps this in turn accounts for the success of a certain kind of "functionalism" in anthropology: the explication of given social relations and customs by their contribution to "social solidarity" or "equilibrium." Primitive
society is at war with Warre. Hence functionalism has unusual power and
appeal as an anthropological theory.

sional intertribal event. It becomes a continuous process, going on within society itself. As much as Warre is an implicit circumstance, that much does peacemaking become an explicit necessity. . . .

And because the condition of Man . . . is a condition of Warre of every one against every one; in which case every one is governed by his own Reason; and there is nothing he can make use of, that may not be a help unto him, in preserving his life against his enemyes; It followeth, that in such a condition, every man has a Right to every thing; even to one another's body. And therefore, as long as this naturall Right of every man to every thing endureth, there can be no security to any man, (how strong or wise soever he be,) of living out the time, which Nature ordinarily alloweth men to live. And consequently it is a precept, or generall rule of Reason, *That every man, ought to endeavour Peace, as farre as he has hope of obtaining it; and when he cannot obtain it, that he may seek, and use, all helps, and advantages of Warre.* The first branch of which Rule, containith the first, and Fundamentall Law of Nature; which is, *to seek Peace, and follow it.*

—Hobbes, *Leviathan.*

Man cannot in fact hope to survive unless Warre is regulated. Hobbes therefore held it a precept of Reason that men seek peace. My point is that peacemaking is the wisdom of tribal institutions. Moreover, because tribal institutions must bear this political load, they are sometimes quite different from analogous institutions of civilizations. For in civilizations, Peace need not be built into, say, economic relations. Here Law and Order are secured by a specialized political organization, Government, and imposed on the economy. So if a man charges "what the traffic will bear," the only licking he risks is the financial one.

Of course, not only tribes have had to control warre. Hunters are at least as much in the state of nature and have been there much longer. Many of the peacemaking arrangements of tribal culture are similar to those of hunters and gatherers. Yet the potential of Warre is, if anything, increased by the advance to tribalism. Tribal techniques of production typically support more people, populations both more dense and more concentrated, than does simple hunting. The sheer number of Brownian contacts, hence of possible conflicts, increases. Uniquely valuable, stable and scarce resources are defined by tribal technologies: arable land, timber lots for forest agriculture, pasturage and water for cattle. Too, there are more goods in society—aside from new techniques of production, the immobility of tribal life makes feasible some accumulation of wealth—hence, more things to steal, loot or otherwise quarrel over. Warre takes on new vistas among tribesmen. The tribal war on Warre is proportionately intense.

Take economic relations. Exchange in tribal societies generally proceeds under certain constraints. Competition and gain are often excluded, either in the attempt to make friendly relations or by the necessity to avoid unfriendly ones.

In an uncommon number of tribal transactions material utility is played down, to the extent that the main advantages appear to be social, the gain coming in good relations rather than Good Things. I refer to the several varieties of "reciprocal gift giving" (so-called), ranging from informal hospitality to the formal exchanges that seal a marriage or a blood brotherhood. These are *instrumental exchanges*, i.e., they establish solidarity between people through the instrumentality of things. (As we say—but on comparatively rare occasions—"it's the sentiment that counts.") In instrumental transactions, two parties may exchange goods with which both are already supplied. Sometimes— in making blood brotherhood, settling feud or arranging marriage—the people give each other equal amounts of identical goods. A waste of time and effort? As the famous anthropologist Radcliffe-Brown observed of comparable dealings among Andamanese hunters: "The purpose . . . was a moral one. The object of the exchange was to produce a friendly feeling between the two persons concerned, and unless it did this it failed of its purpose." [4] Material benefit is not the issue, except it be the other party's benefit, for sacrifices may be made—in the interest of peace. The issue is peace.

4. A. R. Radcliffe-Brown, *The Andaman Islanders.* (New York: The Free Press, 1948, p. 84.)

And even where utilities are sought through exchange, due regard for the other person is usually politic. A transaction always has an instrumental coefficient: It is socially negative or positive, depending on how far material advantage is pressed or how much is given in return for favors received. An exchange is inevitably a social strategy. In Warre the strategic alternative is to be nice—or be prepared to fight. Therefore, *reciprocity,* or some approximation to it, dominates tribal economics. Reciprocity in exchange is economic diplomacy: The mutuality of the material flow symbolizes willingness to consider the other party's welfare, a disinclination to selfishly prosecute one's own. Here again Hobbes anticipates ethnography. In a time of Warre, he divined, reciprocity is a law of nature, consequent on the first law, which enjoins men to seek Peace:

As Justice dependeth on Antecedent Covenant; so does GRATITUDE depend on Antecedent Grace; that is to say Antecedent Free-gift: and is the fourth Law of Nature; which may be conceived in this Forme, *That a man which receiveth Benefit from another of meer Grace, Endeavour that he which giveth it, have no reasonable cause to repent him of his good will.* For no man giveth, but with intention of Good to himselfe; because Gift is Voluntary; and of all Voluntary Acts, the Object is to every man his own Good; of which if men see they shall be frustrated, there will be no beginning of benevolence, or trust; nor consequently of mutuall help; nor of reconciliation of one man to another; and therefore they are to remain still in the condition of *War;* which is contrary to the first and Fundamentall Law of Nature, which commandeth men to *Seek Peace.*
                                                                    —Hobbes, *Leviathan.*

Exchanges become peace treaties. The transactions show a willingness to live and let live. Marcel Mauss, in his well known "Essay on the Gift," having recognized the Hobbesian circumstances, suggested there was little else for it—the people have to "come to terms":

In these primitive and archaic societies there is no middle path. There is either complete trust or mistrust. One lays down one's arms, renounces magic and gives everything away, from casual hospitality to one's daughter or one's property. It is in such conditions that men, despite themselves, learnt to renounce what was theirs and made contracts to give and repay.

But then they had no choice in the matter. When two groups of men meet they may move away or in case of mistrust or defiance they may resort to arms; or else they can come to terms.[5]

Nor are primitive peoples themselves unaware of the peace in their trade. In certain East African languages, "trade" or "barter" means also "peace." Perhaps this Bushman said it best:

Demi said, "The worst thing is not giving presents. If people do not like each other but one gives a gift and the other must accept, this brings a peace between them. We give to one another always. We give what we have. This is the way we live together." [6]

Now take tribal social relations in general. They are, as the evolutionary proverb has it, dominated by kinship. Kinship is a social relation of cooperation and nonviolence (ordinarily). "Kindred" has the same root as "kindness," two words—as E. B. Tylor said—"whose common derivation expresses in the happiest way one of the main principles of social life." [7] Languages of tribesmen embody similar correspondences. Among the Nuer of East Africa, "kinship" is the word for "peace." In Fijian, the phrase *tiko vakaveiwekani*, "to be as (or live as) relatives" is applied to the establishment and condition of "living in peace." A term meaning "to be acquainted, to know one another" is the synonym of "to be related." On the other hand, "stranger" means also "not related" and for Fijians as for many other tribal peoples has a sinister connotation, if not the denotation of "enemy"— someone you can eat. Kinship is a fundamental ground of peaceful human discourse. The wide extension of kinship idioms, relations and groups in tribal societies represents another way they seek peace.

This is not to claim that kinship prevails in tribal society just because of its political functions. The economic cooperation it sustains is equally vital and perhaps decisive. Also, I do not wish to claim that kinship is the sole tribal principle. Military, reli-

5. Marcel Mauss, *The Gift*. London: Cohen and West, 1954, p. 79.

6. Marshall, Lorna, "Sharing, Talking, and Giving: Relief of Social Tensions Among Kung Bushmen," *Africa*, XXXI (1961), p. 245.

7. Tylor, Sir Edward B., *Anthropology* (Ann Arbor: Ann Arbor Paperbacks, U. of Michigan Press, 1960), p. 249.

gious, and age-grade associations not organized as kinship groups
are widely distributed in Africa, Oceania, and aboriginal America. It might be observed, however, that these are often institutionally subordinate to the kinship design, that personal kinship
with a member of the association is a common basis of recruit-
ment, and that the idiom of group solidarity is frequently kinship—the associations are "brotherhoods." The last exemplifies
the general propensity of tribal peoples to cloak alliances of
convenience in kinship garb. Where peace is necessary or desirable, kinship is extended to effect it.

On the interpersonal level, kinship is widely extended
through the tribe. Perhaps you are familiar with "classificatory
kinship." It is characteristic of the very great majority of tribes.
In classificatory schemes, certain people related to oneself in a
direct line of descent are in a class with collateral relatives. Thus
in a common classificatory usage, the brother of my father is related to me in the same way as my father: I call them both by
the same term—translated, "father"—and behave more or less the
same way to both. Said differently, relatives of the same broad
social status are classed together. My father and his brother may
be in critical social attributes the same: males of my lineage of
the same senior generation. The social similarity is embodied in
a common kinship designation. Now, the important thing is that
once kinship categories are thus widely defined they are widely
extendable. If my father is socially equivalent to his brother, the
latter's son is logically equivalent to my brother; hence FaBrSo =
Br. By the same principles, my father's father and his brother are
equivalent, my father's father's brother's son is "father," his
son is "brother," and so on. Classificatory kinship has a logic
of expandability. However remote genealogically, kinsmen are
not lost track of, nor the fact conceived remote in kinship class.
Of course the people can and do make distinctions between
a mother's husband ("own" father) and other "fathers," and between "near" and "distant" kinsmen of a given class. But the
expandability of kinship classes, and their manifest designation
as familial categories, is an obvious help to peacemaking.

On the level of group organization, beyond the interpersonal level, tribes have made a main contribution to the repertoire of kinship. *Descent groups* are perhaps original with tribes: certainly not characteristic of hunters, yet run-of-the-mill in the tribal range. A descent group is a body of kinsmen united by common ancestry. Tribal descent groups vary extremely—e.g., in the mode of reckoning common descent, which may be through males only (*patrilineal*), females only (*matrilineal*) or males and

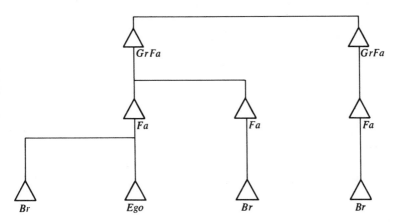

CLASSIFICATORY KINSHIP CATEGORIES
(based on *The equivalence of brothers*)

females (*cognatic*). We are concerned at the moment with those that are *corporate,* in the sense of perpetual units of the tribal system, existing forever although individual members come and go through birth and death. The group has a destiny and a reality that transcend the mortal span of persons. It is a super-person, and its members are as one—so close perhaps as to be reckoned "brothers" and "sisters" if of the same generation, and perhaps forbidden to marry. Within such groups a Warre of *every* man against *every* man cannot materialize. To proceed by force against a fellow clansman is to proceed against oneself, which is contrary even to Laws of Nature, a sin, possibly subject to dire consequences of ancestral wrath. In some tribes the only safe conduct is in those places where clanship can be established. Otherwise, except to make war people are well advised to stay home. In thus assuming protection of its members and precluding internal violence, descent groups push outwards the sphere of Warre, at the minimum to some intergroup sector.

Yet even here diplomatic arrangements are possible. By further permutations of kinship principle, descent groups themselves can be allied by kinship. Intermarriage effects *alliance,* i.e., insofar as each group is a cohesive entity, marriages between members of different groups can be translated into marriages between the groups themselves. Kinsmen are made as well as born; they are made by marriages. And marriages are not made in heaven; they are made according to rules. A rule against marriage in one's own group enjoins marriage with another group. Beyond this, the rules may specify the kind of relatives whom one must or should marry; for example, someone related as "mother's brother's daughter." This sort of prescription, as we shall see, systematically relates lineages. Each such rule develops a systematic pattern of alliance between descent groups. Marital maneuvers are typically of consuming interest to tribesmen. For in the tribal war on warre, marriage is an institutional strategy of first importance.

Now the lessons we have taken from tribal economics and kinship could also be drawn from other cultural sectors. Ritual in tribes (as in other types of culture) may be closely engaged in seeking peace. Confucius said: "Ceremonies are the bond that holds the multitudes together, and if the bond be removed, the multitudes fall into confusion." Public, communal rituals become fairly common at the tribal level. These rituals impose at the minimum a ceremonial peace, and by the implication of common dependence on supernatural powers instill a sense of the collectivity and of the *dependence* of every man upon every man. The latter effect may be heightened by a ceremonial division of labor among kin groups, each charged with a special ritual function or performance, such that collaboration becomes necessary to secure supernatural benefits. There are tribes—the Voltaic peoples of West Africa and the Pueblo Indians come to mind—where the burden of peacemaking rests most critically with ritual, as if in these densely populated yet socially fragmented communities the ordinary secular devices of good order must prove inadequate.

But enough said. The meaning is clear and needs no more repetition.

I have tried to show that civilizations differ from tribes by virtue of their specialized political institutions, their governments, which sovereignly assume the power and right to protect the citizenry and maintain Peace within the state. In tribal societies control of force is not withheld from the people; they are in that condition Hobbes called warre, which is a fatal condition if not checked. Lacking *specialized* institutions of law and order, tribes must mobilize the generalized institutions they do have to meet the threat of warre. Economics, kinship, ritual, and the rest are so enlisted. In the process, by undertaking this political function, tribal institutions develop particular forms and particular expressions, different and curious perhaps, but each and all understandable as diplomatic arrangements for keeping a modicum of peace. Such is the wisdom of tribal institutions.

JULES HENRY

The Term "Primitive" in
Kierkegaard and Heidegger

In *The Phenomenology of Mind* Hegel says:

Knowing as it is found at the start, mind in its immediate and primitive stage, is without the essential nature of mind, is sense-consciousness. To reach the stage of genuine knowledge, or produce the element where science is found—the pure conception of science itself—a long and laborious journey must be undertaken. This process towards science, as regards the content it will bring to light and the forms it will assume in the course of its progress, will not be what is primarily imagined by leading the unscientific consciousness up to the level of science: it will be something different, too, from establishing and laying the foundations of

This paper was prepared during the author's tenure as Fellow at the Center for Advanced Study in the Behavioral Sciences, Stanford, California.

science; and anyway, something else than the sort of ecstatic enthusiasm which starts straight off with absolute knowledge, as if shot out of a pistol, and makes short work of other points of view simply by explaining that it is to take no notice of them.

The task of conducting the individual mind from its unscientific standpoint to that of science had to be taken in its general sense; we had to contemplate the formative development of the universal individual, of self-conscious spirit.[1]

Unless one knows about Hegel's contempt for intuition—about his scepticism, amounting to scorn, of the virtues of immediate perception, one does not understand why Kierkegaard attacks him so; for Kierkegaard believes in the primitive, the untouched, really innocent approach to truth. In Kierkegaard the primitive is exalted: Through primitiveness, he argues, one attains to God. To Hegel, primitive perception is "*sense*-consciousness" only, while scientific perception comes through *self*-consciousness, awareness of the process through which consciousness goes in attempting to establish the truth. Truth cannot be an immediate experience; one has to know not only all sides of phenomena, but also how they are in a constant state of flux, negating one another, becoming one another, being necessary to one another. This process is *Life,* and comes to the understanding only after the most rigorous training. Science supersedes immediate sense-perception and is superior to it.

The *Concluding Unscientific Postscript* is Kierkegaard's monumental reply to Hegel. Actually, in spite of its demanding intellectual quality it is a very anti-intellectual document. The best expression of this is the following:

> If one can sometimes remember with a certain sense of relief that Caesar burned the entire Alexandrian library, one could also in all good will wish that our superfluity of knowledge could be taken away, in order that we might again learn what it means to be a human being. (p. 229) [2]

1. G. W. F. Hegel, *The Phenomenology of Mind,* translated with an introduction and notes by J. B. Faille. Macmillan Company, New York, 1931.
2. Translated from the Danish by David E. Swenson. Princeton University Press, 1941.

In 1846, the year he wrote the *Concluding Unscientific Post-script*, Kierkegaard made the following entry in his Journal: [3]

Almost everything that nowadays flourishes most conspicuously under the name of science (especially as natural science) is not really science but curiosity. *In the end all corruption will come about as a consequence of the natural sciences.* . . . But such scientific method becomes especially dangerous and pernicious when it would encroach also upon the sphere of the spirit. Let it deal with plants and animals and stars in that way; but to deal with the human spirit in that way is blasphemy, which only weakens ethical and religious passion. Even the act of eating is more reasonable than speculating with a microscope upon the functions of digestion. . . . A dreadful sophistry spreads microscopically and telescopically into tomes, and yet in the last resort produces nothing, qualitatively understood, though it does, to be sure, cheat men out of *the simple, profound and passionate wonder* which gives impetus to the ethical. . . . *The only thing ethical is the ethical religious.*

Thus Kierkegaard equates ignorance of conventional knowledge, including science, with being human. Kierkegaard scorned science, not only because he was a man of faith but particularly, I think, because he had a dread of losing his own: [4]

What I therefore fear and shrink from, more than I fear to die and lose my sweetheart, is to say about Christianity that it is to a certain degree true. If I lived to be seventy years old, if I shortened the night's sleep and increased the day's work from year to year, inquiring into Christianity—how insignificant such a little period of study, viewed as entitling me to judge in so lofty a fashion about Christianity!

Kierkegaard turned in dismay from intellectual sophistication toward what he called the primitive, as part of a tremendous— and successful— effort to regain his faith. I will now examine

3. This is taken from p. xv of Walter Lowrie's introduction. With the exception of "the simple, profound and passionate wonder" all other italics are in the original. I have italicized those words because they seem to me to contain the very essence of "primitive" as Kierkegaard uses the word.
4. For much better evidence than this the reader is referred to Walter Lowrie's *A Short Life of Kierkegaard*, Princeton, 1942; and to T. H. Croxall's "Assessment" in his translation of Kierkegaard's *Johannes Climacus*, Stanford University Press, 1958.

rather systematically his use of the term primitive. For example, in the second paragraph of the following:

> The worldly view always clings fast to the difference between man and man, and naturally it has no understanding of the one thing needful (for to have that is spirituality), and therefore no understanding of the narrowness and meanness of mind which is exemplified in having lost one's self—not by evaporation in the infinite,[5] but by being entirely finitized, by having become, instead of a self, a number, just one man more, one more repetition of this everlasting *Einerlei*.
>
> Despairing narrowness consists in the lack of primitiveness, or of the fact one has deprived oneself of one's primitiveness; it consists in having emasculated oneself, in a spiritual sense. For every man is primitively appointed to be a self, appointed to become oneself; . . . not that for fear of men it has to give up entirely being itself, nor even that for fear of men it dare not be itself. . . .[6]

So here to be primitive means to be unafraid to be oneself; to not fall into the common patterns of existence offered by "the multitudes of men . . . by getting engaged in all sorts of worldly affairs, by becoming wise about how things go in this world"; to "dare to believe in himself." The reader will have observed that here Kierkegaard's "primitive" resembles Heidegger's "authenticity" and Erikson's "ego identity."

In *The Concept of Dread* Kierkegaard speculates about the quantity of sin born by early man and "in the later individual" and concludes that in the latter the dread must be greater because the history of the race is longer. Yet, since not all people have the same consciousness of sin, not all feel equal dread. It is the primitive one, says Kierkegaard, who has the deeper dread:

> . . . one may say that the more primitiveness man has, the deeper is the dread, because the supposition of sinfulness, which his individual life supposes, since he enters indeed into the history of the race, must be appropriated. (p. 47)

5. A dig at Hegel, no doubt.
6. From *Fear and Trembling*, and *The Sickness Unto Death*, Doubleday: Anchor Books, 1941, 1954, pp. 166–7.

Thus the man who is not afraid to be "oneself", whose spiritual life has not been emasculated, etc., is also one with a deeper sense of sin than the multitude.

We now have a pretty good beginning notion of what Kierkegaard means by primitive. Actually his primitive man is one who, close to God, looks out upon existence with the flower-eyes of innocence, yet, at the same time, has a deep sense of primordial guilt. A strange contradiction. I continue the examination of quotes.

On pages 39 and 40 of SP [7] Kierkegaard argues that it is impossible to prove that the *same* (Christian) Church "has persisted for eighteen centuries" and that an "introductory discipline becomes necessary" to prove it and that "This discipline would have the task of proving the primitive character of the confession of faith, its identity of meaning everywhere and in every moment through eighteen centuries (where criticism will stumble on difficulties . . .); and so again there will be nosing about in ancient documents." Here again we have the primitive as immediate, intuitive, unreflective, contrasted with the dust and ashes of scholarship that tries to prove the unprovable.

Continuing with his attack on philosophy and theology Kierkegaard rhapsodizes over Lessing,[8] about whom he says, in profoundest appreciation:

. . . his merit consists precisely in his having . . . religiously shut himself up within the isolation of his own subjectivity; that he did not permit himself to be deceived into becoming world-historic and systematic [9] with respect to the religious, but understood and knew how to hold fast to the understanding that the religious concerned Lessing, and Lessing alone, just as it concerns every other human being in the same manner. . . .

But now to his result– Has Lessing accepted Christianity or has he rejected it, has he defended it or has he attacked it—in order that I too may adopt the same conclusion, in reliance upon him, this man who had

7. This abbreviation will be used for the *Concluding Unscientific Postscript.*
8. Whose ideas Hegel attacks in the *Phenomenology.*
9. Another slap at Hegel.

poetic imagination enough to make himself at any moment contemporary with the event that occurred now 1812 [10] years ago, and that in so primitive a manner as to exclude every historical illusion, every perverse objective [11] falsification. Aye, take Lessing there! No, he had the sceptical ataraxy [12] and the religious sensibility necessary in order to become aware of the category of the religious (SP, p. 61).

Primitiveness, in Kirkegaard's system, is now seen clearly as a specifically religious quality. It includes the capacity of the soul to fly back in time to the first moments of the emergence of Christianity—to have the same immediate experience of faith as those who saw and heard Jesus. What else does having "poetic imagination enough to make himself at any moment contemporary with the event" (Jesus) mean? New characteristics are now added to primitiveness: (religious) subjectivity, which means direct, personal approach to God; rejection of all (organized) mediation; the ability to feel faith as a primordial experience.

Kierkegaard views the ethical also in the dual context of his attack on philosophy, particularly on Hegel, and the cherishing of the primitive capabilities of the unspoiled individual.

The more simplified the ethical, the more perspicuous does it become. It is therefore not the case, as men deceitfully try to delude themselves into believing, that the ethical is more clearly evident in human history, where millions are involved, than in one's own poor little life. On the contrary, precisely the reverse is true, and it is more clearly apparent in one's own life, precisely because one does not here so easily mistake the meaning of the material and the quantitative embodiment. The ethical is the inwardness of the spirit, and hence the smaller the circumstances in which it is apprehended in its infinitude, the more clearly it is perceived; while whoever needs the world-historical accessories in order, he thinks, the better to see it, proves thereby precisely that he is immature. . . .
[Under these circumstances] the ethical is thus not the primitive, the

10. Since Lessing died in 1781 and Kierkegaard was born in 1813 and wrote SP in 1846 it is difficult to imagine what event in New Testament history he could be referring to.
11. The asterisk will be used hereafter to denote attacks on Hegel. Here Kierkegaard attacks objectivity.
12. In the *Phenomenology* Hegel explains "ataraxia" as "self-thinking thought, the unalterable and genuine certainty of its self."

most primitive of all that the individual has within him, but rather an abstraction from the world-historical experience. [Under these circumstances] we contemplate universal history, and seem to see that every age has its own moral substance. We become objectively puffed up, and, though existing [13] individuals, we refuse to be content with the so-called subjective ethical. No, the now living generation, while still in the midst of its allotted span of life, desires to discover its own world-historical moral idea, and to act out of a consciousness of this. Alas, what will the Germans not do for money—and the Danes do afterwards, when the Germans have done it first! (SP, 127-9)

This is the third time we have come across words like "cheat," "deceive," and "deceitful." Kierkegaard believes that science and philosophy are cheats; and here he applies the point of view to ethics, in the argument that the attempt to arrive at ethical conceptions through "world-historical" sweeps, obscures the reality of the ethical problem in simple, intimate, everyday relations. One does not arrive at ethical conduct through learned divagations through the ethical codes of the world but through concentrating on the actual relations between existing, i.e., real, standing-before-one, breathing, suffering, loving people. Philosophical sweeps are a mere excuse for avoiding the personal issues that confront us all, every day, with those around us. These can be met only through the capacity of the individual to confront the concrete, rather than the abstract, the immediate, not the historical or the remote. Thus another quality of the primitive: preference of the actual and the real in ethics for the hypothetical and the historical.

Out in the country, where peace dwells under the shade of the leafy canopy, when . . . the little family sits down to dinner with a fowl on the table, and there is plentiful sufficiency for the few: is then this dinner not a rich abundance compared with the great dinner where indeed an entire ox was set forth . . . ? (SP, p. 130)

But, of course, Kierkegaard does not think there are many ethical personalities; people have been corrupted and *know* they have lost the capacity to be ethical along with their primitiveness.

13. In the sense of real; experiencing, as individuals, love, hope, despair and so on.

Falstaff says somewhere [14] that he once had an honest face, but the year and date of its existence have been erased. . . . Perhaps the poet [15] wishes to teach us that it is rare to find an individual on whom that eternal mark of the divinity which expresses itself in the ethical, stands out pure and clear and distinct as once it did; that it is rare to find a personality for whom time does not lie like an eternity between him and this remembered impression [of honesty], but for whom the longest life is but a yesterday with respect to this mighty eternal presence; a personality . . . who day by day strives to reinstate the primitiveness which was his eternal origin! How rare it is to find a personality for whom the ethical preserves this chastity, infinitely inaccessible to even the most distant hint of every foreign admixture; a personality that preserves, yet no, let us speak ethically, that *acquires,* that in this life acquires this virgin purity of ethical passion, in comparison with which the purity of childhood is but an amiable jest! For aesthetically a man may have a primitiveness, a wealth, a little of which he may even endure to lose in life; but ethically understood he possessed it, and if he does not acquire anything, all is lost! (SP, 136–7)

Primitiveness is a "virgin purity of ethical passion" that is not an original gift, but must be *acquired.* This brings us to *striving,* another idea central to Kierkegaard's thought.[16] Kierkegaard emphasizes that to be Christian, as well as to be ethical, requires unremitting work—striving. So one is not ethically pure nor Christian by being born so, but by working for it. He has no use for the innocence of childhood:

What is baptism without personal appropriation? It is an expression for the possibility that the baptized may *become* a Christian, neither more nor less. A parallel is, that one must be born and must exist in order to become a human being (for a child is not yet a human being). . . . [Italics supplied.] (SP, 327)

Primitiveness is thus an acquired characteristic and requires work —striving.

14. The editor's notes say, "It seems that such an utterance is not to be found in Shakespeare"; yet it does not make any difference for the understanding and power of Kierkegaard's argument.

15. Presumably Shakespeare.

16. People interested in indexes may be interested to learn that neither of these two ideas is found in the index of SP. Let this be a warning to people who are thinking of having their indexes made by a "professional."

I give one more example illustrating the nature of Kierkegaard's quarrel with philosophy and science:

The scientific movement of thought is from lower to higher, and thought is designated as the highest stage. In the interpretation of the historical process there is similarly a movement from lower to higher, and thought is designated as the highest stage. In the interpretation of the historical process there is similarly a movement from lower to higher; the stages of *imagination and feeling* have been left behind, and thought as the highest stage is also the last. Everywhere it is decisively concluded that thought is the highest stage of human development; philosophy moves farther and farther away from contact with primitive existential impressions, and there is nothing left to explore, nothing to experience. Everything has been finished, and speculative thought has now to rubricate, classify, and methodically arrange the various concepts. One does not live any more, one does not act, one does not believe; but one knows what love and faith are, and it only remains to determine their place in the system. (SP, 307)

This is humanism; perhaps humanism's most eloquent defender against the march of the science that men feel threatening them. In this context, perhaps, primitiveness becomes humanism. To feel the dew of the morning, the morning air; to see the flowers; to dine beneath a tree with those one loves; to feel and know that one feels the presence of God—this is primitiveness. And the man or woman who can feel these things and be absolutely sure that there is nothing between him and the immediate impression of, of . . . of whatever is outside of him, but also inside, like the presence of God, has primitiveness.

At times Kierkegaard uses the terms "simple" and "plain" to cover the same ground. I give a few examples:

Now if I could only contrive an opportunity to speak with the wise man. . . . I would gladly be content to be the plain man who asks him to pause a moment over the following simple remark: *Is it not the case that what is most difficult of all for the wise man to understand is precisely the simple?* The plain man understands the simple directly, but when the wise man sets himself to understand it, it becomes infinitely difficult. . . . And yet he feels himself gripped by a profound humanity, which reconciles him with the whole of life: that the difference between the wise man and the simplest human being is merely this vanishing little distinction, that *the simple man knows the essential,* while the wise man little by little learns *to know that he knows it,* or learns *to know that he does not* know it. [Italics in the original.] (SP, 143)

What is developed in these pages does not concern the simpleminded, who bear feelingly the burdens of life, and whom God wishes to preserve in their loveable simplicity, which feels no great need of any other sort of understanding. Or in so far as such need is felt, it tends to reduce itself to a sigh over the ills of life, the sigh humbly finding solace in the thought that the real happiness of life does not consist in having knowledge. [Note the anti-intellectual emphasis again.] (SP, fn. 152)

What now is the absurd? The absurd is—that the eternal truth has come into being in time, that God has come into being, has been born, has grown up, and so forth, precisely like any other human being. . . . For the absurd is the object of faith, and the only object that can be believed.

Or suppose a man who says he has faith, but desires to make his faith clear to himself, so as to understand himself in his faith. Now the comedy again begins. The object of faith becomes almost probable, as good as probable, extremely and emphatically probable. He has completed his investigations, and he ventures to claim for himself that he does not believe as shoemakers and tailors and other simple folk believe, but that he has understood himself in his believing. On the contrary. . . . (SP 188–9)

The *Concluding Unscientific Postscript* but principally the *Philosophical Fragments* is deeply—one might say, emotionally—concerned with the paradox that the eternal, the infinite, is embodied in what was finite—Christ. In Kierkegaard—in contrast to Camus—the absurd is the unbelievable; and primitiveness, simplicity, and faith itself consist in the ability to believe the unbelievable. While in the *Postscript* and the *Fragments* the absurd is the embodiment of the infinite in the finite, in *Fear and Trembling* it consists in God's asking Abraham to sacrifice his own son. Much of *Fear and Trembling* is taken up with a tormented analysis of this "absurdity." Fundamentally, then, religiousness consists in being able to believe the absurd true—which makes us think again that perhaps Kierkegaard, like Descartes, protests too much! At any rate, sooner will a simple, a primitive shoemaker or tailor acquire the capacity to believe the absurd than the man who engages in "objective inquiry"—which is true enough. And as far as that's concerned, aren't all of us asked, from birth, to believe the unbelievable? My definition of the perfectly socialized individual, as a matter of fact, would be *one who believes the unbelievable*.

Let us have done now with Kierkegaard and go on to Heidegger.

THE TERM "PRIMITIVE" IN
MARTIN HEIDEGGER

If we were to remove Hegel, Husserl, Kierkegaard, and Plato from Heidegger there would not be much left. *Being and Time* is very much a phantasmagoric teutonization of Kierkegaard, whom Heidegger regards with the greatest reverence and often cites. What Heidegger has really done, so it seems to me, is grind up Kierkegaard in a German metaphysical machine so that he comes out looking like something different. Among the ideas of Kierkegaard that are treated in this way by Heidegger is *primitive*, which turns up in *Being and Time* as "authentic" (*eigentlich*). Compare the following from *Being and Time* with the extract from *The Sickness Unto Death* quoted on page 215:

And because Dasein is . . . essentially its own possibility, it *can*, in its very Being, "choose" itself and win itself; it can also lose itself and never win itself; or only "seem" to do so. But only in so far as it is something which can be *authentic*—that is, something of its own—can it have lost itself and not yet won itself.

Since this paper is not intended as a polemic against Heidegger, I will merely point out that if one will examine the relationship between the self and choice in Kierkegaard's *Either/Or* [17] and the relationship between "individuality" and ownness in Hegel,[18] he will have the sources of the notion of the "authentic" in Heidegger.

17. Especially pp. 219–20 of Volume 2.
18. See p. 336 of the *Phenomenology*.

I turn now to Heidegger's own use of the term primitive, which is more or less the way anthropologists use it. In examining the term in Heidegger, however, we uncover also his attitudes toward modern anthropology.

The word "Primitive" in *Being and Time* [19]

The Interpretation of Dasein in its everydayness, however, is not identical with the describing of some primitive stage of Dasein with which we can become acquainted empirically through the medium of anthropology: *Everydayness does not coincide with primitiveness,* but is rather a mode of Dasein's Being, even when that Dasein is active in a highly developed and differentiated culture—and precisely then. Moreover, even primitive Dasein has possibilities of a Being which is not of the everyday kind, and it has a specific everydayness *of its own.* To orient the analysis of Dasein towards the "life of primitive peoples" can have positive significance [Bedeutung] as a method because "primitive phenomena" are often less concealed and less complicated by extensive self-interpretation on the part of the Dasein in question. Primitive Dasein often speaks to us more directly in terms of a primordial absorption in "phenomena" (taken in a pre-phenomenological sense). A way of conceiving things which seems, perhaps, rather clumsy and crude from our standpoint, can be positively helpful in bringing out the ontological structures of phenomena in a genuine way.

But heretofore our information about primitives has been provided by ethnology. And ethnology operates with definite preliminary conceptions and interpretations of human Dasein in general, even in first "receiving" its material, and in sifting it and working it up. Whether the everyday psychology or even the scientific psychology and sociology which the ethnologist brings with him can provide any scientific assurance that we can have proper access to the phenomena we are studying, and can interpret them and transmit them in the right way, has not yet been established. . . .

We shall not get a genuine knowledge of essences simply by the syncretistic activity of universal comparison and classification. Subjecting the manifold to tabulation does not ensure any actual understanding of what lies there before us as thus set in order. If an ordering principle is genuine, it has its own content as a thing [Sachgehalt], which is never to be found by means of such ordering, but is already presupposed in it. So if one is to put various pictures of the world in order, one must have

19. References are all to pages in the English translation of *Being and Time* by John Macquarrie and Edward Robinson, Harper & Row, 1962.

an insight into Dasein's basic structures in order to treat the world-phenomenon conceptually (pp. 76–7).

Primitive man is not equivalent to the average, everyday man in our culture. Primitive man, says Heidegger, is capable of a Being beyond the everydayness of his own peculiar existence; and study of primitive man, in the anthropological sense, may be helpful, he suggests, in understanding the general problems of Being. Heidegger has the usual notion of primitive man's "primordial absorption in phenomena" but he adds something new to this *usual* notion in suggesting that primitive man is less given to "extensive self-interpretation." Actually anthropologists know practically nothing about this, and will continue to know nothing —glorying, as a matter of fact, nowadays, in a "know-nothing" attitude toward the inner life—as long as all psychological investigations—except the presently sanctified ones of ethno-science— are depreciated. Etho-science does not point toward the inner life, as most educated people understand it, but rather toward the arid elucidation of categories.[20] Meanwhile the last sentence of Heidegger's first paragraph above is not to be understood in terms of phenomena in *general*, but rather in terms of primitive Dasein, for the reason that at this point Heidegger is not interested in phenomena in general.

In pointing out that anthropology "operates with definite preliminary interpretations of human Dasein in general," Heidegger underscores a weakness in our researches into the inner life of exotic peoples, and casts doubt on our ability to give reliable descriptions of it. It seems to me that no logical disproof of Heidegger's stricture can be given; and indeed, we cannot step out of our culturally determined natures. Thus we encounter, in Heidegger's objections, the principle of indeterminacy in our own work; and we cannot conduct critical experiments in ethnography. Even writing a particular ethnography so that it is internally consistent is no proof that the ethnographer is right.

On the other hand, it is equally impossible to prove that our

20. Not at all to be confused with phenomenological studies.

"preliminary interpretations of human Dasein in general" are incorrect, for it would be necessary, as a "preliminary," to prove that mankind has no psychic unity. Ethnography, however, rests its case for the validity of its interpretations of the inner life of exotic peoples precisely on the assumption of the psychic unity of mankind.

The question is, In what does this psychic unity consist? Or, what psychic unity is assumed? I give a non-exhaustive list of components of psychic unity.

1. Culture, that everywhere has the same basic elements: economic system, role differentiation, technology, religion, systems of reward and punishment, social organization, including role differentiation, language.
2. Use of rewards as well as punishments for social control.
3. The following "inner mechanisms": phantasy, inhibition, and probably all the mechanisms of defense such as reaction formation, compensation, repression, projection, displacement, substitution, and symptom formation.
4. Unity of the physical and the psychic (the "psychosomatic reaction").
5. The capacity for deductive as well as for inductive reasoning.
6. The capacity to attach connotative meanings to all phenomena.
7. Systematic attention to subjects rather than to predicates [21] in all discourse.
8. The capacity to link time, space, motion, objects, people, and symbols into complex systems.

21. On this subject see E. von Domarus' essay "The Specific Laws of Logic in Schizophrenia" in *Language and Thought in Schizophrenia* edited by J. S. Kasanin, University of California Press, 1944. A good example of attention to the predicate rather than to the subject is the following from Dylan Thomas' *Adventures in the Skin Trade*: "Now the woman in the fur coat would be telling a policeman, 'I have just been winked at by a short boy wearing a wet hat.' 'But it isn't raining, madam.' That would settle her." The humor consists in emphasis falling on "wet hat," the predicate, rather than on "boy," the subject.

Thus it is the psychic unity of mankind that gives reason-
ableness to interpretations of the inner life of exotic peoples. It
seems to me that in the last of the above paragraphs Heidegger
is saying that no essences are to be discovered by comparisons.
To us, this means cross-cultural comparisons, including correla-
tional and factor analysis. "Tabulation," he avers, is no substitute
for insight—into the nature of Dasein, or, apparently, of anything.
Does his emphasis fall on the word "ensure," or does he want
to throw all "tabulation" out the window? I think he intends the
latter. No "ordering principle," he says, "is . . . to be found by
means of . . . ordering," for obviously, this leads to tautology.
He confronts us again with the harrowing truth of the indeter-
minacies and tautologies with which we constantly struggle.

On pages 112–113, in discussing the problem of signs,
Heidegger refers to the commonly held belief that

. . . for primitive man, the sign coincides with that which is indicated.
Not only can the sign represent this in the sense of serving as a substitute for what it indicates, but it can do so in such a way that the
sign itself always *is* what it indicates.

He therefore believes that the kind of ontological analysis that
is useful in understanding the relationship between sign and
signified in our culture is not directly applicable to cultures in
which sign and thing are so closely linked as he—along with
others influenced by Lévy-Bruhl—thinks they are in the primitive world. Nevertheless, he believes that formal attention to
the way the primitive world intuitively construes the relationship between sign and thing will illuminate the general ontological problem of the way signs enter into the relation between
Dasein and things.

Finally we may consider Heidegger's reference to the primitive world's attitude toward death:

. . . the ways in which death is taken among primitive peoples, and
their ways of comporting themselves towards it in magic and cult, illuminate primarily the understanding of *Dasein;* but the Interpretation of
this understanding already requires an existential analytic and a corresponding analytic of death.

Thus Heidegger tells us, with consummate insight, that we do not understand primitive peoples' attitude toward death unless we know their conception of the self: what a person's attitude toward his past and his present and his (living) future are; what it means to become a self (*Dasein*); and what all this means to him in relation to his dying. We have mountains of data on funeral rites, on sociological interpretations of them and sometimes even some references to the *personal* feelings of the survivors. But how primitive *Dasein* confronts death (i.e., in terms of his feelings about his self), we do not know. It is interesting that we have so much data in anthropology about peoples' beliefs about the after life; but we have little about how they feel about being there. Even less, however, and more importantly, we have practically no data about the bearing his own death has on the present life of the existing, real individual who plans his life, looks back on his past and has hopes for his future. In anthropology the data from the Plains Indians gives us some idea of the way awareness of death, the necessity of constantly confronting it, shapes the existence of the living.[22] Tacitus' *Annals of Imperial Rome* is a pretty good example from history; although in the *Annals* we have to infer too much.

Thus Heidegger has made some penetrating observations about anthropology, has pointed to areas badly in need of study and suggests various kinds of collaboration between existentialist philosophers and ethnographers.

CONCLUSIONS

Man-in-the-west has always had to have a baseline for his thinking about himself. Whether it was Tacitus,[23] during the darkness of the Imperial period, assuming some age of primordial

---

22. Possibly the Plains Indian material, which is inseparable from warfare and death, enables us to form an impression of the way in which, in one area of the world, the awareness of death shapes the attitudes of the living.

23. *The Annals of Imperial Rome*, Penguin Classics, p. 129.

cleanliness and innocence, Hegel needing a starting point for a theory of the development of reason, Kierkegaard longing for a form of self that could put itself in immediate contact with God, the early anthropologists searching for a starting point for a theory of evolution that would put contemporary man at the top of the tree, or Karl Marx searching for an archetype of simple sharing, Man-in-the-west has had to have some kind of primordial anchor point for his intellectual systems. Even logic talks of "primitive postulates." I infer, therefore, that a long, persisting trait of the western cultural manifold is to seek to anchor all intellectual endeavors in a fixed point. Or perhaps one should say "has been" rather than "is," for it seems to me that the theory of relativity blew the fixed point of reference away definitively. Of course, the principle of relativity did not alone accomplish the dissolution of the anchor point; the growth of knowledge and the acid of worldly scepticism about fixity, innocence and system, helped. Relativity gave the ultimate proof.

Mankind cannot, therefore, look back with certainty on any beginning. Nobody knows how anything began; nobody knows where the origins of anything are; nor does he know about their ends. Logic has passed from the assumption of something primitive to the "operational definition." And so life has become an operational definition of existence.

EDWARD P. DOZIER

The Concepts of "Primitive" and

"Native" in Anthropology

INTRODUCTION

THIS PAPER considers the views of anthropologists toward the societies they have traditionally studied—"primitive" and "native" peoples. These views are considered in terms of the main currents of anthropological theory, because such views and the development of theory bear important relations to one another.

Reprinted from *Yearbook of Anthropology 1955*, New York, Wenner-Gren Foundation for Anthropological Research Incorporated, 1955, pp. 187–202.

A sketch on field methods and techniques has also been included, again because the approach to field work appears largely to be the result of the specific concepts and attitudes that anthropologists have toward nonliterate societies. Finally, the terms "primitive," "native," and the like, are analyzed for their validity as descriptive and taxonomic designations and with reference to their reception by the public-at-large and the peoples so designated.

The problem of terminological designations for nonliterate societies is an especially serious one. The fact that "primitive," "native," and similar terms are often placed within quotation marks indicates the shaky and unsure ground upon which they rest as designations for the societies which anthropologists study. That these terms are not used in a definitive and precise fashion reflects the growing and changing science of anthropology and also a changing world situation. As a science grows and matures it revises and regulates its terminology. More appropriate terms, both in a descriptive and taxonomic sense, replace the older and less appropriate designations. Among anthropologists there is an increasing awareness that these terms are unsatisfactory and inadequate.

Appropriate taxonomic and descriptive designations are more difficult in anthropology than in most other sciences. Students of the physical and biological sciences logically can be concerned only with proper descriptive and classificatory designations, but anthropologists, because they deal with human phenomena, must take into consideration the reception of these terms by the peoples they purport to identify. Anthropologists are thus in the precarious position of having to select terms which are adequate taxonomic and descriptive designations as well as terms which do not evoke a clamor of negative reaction from the public-at-large. This is felt more keenly today because the societies which anthropologists traditionally have studied are themselves in a ferment of change. The impact of industrialized civilization is penetrating into the most marginal and isolated areas of the world. In the process, large numbers of "nonliterates" are becoming literate and participants in "non-primitive" cultures. Anthropologists, therefore, have the task of selecting designations which satisfy the requirements of their science and which do not offend the sensibilities of large numbers of people.

THE ANTHROPOLOGISTS' "LABORATORY"

Anthropology, or more specifically ethnology, has now and in the past depended for much of its basic data on descriptive studies of nonliterate societies. These societies, as generally agreed among anthropologists, have the following characteristics: (1) absence of a written language; (2) a relatively simple technology; (3) social institutions which are cast in a simpler mold; (4) smaller numbers; (5) relative isolation; and (6) societies whose cultures are in general characterized by a slower rate of change. The contrast is made, of course, to social entities with large populatons, a written tradition, a complex technology and varied social institutions, and whose cultures are rapidly changing. Benedict's characterization (1934, p. 17) of nonliterate societies and her justification of them as an anthropological "laboratory" is worth quoting here:

> . . . the most illuminating material for discussion of cultural forms and processes is that of societies historically as little related as possible to our own and to one another. With the vast network of historical contact which has spread the great civilizations over tremendous areas, primitive cultures are now the one source to which we can turn. They are a laboratory in which we may study the diversity of human institutions. With their comparative isolation, many primitive regions have had centuries in which to elaborate the cultural themes they have made their own. They provide ready to our hand the necessary information concerning the possible great variations in human adjustments, and a critical examination of them is essential for an understanding of cultural processes. It is the only laboratory of social forms that we have or shall have. . . .

As a "laboratory," nonliterate societies provide other advantages as well. The investigator, who is most often an alien, can approach his work with detachment and objectivity—a difficult and often impossible task in the study of his own society and culture. The very complexity of literate societies also prevents comprehensive studies. Rapid communication systems such as telephones, radio, and television have complicated the situation further. The factor of size makes for divergent sub-groups with their own special kinds of values, social goals, and ethics, where the interrelation is so complicated that proper analysis presents in itself a methodological problem of considerable magnitude. In nonliterate societies, on the other hand, the cultures tend to be more homogeneous. There are fewer individuals involved, the patterns in the culture are comparatively regular, so that fewer variables must be dealt with. Moreover, the study of non-European, nonliterate societies helps us to understand the more complex ones. As Linton (1945, p. 12) writes:

> . . . It is a general rule of science that research should proceed, when possible, from the simple to the complex and the ethnologist has been doing just this in his social and cultural investigations. . . .

Benedict's statement as to the importance of nonliterate societies as a laboratory, however, is quite inadequate, since they are by no means the only social laboratory we have or shall have. Even when she wrote, those in the fields of personality-and-culture and community studies were exploiting other areas of research. Acculturation and "culture-contact" studies have long concentrated on essentially different kinds of situations, especially where industrialized literate societies have interacted with non-literate ones. The contemporary tendency of certain anthropologists to drift away from their traditional "labortory" will be discussed later in more detail; first we review briefly the historical development of the study of nonliterate societies.

HISTORICAL SURVEY

The early pioneers of anthropology, Morgan and Tylor, were among the first to use data from nonliterate societies in a systematic fashion. These writers secured their information about societies different from their own wherever they could get it: from the accounts of travelers and missionaries for the most part. In the vogue of the day, when "unilinear evolutionistic" hypotheses dominated investigation, nonliterate societies were considered "survivals," or degenerated societies. Such societies were most often and most consistently thought to represent "stages" in the cultural growth of mankind that culminated in the so-called "advanced" traditions of Europe. "Psychic unity" also characterized the thinking of the day so that the work of the early anthropologists was done largely in the belief that primitives represented the back-waters in the historical stream. The specific attitudes toward nonliterate societies as held by Morgan and Tylor are germane to report. Morgan writes in his *Ancient Society* (1877, p. 41):

> The inferiority of savage man in the mental and moral scale, undeveloped, inexperienced, and held down by his low animal appetites and passions, though reluctantly recognized, is, nevertheless, substantially demonstrated by the remains of ancient art in flint, stone and bone implements, by his cave life in certain areas, and by his osteological remains. It is still further illustrated by the present condition of tribes of savages in a low state of development, left in isolated sections of the earth's monuments of the past. . . .

The attitudes of Tylor toward nonliterate societies are almost identical with those of Morgan. Indeed, in the quotation below (Tylor, 1891, p. 31), something akin to Morgan's three-fold classification of the world's societies into savagery, barbarism, and civilization is evident:

> . . . We may, I think, apply the often-repeated comparison of savages to children as fairly as to their moral as to their intellectual condition. The better savage social life seems in but unstable equilibrium, liable to be easily upset by a touch of distress, temptation, or violence, and then it becomes the worse savage life, which we know by so many dismal and hideous examples. Altogether, it may be admitted that some rude tribes lead a life to be envied by some barbarous races, and even by the outcasts of higher nations . . . while the general tenor of the evidence goes far to justify the view that on the whole the civilized man is not only wiser and more capable than the savage, but also better and happier, and that the barbarian stands between. . . .

The well-known fact that Tylor and Morgan examined a wide range of available literature on nonliterate cultures in their day must be re-emphasized, for they were scholars in every sense of the term. This is evident from their writing, rich in documentation. And while both of these men have been accused of being "armchair anthropologists," they had high regard for empirical data and each had had field experience. Tylor had traveled in Mexico, while Morgan is considered the first comprehensive field worker. His studies on the Iroquois of New York must be regarded as setting new standards for the investigation of nonliterate cultures.[1] Morgan also made several brief trips to the western United States at considerable expense and sacrifice to collect data at first hand (White, 1942, pp. 1–26). In addition, Morgan was in correspondence with large numbers of people throughout the world to obtain information about other nonliterate peoples (Lowie, 1937, p. 62).

Tylor, too, valued field work. As Lowie (1937, p. 71) put it:

> Tylor was not technically a field worker, yet he was the very opposite of an armchair anthropologist. That he saw Mexican natives in his early manhood and later (1884) paid a brief visit to Pueblo villages counts for something, but more important is his unremitting tendency to study culture in the very heart of a metropolis. He receives a Tasmanian skin-scraper and forthwith has it tested by his butcher; he peers into shop windows for a parallel of the Oceanian pump-drill; in Somersetshire he watches a weaver throw her shuttle from hand to hand; and discerning a problem in aboriginal gesture languages, he learns hundreds of signs in the Berlin Deaf and Dumb Institution.

We no longer hold with Tylor's view that human societies can be placed in a series of strata substantially uniform throughout the world. Nor do we go along with Morgan's axiom that all social institutions can be classed into neat stages of savagery, barbarism, and civilization. The writings of Morgan and Tylor are significant, however, in the development and use of an important methodological approach in anthropology—the comparative method which both applied assiduously to their data. In their efforts to fit nonliterate societies into the evolutionary ladder they

1. Lowie, R. H., 1937, pp. 54–67; White, Leslie, 1951, pp. 11–17.

posited, they carefully combed the literature. They erred by forcing data into categories established on the bases of single criteria (social, political or whatever) or, in other cases, criteria heavily overweighted.

It is important to keep constantly before us the fact that anthropological studies were in their infancy when Morgan and Tylor wrote. The intellectual climate of their day made imperative the classification of phenomena into uniform, orderly sequences. Most important was the fact that studies of nonliterate societies were lacking for large areas of the world, and those that existed were of questionable validity. In view of these limitations, their impressions of "primitives" and their essentially untenable scientific and speculative assumptions become less grievous.

Morgan and Tylor have exerted considerable influence on several contemporary anthropologists, as is seen in the recent reexamination of their theories and assumptions by such students as White (1949) and Steward (1949). Though proof has not as yet been given, the evolutionary framework, through the use of more refined and controlled methods and in combination with historical and functional points of view, may give us more acceptable results.

After the turn of the century, anti-evolutionistic views emerged in both Europe and America. The most radical of these stressed the uninventiveness of man and tried to explain cultural content as ultimately derived from a single source. This extreme position was maintained by the British anthropologists, Smith (1929) and Perry (1923). These two writers, whose views were never accepted by the majority of anthropologists, attempted to explain the derivation of almost all cultural elements from one source—Egypt. Their postulations were based almost wholly on philosophical and speculative thinking. Their views of nonliterate peoples, therefore, were vague and undefined.

W. H. R. Rivers, the psychologist, whose anthropological interests dominated his later life, eventually affiliated himself with Smith and Perry as an extreme diffusionist (Smith, 1924, pp. v–vii). Rivers did ethnographic research of a high caliber. The publications of his investigations among the Todas and to a lesser extent among the Melanesians constitute genuine contributions to descriptive studies of nonliterate societies. Heralding a view later made more explicit by Boas was Rivers' concept (1924, pp. 52–53) of "primitive" thought:

> There can be no greater hindrance to progress in our attempts to understand the mind of man of lowly culture than the belief so widely held, that his actions are determined by motives having that vague and lawless character ascribed by many to the thought of savage man. There are even those who hold that such peoples as the Papuan and Melanesian have not yet reached the logical stage of thought. I believe there is no single department of social life in which it cannot be shown that this view is false . . . I hope the facts brought forward here are sufficient to show that, in the department of his activity in which he endeavors to cope with disease, savage man is no illogical or prelogical creature, but that his actions are guided by reasoning as definite as that which we can claim for our own medical practices.

More significant for the purposes of this paper are the contributions of the so-called Kulturkreis school of Fritz Graebner, Father Wilhelm Schmidt, and others. These anthropologists consider the peoples of the world as products of several core cultures which spread over the entire world after attaining essential characteristics in the Old World, especially in Asia. As these basic cultures spread, new elements were added and others lost, but in every case enough of the original complex remained so that each could be identified (Schmidt, 1939).

The views of the Kulturkreis school regarding the peoples they study, however, appear to be substantially the same as those of their predecessors and contemporaries, and representative of an older stratum. Their attitudes thus differ from the present view toward nonliterate peoples held by American anthropologists, which was established by Boas and is discussed in detail below.

It is now important to consider the views of Boas and his students who are responsible for much of the present attitude toward nonliterate peoples and a novel approach to field investigations. The so-called American historical school emphasized the study of nonliterate cultures and rigorous field techniques. Boas insisted that all aspects of these societies be studied, and that cultural groups be described from within, from the viewpoint of the members of the society rather than from that of the ethnographer. He promoted the learning and use of native languages; where this was impossible he suggested recording of native terms, the collection of texts, and the teaching of natives to write their own language so that they themselves could record significant aspects of their culture.

For Boas and many of his students, nonliterate societies provided the only data for anthropological research. So much were such societies considered the legitimate laboratory of the anthropologists that the acculturation and extinction of nonliterate societies as such were viewed with alarm. Thus, for example, Linton (1945, p. 10) remarks:

> . . . Until very recent times, ethnologists have limited their fact-finding activities to the so-called "primitive" peoples, those living outside the scope of the few rich and complex cultures which we call civilizations. The more isolated such groups and the more widely their cultures differed from our own, the greater has been the interest in them. The old line ethnologist is in the seventh heaven if he can find a group which has never seen a white man before and he views the current opening up of the far corners of the earth with all the alarm of any craftsman whose livelihood is threatened. . . .

The conception of the nonliterate as mentally inferior and as an individual incapable of surmounting his "lowly level" of culture was specifically challenged by Boas in *The Mind of Primitive Man*. In this collection of essays Boas showed conclusively that the mentality of "primitive" man was not substantially different from that of "civilized" man. Boas demonstrated that the lowly station and inferior position in which a member of a nonliterate society is placed is merely the result of an ethnocentric comparison on the basis of one standard—the yardstick of the anthropologist's own culture. He insisted that investigations be made without such preconceived notions.

In terms of theory, Boas severely criticized the comparative method as it was employed by the classical evolutionists. In a paper condemning the comparative method, Boas (1940, pp. 276–280, 633–634) formulated two imperatives for anthropologists: (1) detailed studies of specific tribes in their cultural and regional context as a means to the reconstruction of the histories of tribal cultures and regions, and (2) the comparison of these tribal histories, with the ultimate objective of formulating general laws of cultural growth.

As is well known, Boas' first imperative was carried out in an admirable fashion by Boas himself and his students. The second task, the application of the comparative method, was largely ignored in the intense preoccupation of describing indigenous societies (Ackerknecht, 1954; Eggan, 1954).

Although the use of the comparative method was minimized by Boas and his students, they produced excellent descriptions of nonliterate societies. That so-called primitive societies were the "laboratory" of the cultural anthropologists was not doubted during this period. Most important in terms of this paper are the attitudes toward nonliterates and the efforts of the investigators to describe cultures in terms of the societies studied. This was true of all aspects of culture—the forms and categories were not to be imposed from without; they were to be "discovered." Bidney (1953, pp. 688–689) ascribes the attitude toward "primitives" and the reluctance to evaluate cultures of Boas and his students as an expression of the liberal and democratic climate of their culture:

. . . As liberals and democrats, they merely accentuated tendencies inherent in their culture but professed to have derived their "higher tolerance" from a comparative study of primitive cultures. The idea of an "ethics of violence" . . . and of perpetual crises brought about through the conflict of social classes and national interests, which Marx and Sorel taught, did not enter into their peaceful scientific perspective at all. Had they thought in terms of the possible incompatibility and conflict of ideologies and of the doctrine of social revolution rather than of social evolution, they would not have labored under the naive optimism of cultural laissez-faire. It has taken the impact of the second World War to shake this romantic cultural optimism and to awaken anthropologists to the reality of cultural crises and to the need for cultural integration on a world scale.

In criticizing Boas and his students for their reluctance to evaluate cultures, Bidney also appears to reject the anthropological approach to the analysis of nonliterate cultures. This approach in itself does not condone culture relativism; it advocates, rather, the need for discovering or ascertaining the unique cultural systems of nonliterate societies. It specifically emphasizes that one cultural model cannot be used in the study of another; for the standards and categories vary tremendously among diverse cultural groups. It is true that cultural relativism arose as a byproduct of this approach but it is not inherent in the approach itself.

Whether the scientific attitude of Boas and his students was derived from the study of nonliterate societies or from the values inherent in their own culture is unimportant within the limits and purposes of this paper. The approach of Boas and his students is significant, however, in establishing the fact that cultures of nonliterate societies are adequate and consistent systems. And most important, the approach has destroyed a former view of "primitives" as inferior, child-like beings or men incapable of rising above their assigned cultural level.

The contemporary British social anthropologists tend to regard their discipline as completely concerned with the study of nonliterate societies. This point was made by Evans-Pritchard (1951, pp. 10–11) when he reported: "Social Anthropology . . . can be regarded as a branch of sociological studies, that branch which devotes itself to primitive societies." The views of British anthropologists regarding the methods of studying these societies appear to be similar to those already sketched for contemporary American anthropologists, since they share with Americans an emphasis on field studies and, at least with Boas, the desirability for learning native languages (Firth, 1951, p. 474; Evans-Pritchard, 1951, pp. 76–77).

British social anthropologists differ, however, from their American colleagues in other significant ways. The most important difference, perhaps, is that they restrict themselves to a narrow range of cultural phenomena and, though they no longer reject history, they rarely engage in historical analyses. As Murdock (1951, p. 471) points out, "They are interested primarily in social groups and the structuring of interpersonal relationships rather than in culture, and in synchronic rather than diachronic correlations." Murdock concludes (1951, p. 472) that "British social anthropology [is actually] a specialized school of sociologists." With these statements Firth (1951, p. 477) is in substantial agreement.

Returning again to America, there is today—at least among many anthropologists—a trend away from the study of nonliterate societies to a study of modern communities and communities in transition. This is due, as one group of anthropologists sees it, to the disappearance of nonliterate peoples and therefore to the need to find a new "laboratory." Another group of anthropologists feels that the methods and techniques perfected on nonliterate societies can be applied with effectiveness to other types of communities. The former view is espoused by Kroeber (1953, p. 360) in commenting on community studies:

> . . . It is plain that the present-day community study of a more or less isolated group within a larger society, and its particularities of culture, is merely a substitute for the old-fashioned holistic tribal study on which ethnography cut its teeth. Primitive persistencies just got to be fewer and fewer and became so remote that where formerly for a few hundred dollars one could study a tribe for a summer, now one has to go off for most of a couple of years and it is a matter of thousands of dollars to do field work—and many native cultures are wholly gone, even as memories. So anthropologists faced with a shrinking material . . . have turned to the modern type of community study, which you can sometimes make by paying a dime and taking the subway somewhere downtown. In these community studies one can still use the traditional face-to-face methods, the familiar personal-relation-with-informants methods, which have been distinctive of anthropologists as compared with most sociologists and all economists.

Ralph Linton (1945, p. 10) emphasizes the utility of the traditional techniques and methods of ethnologists on modern communities and he reports:

> . . . Ethnologists of the younger generation are less worried by the march of events [than old line ethnologists about disappearance of nonliterate societies]. The study of cultures widely different from our own

has led to the development of techniques for fact finding and, above all, of attitudes of detachment, which lose none of their value when they are applied to civilized societies and cultures in transition. It is more romantic to study the natives of a South Sea island than a community of Iowa farmers, but the same scientific methods can be used with both and both can yield significant results. As long as human beings continue to live in communities and to develop special ways of life to meet special conditions the ethnologist will not be threatened with technological unemployment. . . .

Kroeber, in his concluding review of *Anthropology Today* (1953, pp. 366–367), is frankly concerned about the survival of ethnology as a discipline devoted to the study of nonliterate societies: "I am about ready to abandon this baby [ethnology] to the wolves—to a premature fate or to a senescent death as one may see it." He then indicates why he believes ethnology appears to be vanishing: the decrease in primitives, the failure to make classifications and comparisons, and the tendencies to leap directly into large-scale speculations.

In answer to Kroeber's statements, Eggan (1954, p. 756) calls attention to cultures as yet untouched in the interior of New Guinea. He also points to untapped resources of peoples in Africa, India, Southeast Asia, Indonesia, and Melanesia. These last are cultures under change, a challenging "laboratory."

Beals' remarks (1953b, p. 65) in the introduction of a paper describing a community under the impact of industrialized civilization are also pertinent:

. . . Statistics are poor or nonexistent for many parts of the world, but by the most conservative estimate more than two-thirds of the world's people live in villages; the figure may well be seventy-five or eighty per cent or more. Moreover, the village is a conveniently small unit for the study of many problems of theoretical importance.

Numbers and convenience are not the only reasons to study the village. Today the village world is in a ferment of change under the mounting impact of industrial civilization, and gives rise to some of the most critical problems of our times. The varied conditions of change likewise provide as near an approach to laboratory conditions as the student of man is likely to find. Both the needs of science and urgent practical affairs call for study of the village. . . .

As for Kroeber's second point, the failure to make classifications and comparisons, Eggan points to the need of borrowing the methods and techniques of the British social anthropologists and for following the lead of Murdock as exemplified in his *Social Structure* (1949). Eggan suggests that we return to the basic problems American ethnologists were tackling in the 1920's and 1930's with new methods and points of view and greater range of concepts. He feels that the tendency to leap directly into large-scale speculations is diminishing. Eggan points to such investigations by Kluckhohn, Opler, Hoijer, Goodwin, and others among Southern Athapascan-speaking peoples as fruitful kinds of research. As other examples of effective utilization of the comparative method, he mentions Spoehr's researches in the Southeast and Redfield's studies in Yucatan.

Eggan (1954, p. 759) concludes his answer to Kroeber:

I have suggested there may be some virtues in combining the social anthropological concepts of structure and function with the ethnological concepts of process and history. If we can do this in a satisfactory manner we can save the "ethnological baby" from the fate to which Kroeber has consigned it. . . .

The interest in nonliterate peoples still is very much alive. The cultural anthropologist or ethnologist is vitally concerned with these societies although it may be difficult in some cases to tell the modern versions—the changed and acculturated communities. Yet the "laboratory" is rife with problems of theoretical importance, whether it involves a community in the traditional sense or the modern, changed variety.

FIELD TECHNIQUES AND METHODS

The inclusion of the following brief account on field techniques and methods is deemed appropriate because the approach to field work is to a large extent influenced by the view of non-literate societies, especially as established by Boas.

The most recent and full accounts are those of Lounsbury on linguistics; Henry and Spiro on psychological techniques; Paul on interview techniques and field relationships; and Lewis on controls and experiments in field work.

What characterizes the work of anthropologists among nonliterate groups from investigations carried out by other disciplines is that of observation and interview. While working in a nonliterate society the anthropologist participates to a greater or lesser extent in the lifeway of the people. Among some groups this is essentially impossible, of course. White, for example, was unable to take part in Keres life, though he visited the various pueblos and observed public ceremonies when circumstances permitted him to do so. This was because of the intense reticence of the Rio Grande Pueblo Indians toward being studied. White (1935, p. 7) reported the peculiarities of field work among these peoples:

> . . . To the reader unfamiliar with the pueblos of New Mexico it should be said that in most of them it is utterly impossible to do ethnological work in the open. The ideal of going out and "living the life of the people" is utterly impossible among the pueblos along the Rio Grande. On the contrary, these pueblos are very strongly opposed to telling outsiders anything pertaining to their customs and beliefs. Children are taught from infancy to tell outsiders nothing. Strict watch is kept over all that none may betray the pueblo's secrets.

Complete participation of an alien in a society unlike his own where physical characteristics set him apart from others in the community is probably impossible. The nearest approach to complete participation may have been achieved by Florence Kluckhohn. The varied kinds of participation and their advantages are fully discussed by Kluckhohn (1940) in her excellent paper.

"Going native," granting the possibility, has serious difficulties of emotional involvement and identity. Paul indicates that in such cases the investigator often ceases to be an observer and can no longer be counted within the fold of anthropologists. He cites (1953, p. 435) the instance of Frank Cushing at Zuñi who became so emotionally identified with the people that he refused to continue publishing his Zuñi data.

Another desideratum of the field worker among nonliterate societies is learning the language. In the earlier days this was almost a necessity when communities were wholly or largely monolingual. In more recent years the language problem has been circumvented by the use of bilinguals as informants or as interpreters. Kluckhohn (1945, pp. 111–114) indicates that some knowledge of the language is indispensable even if natives are bilingual or interpreters abundant.

The collection of texts in the native idiom was stressed by Boas and was essentially characteristic of his monographs and those written by his students. Texts are always helpful but perhaps more to the linguist and for the specialized interests of the student in culture and personality. Mechanical aids such as wire and tape records may be used in a variety of useful ways and are becoming standard equipment in the field. This statement also applies to photographs, either black and white or color. Motion pictures of various aspects of native life are extremely desirable, but the high cost of film and cameras and the equally important consideration of their possible rejection by the people to be studied, tend to restrict their use.

Rigorous sampling procedures are usually not utilized by anthropologists interested in the general cultural patterns of nonliterate societies. As Mead (1953a, pp. 654–655) points out, sampling in anthropology is of a different kind, viz.: ". . . in which the validity of the sample depends not so much upon the number of cases as upon the proper specification of the informant, so that he or she can be accurately placed, in terms of a very large number of variables—age, sex, order of birth, family background . . . etc." This statement is based on the view of culture as an integrated system (especially relevant in a small, fairly homogeneous group), and a few informants, as long as they are full participants in the culture, should be able to give you the general cultural patterns of the society. Essentially this is what Herskovits means when he reports (1954, p. 16) that an informant cannot invent a culture, any more than he can invent a language. However, Mandelbaum (1953, p. 185) has pointed out significantly that, when one is interested in the variations of cultural patterns, more careful sampling methods are essential.

THE NON-PROFESSIONAL PUBLIC AND THE "NATIVE"

But what of the readers of anthropological literature outside of our professional, select circle, for we cannot escape the impact of the study of anthropology on the lay public. Not only do we consider this a valuable and natural course of a science devoted to the understanding of behavior, of man understanding man, but in recent years a number of "popular" books and articles have been aimed directly at the non-professional public. Furthermore, we must realize that this literature reaches not only large numbers of literate peoples of industrialized societies, but also members of societies which have been the subject of anthropological study. Indeed, many of these people are themselves in professional positions, such as teachers, lawyers, medical doctors—even anthropologists. In other words, it is important to recognize the fact that large numbers of "natives" are now full participants in literate, industrialized cultures and contributors to a way of life which has been considered alien to them. They are strongly affected by the work of anthropologists, especially with the literature devoted to them and most particularly with the terminology used.

Any anthropologist who has addressed a large audience composed of persons of mixed backgrounds has realized that he has had to choose his words with extreme care when he talked of his "laboratory." Even the professional anthropologist most inclined to use such terms as "primitive," "backward," "savage," and the like has had to grope for substitute words. The problem of choosing proper and unoffending terminology has become increasingly difficult in professional publications, in the classroom, and in public lectures.

The lay public of non-"native" origin accepts for the most part the negative connotative values of anthropological terminology with respect to nonliterate societies. Since "racial," "mental," and cultural attributes of a people are ordinarily conceived as a *gestalt* by the public-at-large, the anthropologist's terms are accepted as characterizations of nonliterates in all three categories. Thus, when the term "primitive" is used to designate a particular nonliterate society, the popular assumption is that such people are racially, mentally, and culturally retarded. This concept of nonliterates appears crucial in the unfavorable reception often accorded anthropologists in their attempts to study modern communities. The objection to being studied by an anthropologist is apparently because the members of modern communities feel that they are being relegated to the category of "primitives" with all of the unpleasant attributes associated with this term and similar designations. The reaction of Hollywood to Powdermaker's study (1950) is evidence on this point. Hollywood raised a hue and cry about being classed as "savages"—this reaction was expressed profusely and with great emotion in newspaper and magazine articles. Hollywood's response is thus a good index of what the lay public thinks about anthropology and the societies anthropologists study. Those anthropologists interested in modern communities are of course aware of this problem. The anticipated difficulties of entree and rapport have led to the assumption of more familiar and more "respectable" roles, such as those of teacher (Powdermaker, 1939), or "historian" (Paul, 1953, pp. 432–433).

To the public-at-large, it seems, then, anthropologists are those who study backward, crude, uncivilized, or savage people. It also should be emphasized that the terms used by anthropologists are interpreted by the lay public generally to apply to the physical, mental, and cultural characteristics of nonliterates. Anthropologists may present the case of these societies clearly and emphasize the contemporary point of view that there is no evidence to demonstrate the physical and mental inferiority of any people; but so long as they use terminology which has a popular etymology and belies scientific usage, just so long will the non-professional public consider and think of "primitives" and "savages" as such.

It is remarkable how term-conscious social scientists can be when they study literate communities. It is obvious that in the study of modern communities the positive or negative reaction of such communities is anticipated. Observe, for example, the fictitious place-names used in the published reports of: *Middle Town, Yankee City, Plainville, U. S. A.* In the last of these publications the writer even found it expedient to use a pseudonym. Sociologists, because they deal wholly with literate societies, consistently have been aware of terminology and have refrained from using emotionally or negatively charged terms in setting up classificatory or taxonomic systems. Thus dichotomies like "gemeinschaft-gesellschaft" and "urban-rural," do not carry the negative connotations that characterize anthropological designations. This is true of the essentially sociological studies of Redfield in Yucatan. His "tribe," "folk," "urban" designations do not connote negative meanings.

Except for a few notable exceptions, anthropologists have not taken the trouble to hide the identity of the nonliterate societies they have studied.[2] It should be emphasized, however, that many anthropologists have gone to considerable trouble in their published reports to safeguard informants, but for the most part these precautions have not been extended to whole societies. Even more rarely have anthropologists attempted to choose less offensive terms for the characterizations of nonliterates generally. Yet it is encouraging that even this censure must allow for exceptions. A few anthropologists, for example, have circumvented the more derogatory terms or those which have ambiguous designations. Thus, for instance, the recent introductory textbook on anthropology by Beals and Hoijer (1953) avoids the use of the term "primitive," yet lucidly documents achievements and developments in selected societies. Others use the more offensive terms

2. For exceptions see Clyde Kluckhohn, 1951; Margaret Mead, 1932.

in quotes or preface them with "so-called," indicating dissatisfaction and disapproval of such designations. Herskovits in *Man and His Works* (in which the use of "primitive" was first specifically rejected) makes a strong case (1948, pp. 74–75) for *nonliterate* as the appropriate term:

> . . . Several terms to replace "primitive" have been suggested. "Nonhistoric" which is one of these, has not found much acceptance. It implies that absence of written history is the equivalent of having no history at all, which, of course, cannot be said of any people who exist in time. "Preliterate" has found more favor, but the objection to be raised here is that the prefix *pre-* carries a meaning of time that infers prediction. It is, in essence, a carry-over of the "contemporary ancestor" concept since it implies that peoples without written languages are at a stage antecedent to the one in which, presumably, they will devise, or at least acquire, writing. The third form, nonliterate, simply describes the fact that these people do not have written languages. It is sometimes confused with "illiterate," but the use of this latter word should be guarded against, since it carries a distinct connotation of inferiority in ability or opportunity, or both. Nonliterate, because it is colorless, conveys its meaning unambiguously and is readily applicable to the data it seeks to delimit, is thus to be preferred to all the other terms we have considered. . . . It is to be recognized that commonly certain other characteristics go with an absence of writing. Nonliterate peoples are found on observation to be relatively more isolated, to have smaller numbers, and to be less addicted to rapid change in their sanctioned modes of behavior than those that have writing. In recent generations, moreover, Euro-American culture has had to be set off not only from nonliterate cultures, but from the literate cultures outside of Europe and America as well, because of the presence in European and American culture of a technology based on power machinery and the scientific tradition. But it must be recognized that none of these differences, except perhaps this last, is as clearly manifest as is the presence or absence of writing.

Agreement on an adequate term or terms, appropriate both as a classificatory designation and one free of unpleasant connotations is admittedly difficult. Although the term "nonliterate" has been used in this paper it is not a completely satisfactory term. Its possible confusion with "illiterate" makes it an unfortunate term to use. Moreover it is no better than the more negatively charged terms as a classificatory designation. Anthropologists however can seek better terms and in the meantime guard against using the more offensive terms like "primitive," "savage," and other similar designations. Terms like "tribe" or "tribal," "simple" or "simpler," "complex" or "less complex," and others carry less derogatory connotations. Such terms could be used interchangeably. It is true, of course, that any one of these terms under local or special cases might carry or acquire negative meanings; in such instances other more neutral terms should be substituted. In specific cases the term "folk" might be used although this has been given specialized meaning in the writings of Redfield and others [3] may not be appropriate under all circumstances.

The reasons for selecting terms which do not offend and degrade nonliterates are essentially ethical, but in view of the world situation, can be practical as well. It is appropriate to quote again from Herskovits, who is keenly aware of the problem. In the preface of his revised edition of *The Economic Life of Primitive Peoples,* recently reissued under the title of *Economic Anthropology,* Herskovits (1952, pp. v–vi) remarks:

. . . The change in title presents a reorientation in point of view that goes far beyond the question of mere terminology. Ten years ago, the word "primitive" came easily to lips. It is only with the rapid development of communications of the past decade, and the growing integration of peoples of the most diverse cultures into the world scene, that the essentially pejorative and tendentious character of this designation, like others such as "savage," "backward," or "early" when applied to any functioning way of life, became apparent. This is not the place to analyze the cultural or psychological problems of the emergent nationalisms found in expanding and newly literate communities of Africa and Asia and of other non-machine societies. Yet when their story is told, the role played by reaction of their leaders against designations of this order will be found to be a major factor in the latent or explicit hostilities of which these movements are in many cases the expression. . . .

A similar objection was voiced by Mead (1953b, p. 351) in the discussion of the papers in *Anthropology Today:*

. . . [we must avoid value-laden terms] like "native," "vernacular," and "primitive," [which antagonize non-Europeans]. We have to watch at every turn that we do not compromise our capacity to work in the

3. Robert Redfield, 1947. For criticism of the "folk" concept see George M. Foster, 1953, pp. 159–173; Julian H. Steward, 1950, p. 113.

international scene in which each people makes a contribution to the science of anthropology, and recognize that only after each major culture area of the world has made its contribution can we have man commenting on man in terms of man's whole history of thought.

Professor Lips in *The Savage Hits Back* presents a well-documented account of the rise of nonliterate peoples throughout the world and paints a frightening picture of the awakening of millions of "primitives" to white exploitation and injustices. A brief quotation (1937, pp. 25–26) from his book is important:

> The predominance of the white race is still an existing fact, but it has long since been undermined. It consists chiefly in the strength of the British Empire and the solidarity of Europe. We cannot in the future reckon with absolute certainty upon either of these factors. It is impossible to foretell here what the consequences of a new European war [World War II] would be. But one fact is certain: after such a war the white race will have lost the upper hand. Coloured nations will be employed in far greater measure than in the last world war to combat white enemies, and their racial feeling is being cultivated to a pitch whence it is turning against their own white masters. The white man has long ago ceased to be a God, especially since war strips the last shreds of mystery from the technical secret of his superiority. And Gods without secrets, especially Gods whose internal dissension supports them on feet of clay, are rapidly dethroned.

Much of Professor Lips' prophecy has been borne out. There is certainly greater race tension in the world at present than before the war. Asia and Africa are rife with "native" problems and white supremacy specifically is being challenged.

It is clear that the anthropologist no longer can hold out in his academic shell and be immune to the reactions of large numbers of nonliterates who deeply resent negatively charged terminology by which they often are characterized. Especially is this significant when the terms as used by the anthropologist often have no relevance to the connotative value given them by popular usage. Moreover the negative terms used for nonliterate societies do not have a precise descriptive or classificatory value. When the term "primitive" may apply equally to the native of Tierra del Fuego and the Inca of the Andean highlands; to the

Bushman of South Africa and to the Yoruba of West Africa, what scientific justification is there for using it?

Anthropologists are aware of the inadequate descriptive and taxonomic designations used in their discipline. Steward, among others, discusses these problems significantly and extensively in his monograph on Area Research (1950, pp. 106–114). The remarks of White (1949, p. 21) are also germane; in arguing for more precise scientific terminology, he reports:

. . . The maturity of science in any field can be rather accurately gauged by its vocabulary: as "a science" matures it develops its own terminology. This has taken place extensively in the physical and the biological sciences. And such words as *instinct, intelligence, race, society,* are now being found so difficult to use that it is likely they will give way soon to a more effective terminology.

To the list White might have added "primitive," "backward," and the like. We need a more appropriate taxonomic terminology, it is clear; but we must be careful to select terms which do not insult the status and sensibilities of the large numbers of people they purport to identify.

This plea for a more appropriate classificatory and a less derogatory-tainted terminology is not intended to suggest that anthropologists should not seek order, development, and even former conditions of society among nonliterate societies. There is no reason why we cannot have an adequate developmental classificatory scheme and still avoid terms which assign large numbers of the world's population into inferior, degraded statuses.[4]

4. Grateful acknowledgment is made to the Graduate School, Northwestern University, for the aid provided in the preparation of this article. The author also wishes to express his thanks for helpful comments and suggestions by Dr. Fred Eggan, University of Chicago; Dr. William Bascom, Mr. Warren d'Azevedo, and Dr. M. J. Herskovits, Northwestern University. None of them, however, is to be considered as having endorsed or agreed, necessarily, with the organization, contents, or views expressed in the paper; for the latter, the author alone is responsible.

REFERENCES

Ackerknecht, Erwin H. 1954. "On the Comparative Method in Anthropology," pp. 117–125 in Spencer, R. F. (ed.), *Method and Perspective in Anthropology*. Minneapolis: The University of Minnesota Press. 323 pp.

Beals, Ralph L. 1953a. "Acculturation," pp. 621–641 in Kroeber, A. L. (ed.), *Anthropology Today*. Chicago: University of Chicago Press. 966 pp.

———. 1953b. "The Village in an Industrial World," *The Scientific Monthly*, Vol. LXXVII, No. 2, pp. 65–75.

Beals, Ralph L. and Hoijer, Harry, with the collaboration of Roediger, Virginia More. 1953. *An Introduction to Anthropology*. New York: The Macmillan Co. 658 pp.

Benedict, Ruth. 1934. *Patterns of Culture*. Boston: Houghton Mifflin Co. 290 pp.

Bidney, David. 1953. "The Concept of Value in Modern Anthropology," pp. 682–699 in Kroeber, A. L. and others, *Anthropology Today*. Chicago: The University of Chicago Press. 966 pp.

Boas, Franz. 1938. *The Mind of Primitive Man*. New York: The Macmillan Co. 285 pp.

———. 1940. *Race, Language and Culture*. New York: The Macmillan Co. 647 pp.

Cooper, John M. 1917. *Analytical and Critical Bibliography of the Tribes of Tierra del Fuego and Adjacent Territory* (Bureau of American Ethnology, Bulletin 227). Washington: U.S. Government Printing Office. 233 pp.

Eggan, Fred. 1954. "Social Anthropology and the Method of Controlled Comparison" (Presidential paper, 1953, American Anthropological Association), *American Anthropologist*, Vol. 56, No. 5, pp. 743–763.

Evans-Pritchard, E. E. 1951. *Social Anthropology*. London: Cohen and West, Ltd. 134 pp.

Firth, Raymond. 1951. "Contemporary British Social Anthropology," *American Anthropologist*, Vol. 53, No. 4, pp. 474–489.

Foster, George M. 1953. "What is Folk Culture?," *American Anthropologist*, Vol. 55, No. 2, pp. 159–173.

Goodwin, Grenville. 1942. *The Social Organization of the Western Apache*. Chicago: University of Chicago Press. 701 pp.

Graebner, Fritz. 1909. "Die Melanesche Bogenkultur und ihre Vervandten," *Anthropos*, Vol. 4, pp. 726–780, 998–1032.

———. 1911. *Methode der Ethnologie*. Heidelberg: C. Winter. 192 pp.

Henry, Jules and Spiro, Melford E. 1953. "Psychological Techniques: Projective Tests in Field Work," pp. 417–429 in Kroeber, A. L. and others, *Anthropology Today*. Chicago: The University of Chicago Press. 966 pp.

Herskovits, Melville J. 1948. *Man and His Works*. New York: Alfred A. Knopf. 678 pp.

———. 1952. *Economic Anthropology*. New York: Alfred A. Knopf. 547 pp.

———. 1953. *Franz Boas*. New York: Charles Scribner's Sons. 131 pp.

———. 1954. "Some Problems of Method in Ethnography," pp. 3–24 in Spencer, R. F. (ed.), *Method and Perspective in Anthropology*. Minneapolis: The University of Minnesota Press. 323 pp.

Hoijer, Harry. 1938. *Chiricahua and Mescalero Apache Texts*. With ethnological notes by Opler, Morris Edward (University of Chicago Publications in Anthropology—Linguistic Series). Chicago: The University of Chicago Press. 219 pp.

Kluckhohn, Clyde. 1936. "Some Reflections on the Method and Theory of the Kulturkreislehre," *American Anthropologist*, Vol. 38, No. 2, pp. 157–196.

———. 1945. "The Personal Document in Anthropological Science," pp. 79–173 in Gottschalk, L.; Kluckhohn, C.; and Angell, R., *The Use of Personal Documents in History, Anthropology, and Sociology* (Social Science Research Council Bulletin 53). New York. 243 pp.

———. 1949. "The Ramah Project," pp. v–vi in Leighton, Alexander H. and Leighton, Dorothea C. with assistance of Catherine Opler, *Gregorio, the Hand-Trembler* (Papers of the Peabody Museum of American Archaeology and Ethnology, Harvard University, Vol. XL, No. 1). Cambridge. 177 pp.

———. 1951. "A Comparative Study of Values in Five Cultures," pp. vii–ix in Vogt, Evon Z., *Navaho Veterans* (Papers of the Peabody Museum of American Archaeology and Ethnology, Vol. XLI, No. 1). Cambridge. 223 pp.

Kluckhohn, F. R. 1940. "The Participant Observer Technique in Small Communities," *American Journal of Sociology*, Vol. XLVI, No. 3, pp. 331–343.

Kroeber, A. L. 1953. "Concluding Review," pp. 357–379 in Tax, Sol et al. (eds.), *An Appraisal of Anthropology Today*. Chicago: The University of Chicago Press. 395 pp.

Kroeber, A. L. and others. 1953. *Anthropology Today*. Chicago: The University of Chicago Press. 966 pp.

Lewis, Oscar. 1953. "Controls and Experiments in Field Work," pp.

452–475 in Kroeber, A. L. and others, *Anthropology Today*. Chicago: The University of Chicago Press. 966 pp.

Linton, Ralph (ed.). 1945. *The Science of Man in the World Crisis*. New York: Columbia University Press. 532 pp.

Lips, Julius E. 1937. *The Savage Hits Back*. New Haven: Yale University Press. 254 pp.

Lounsbury, Floyd G. 1953. "Field Methods and Techniques in Linguistics," pp. 401–416 in Kroeber, A. L. and others, *Anthropology Today*. Chicago: The University of Chicago Press. 966 pp.

Lowie, R. H. 1937. *History of Ethnological Theory*. New York: Rinehart and Co., Inc. 296 pp.

Lynd, R. S. and Lynd, H. M. 1929. *Middletown*. New York: Harcourt, Brace and Co., Inc. 550 pp.

Mandelbaum, David G. 1953. "On The Study of National Character," *American Anthropologist*, Vol. 55, No. 2, pp. 174–187.

Mead, Margaret. 1932. *The Changing Culture of an Indian Tribe* (Columbia University Contributions to Anthropology, Vol. XV) New York: Columbia University Press. 313 pp.

———. 1953a. "National Character," pp. 642–667 in Kroeber, A. L. and others, *Anthropology Today*. Chicago: The University of Chicago Press. 966 pp.

Mead, Margaret *et al.* 1953b. "Discussion of Anthropology as a Field of Study," pp. 342–356 in Tax, Sol *et al.* (eds.), *An Appraisal of Anthropology Today*. Chicago: The University of Chicago Press. 395 pp.

Merton, Robert K. 1949. *Social Theory and Social Structure*. Glencoe, Ill.: Free Press. 423 pp.

Morgan, H. L. 1877. *Ancient Society*. Chicago: Charles H. Kerr and Co. 570 pp.

Murdock, George Peter. 1949. *Social Structure*. New York: The Macmillan Co. 387 pp.

———. "British Social Anthropology," *American Anthropologist*, Vol. 53, No. 4, pp. 465–473.

Opler, Morris Edward. 1941. *An Apache Life-way*. Chicago: The University of Chicago Press. 500 pp.

Paul, Benjamin D. 1953. "Interview Techniques and Field Relationships," pp. 430–451 in Kroeber, A. L. and others, *Anthropology Today*. Chicago: The University of Chicago Press. 966 pp.

Perry, W. J. 1923. *The Children of the Sun*. New York: E. P. Dutton and Co. 551 pp.

Powdermaker, Hortense. 1939. *After Freedom: A Cultural Study in the Deep South*. New York: Viking Press. 408 pp.

————. *Hollywood, The Dream Factory.* Boston: Little, Brown and Co. 342 pp.

Radcliffe-Brown, A. R. 1931. *The Social Organization of Australian Tribes* (The Oceania Monographs, No. 1). Melbourne: Macmillan and Co. 124 pp.

————. 1952 *Structure and Function in Primitive Society; Essays and Addresses.* Glencoe, Illinois: Free Press. 219 pp.

Redfield, Robert. 1941. *The Folk Culture of Yucatan.* Chicago: The University of Chicago Press. 416 pp.

————. 1947. "The Folk Society," *American Journal of Sociology,* Vol. LII, No. 4, pp. 293–308.

Rivers, W. H. R. 1906. *The Todas.* New York: Macmillan and Co., Ltd. 755 pp.

————. 1914. *The History of Melanesian Society.* Cambridge: University Press. 2 vols.

————. 1924. *Medicine, Magic, and Religion* (The FitzPatrick Lectures delivered before The Royal College of Physicians of London in 1915 and 1916). New York: Harcourt, Brace and Co., Inc. 147 pp.

Schapera, I. 1953. "Some Comments on Comparative Method in Social Anthropology," *American Anthropologist,* Vol. 55, No. 3, pp. 353–362.

Schebesta, Paul. 1933. *Among Congo Pigmies* (trans. by Gerald Griffin). London: Hutchinson and Co., Ltd. 287 pp.

Schmidt, Wilhelm. 1939. *The Culture Historical Method of Anthropology* (trans. by S. A. Sieber). New York: Fortuny's. 383 pp.

Smith, Sir Grafton Elliot. 1924. "Preface," pp. v–viii in Rivers, W. H. R. *Medicine, Magic, and Religion* (The FitzPatrick Lectures delivered before The Royal College of Physicians of London in 1915 and 1916). New York: Harcourt Brace and Co., Inc. 147 pp.

————. 1929. *Human History.* New York: W. W. Norton and Co., Inc. 472 pp.

Spencer, R. F. (ed.). 1954. *Method and Perspective in Anthropology.* Minneapolis: The University of Minnesota Press. 323 pp.

Spoehr, Alexander. 1947. *Changing Kinship Systems* (Anthropological Series, Chicago Natural History Museum, Vol. 33, No. 4). Chicago. 153–235 pp.

Steward, Julian H. 1936. "The Economic and Social Basis of Primitive Bands," pp. 331–350 in *Essays in Anthropology presented to A. L. Kroeber.* Berkeley: University of California Press. 600 pp.

————. 1949. "Cultural Causality and Law: A Trial Formulation of the

Development of Early Civilizations," *American Anthropologist*, Vol. 51, No. 1, pp. 1–27.

———. 1950. *Area Research, Theory and Practice* (Social Science Research Council Bulletin 63). New York. 164 pp.

Steward, Julian H. (ed.). 1946–1950. *Handbook of South American Indians*. (Bureau of American Ethnology, Bulletin 143) Washington, D. C.: U.S. Government Printing Office. 6 vols.

Tax, Sol *et al.* (eds.). 1953. *An Appraisal of Anthropology Today*. Chicago: The University of Chicago Press. 395 pp.

Tylor, Edward B. 1891. *Primitive Culture*. London: J. Murray. 2 vols.

Warner, W. L. *et al.* 1941–47. *Yankee City Series*. New Haven: Yale University Press. Vols. I–IV.

West, James (pseud.) 1945. *Plainville, U. S. A.* New York: Columbia University Press. 238 pp.

White, Leslie A. 1935. *The Pueblo of Santo Domingo* (Memoirs of American Anthropological Association, No. 43). Menasha, Wisconsin: American Anthropological Association. 210 pp.

———. 1942. "Lewis H. Morgan's Journal of a Trip to Southwestern Colorado and New Mexico, June 21 to August 7, 1878," *American Antiquity*, Vol. 8, No. 1, pp. 1–26.

———. 1949. *The Science of Culture*. New York: Farrar, Straus and Co. 444 pp.

———. 1951. "Lewis H. Morgan's Western Field Trips," *American Anthropologist*, Vol. 53, No. 1, pp. 11–17.

Index